CELEBRATIONS OF IDENTITY

CELEBRATIONS OF IDENTITY

Multiple Voices in American Ritual Performance

Edited by
Pamela R. Frese

Foreword by
Emiko Ohnuki-Tierney

BERGIN & GARVEY
Westport, Connecticut • London

Library of Congress Cataloging-in-Publication Data

Celebrations of identity : multiple voices in American ritual
  performance / edited by Pamela R. Frese ; foreword by Emiko Ohnuki-
  Tierney.
      p. cm.
  Includes bibliographical references and index.
  ISBN 0-89789-335-2
  1. United States—Social life and customs. 2. Rites and
ceremonies—United States. I. Frese, Pamela R.
E161.C38   1993
394.2'0973—dc20   92-43387

British Library Cataloguing in Publication Data is available.

Library of Congress Catalog Card Number: 92-43387
ISBN: 0-89789-335-2

First published in 1993

Bergin & Garvey, 88 Post Road West, Westport, CT 06881
An imprint of Greenwood Publishing Group, Inc.

Printed in the United States of America

The paper used in this book complies with the
Permanent Paper Standard issued by the National
Information Standards Organization (Z39.48-1984).

10 9 8 7 6 5 4 3 2 1

To my parents and friends: E.C. and R.J.

With Love and Respect.

Contents

Foreword

Emiko Ohnuki-Tierney

It is almost banal to point out how most academic disciplines have undergone fundamental changes within the past few decades. Such labels as post-colonial, post-structural, post-scientism, and so forth, are not positive labels in that they fail to characterize dynamic and positive developments that are a result of the ongoing dialectic between academic disciplines and the geopolitics of the world at large.

Anthropology, for example, is no longer a "western" scholars' study of the small-scale, the non-literate, the "primitive," or however we have called the anthropological "other" in the past. We have done away with "the divide" which anthropologists had created between "my people" and the generalized "Western" societies.[1] As Marc Augé so poignantly characterized, the divide had produced "the most imperialist of ethnocentrisms," resulting, ironically, from absolute relativism, coupled with a certain kind of anti-ethnocentrism (Augé 1979 [1982]:10-24). The study of not only "primitive" or "minority" pockets of nation-states, but of all nation-states, including the "Western" societies as a whole with all their multiplicities, has become a part of the mainstream anthropology and constitutes a new and healthy development in contemporary anthropology.

A corollary is the blurring of the distinction between the self and other for anthropologists who have started to study their own culture and society. Some older anthropologists have returned home after studying another culture, whereas younger generations of anthropologists have chosen to be "native anthropologists" as their first professional career. As a result, at least in part, there have been healthy dialogues across disciplinary boundaries. Those who wear the professional hat of an anthropologist, as do many of the contributors in this volume, are conversant with historians, literary critics, and scholars in many other disciplines.

This collection of essays on the cultures of the contemporary United States exemplifies this new development. It is a far cry from the picture we used to hold of the dominant Anglos and "minorities." Here we have in one volume, studies of various peoples within the political unit called United States of America whose cultures have woven a rich tapestry of what we have been calling "American culture."

Pluralism, which works at several different levels, is a key concept in contemporary anthropology and related fields. We now recognize diversity and complexity within *any* social group. As a hindsight we see them in societies once thought to be "simple," "small," and so forth. We have indeed wrongly represented a people in a single voice. Every social group is pluralistic, with every individual having multiple cross-cutting social identities arising from but not determined by class, gender, age, ethnicity, and other factors. The essays in this volume capture this "fertile and dynamic interplay . . . among individual, group, and cultural identities," as Pamela Frese puts it in her introduction.

Pluralism operates far beyond multiplicity in terms of social formation. Mikhail Bakhtin's polyphony—multiple voices in power relationships—has alerted us to explore multiple voices embedded in power inequality and has been helpful in understanding the overt or hidden struggles of contestation found in many situations in the past and at present. Even before Bakhtin's concepts became influential, Victor Turner's multivocality of a symbol and ritual performance had a major and enduring impact on the way we think about symbols and rituals. We no longer think of a performance having a singular meaning or structure understood by all participants. Depending upon the context and the social agent, a symbol or a ritual as a whole takes on a different meaning. Furthermore, rituals are performances that have the power to transform the actor and the community. Turner's insistence upon what I would call *symbolic practice* directed us to situate ritual in social interactions. The purpose of ritual studies no longer consists of an analysis of the meaning or structure in the abstract, but the way real social agents perform it.

Having shifted the conceptual locus onto the performative dimensions of ritual, we came to terms with the evocative quality and power of symbols that Turner successfully called attention to on the one hand, and the importance of emotion and feelings of the performing and participating individuals. Rituals, we realize, are not mechanical reproductions and repetitions of formulaic behaviors, verbal and non-verbal.

If the 1960s saw exciting developments in the study of symbols under Claude Lévi-Strauss in France and Edmund Leach in Britain, the 1970s saw the bursting energy of anthropologists and others in the study of rituals. Under Turner's general editorship, Cornell University Press began a new series on Symbol, Myth, and Ritual, and a number of legendary conferences were held. Stanley J. Tambiah's Radcliffe-Brown lecture in 1979 was entitled "A Performative Approach to Ritual," reflecting this development both in the United States and Britain.

"Rituals" and "performance" were no longer confined to a narrowly defined field. *Secular Ritual* (Moore and Myerhoff 1977) and symbols have been identified in the day-to-day lives and in all areas of human experience. This tradition is well and alive today as exemplified in the fine work by the editor of this volume, Pamela Frese, on American culture. For example, she introduces us to "American yard decoration" (1992), telling us about the complex interplay between the individual, who cherishes these objects, and the cultural beliefs about the public and private spheres, gender, marriage, family, class, and other factors. Through her insightful eyes, simple "knickknacks" that escape the notice of many of us become alive, unveiling the lived experience of the individual owners.

Ritual performance is by definition "reflexive" in that the self of the performer or the self of the social group must be contemplated upon—not simply reflected upon. I hesitate to state that a critical distance between the self, who contemplates, and the self, who is mused upon, is necessary, because it might infer some vestige of scientism, or it may seem to overly semiotize the notion of reflexivity. No matter how we might put it, however, reflexivity does require the capacity—not simply cognitive/intellectual but also emotive—to perceive "otherness." But the "otherness" does not have to be located in another culture; it can be right in your culture, as exemplified in this volume.

What is exciting and original about this volume is that the epistemological questions, prompted by the post-World War II geopolitics, have become *naturalized*,[2] portraying the plurality of social and cultural landscapes of the United States as *natural*. Furthermore, the political development arising out of the "colonial situation" (Balandier 1970 [1951]; see also Stocking, Jr. 1991) and the development of the study of ritual and performance in the 1960s and the 1970s have been fruitfully conjoined in this fine series of articles on the multiple voices—at various levels—articulated in daily family, political, religious, and ethnic rituals. The book should appeal to and be read at different levels. Those who are specialists will learn theoretical insights as well as rich ethnography, while others will certainly enjoy American cultures and individuals and their rich experience.

NOTES

1. See Bernard S. Cohn (1980:211), who criticizes the fallacy of using the blanket term "Western" and placing the rest of the world in a "residual category."

2. The term *naturalization* is usually used in a negative sense. Bourdieu (1977:164), for example, uses it in relation to his notion of *doxa*: "Every established order sends to produce . . . the naturalization of its own arbitrariness." His emphasis, then, is the naturalization of *distinction* and other power relations.

BIBLIOGRAPHY

Augé, Marc
   1979 *The Anthropological Circle: Symbol, Function, History*. Cambridge:
   Cambridge University Press. English translation in 1982.

Balandier, Georges
   1970 [1951] *The Sociology of Black Africa: Social Dynamics in Central Africa*. D.
   Garman (trans.) New York: Praeger. Pp. 34-61.

Bordieu, Pierre
   1977 [1972] *Outline of a Theory of Practice*. Cambridge: Cambridge University
   Press.

Cohn, Bernard S.
   1980 "History and Anthropology: The State of Play." *Comparative Studies in
   Society and History* 12:198-221.

Frese, Pamela R.
   1992 "Artifacts of Gendered Space: American Yard Decoration." *Visual Anthropology* 5:17-42.

Moore, Sally Falk, and Barbara G. Myerhoff (eds.)
   1977 *Secular Ritual*. Assen and Amsterdam: Van Gorcum.

Stocking, George, Jr. (ed.)
   1971 *Colonial Situations: Essays on the Contextualization of Ethnographic
   Knowledge*. Madison, WI: University of Wisconsin Press.

Tambiah, Stanley J.
   1981 "A Performance Approach to Ritual." Radcliffe-Brown Lecture, 1979.
   Proceedings of the British Academy 65:113-69.

Acknowledgments

I want to thank my husband Simon Gray for his overall support on this project and for his assistance in producing the final draft of this manuscript. I am grateful to the College of Wooster for their continued support and to my student researchers provided through the Sophomore Research Assistants Program at the College, especially Murray Welsh and Christy Anderson. Carolyn Rahnema did an excellent job of typing an earlier version of this manuscript. I want to thank Dale Catteau and Angie Dobbins for their patience and assistance throughout the entire process.

Excerpts from "Pageantry, Parades and Indian Dancing" by Patricia B. Lerch, were reproduced by permission of the American Anthropological Association from *Museum Anthropology* (16:2). Not for further reproduction.

Introduction

Pamela R. Frese

Americans validate and reinvent their identities as biological, social, and sacred beings through a number of ritualized events. Each ritual is a multifaceted form of cultural performance that serves as a vehicle for legitimizing, perpetuating, and transforming society and the social individual on a number of levels that include racial and ethnic heritage, religious and community identity, and membership in a pluralistic society.

Most ritual theorists agree that ritualized celebrations function to validate and perpetuate religious beliefs and the social structure, serve to enhance group solidarity, work as a vehicle for social control, and act as a means to dispel conflict between social groups. Current scholarship incorporates new perspectives on these conventional anthropological topics, frequently with an increased awareness that ritual must also be viewed as a dramatic performance and as a form of cultural information (see Bauman (ed.) 1992; Bruner (ed.) 1983; Cannadine and Price (eds.) 1987; Damon and Wagner (eds.) 1989; Fernandez 1986; Humphrey and Humphrey (eds.) 1988; Kertzer 1988; Lewis 1988 [1980]; Lincoln 1991; Mahdi, Foster, and Little (eds.) 1987; Morris 1987; Metcalf and Huntington 1992 [1979]; Napier 1992; Neville 1987; Ohnuki-Tierney 1983, 1986 [1984], 1987; Schechner 1985; Schechner and Appel (eds.) 1989; Turner and Bruner (eds.) 1986; Vélez-Ibáñez 1983; Wagner 1986). As epistemological phenomena in their own right, rituals are also cultural performances that involve ethical considerations in fieldwork and the finished product and highlight issues of empowerment (Bell 1992; Faris 1990; Frisbie (ed.) 1989 [1980]; Grimes 1988, 1990a, 1990b; Handelman 1990; Karp and Lavine (eds.) 1991; Karp, Kreamer, and Lavine (eds.) 1992; McLeod 1991a, 1991b; Smith 1987). In the process, ritual may also help to mystify social relations as they are, in favor of an idealized picture of the world, in effect legitimizing the status quo.

A "ritual" may be used to refer to many different kinds of cultural performance: public and private celebrations, sacred and secular occasions, and even as experiential, reflexive play. Some scholars may argue that "ritual" as an all inclusive category of study is problematic and isolate one kind of ritualized act for consideration (Abrahams 1987; Falassi (ed.) 1987; Kinser 1990). However, as this volume shows, a consideration of a variety of ritualized actions in a pluralistic society allows for different kinds of interpretations to be made, especially in terms of understanding the multi-faceted identities of ritual participants.

Important considerations of the role of race, ethnicity, class, and gender in cultural theory and disciplinary epistemology accompany an increased awareness of the cultural pluralism in American society (Alba 1990; Anzaldúa 1987; Asante 1987, 1990; Deegan (ed.) 1989; Frese and Coggeshall (eds.) 1991; Ginsberg and Tsing 1990; Harison (ed.) 1991; Luedtke (ed.) 1992; Marcus and Fisher 1986; Merelman 1991; Minh-ha 1989; Mukerji and Schudson (eds.) 1991; Rose 1989). Accompanying these important issues are the increasing number of works by native speakers about their own version of American culture and the rituals that give them meaning (Allen 1986, 1989 (ed.); Frese 1991; Kertzer 1988; Prell 1989).

This book features a collection of essays that explore a variety of ritual forms in contemporary American society. The contributors are united in approaching ritual as a social phenomenon of shared experience, firmly embedded in human interaction and cultural performance. We explore the fertile and dynamic interplay in ritual celebrations among individual, group, and cultural identities. In particular, we are interested in how these identities are created, validated, and reinvented through ritual performance. The articles in this volume add new dimensions to the anthropology of ritual and contribute to the ethnographic literature on ritual in the United States in exciting ways.

As the complex nature of ritual mirrors the multifaceted identities of an individual, theories about ritual are themselves indicators of the particular cultural orientation of the scholar who interprets ritual for the reader (see Geertz 1983, 1986). By examining the multivocal nature of ritual and the interpretation of ritual experience, the volume can also serve as a lens through which to view the relation between "self" and "other" from a variety of perspectives.

This volume illustrates that ritual performance is indeed "multiplex as a structure of meaning and reflexivity" (Ohnuki-Tierney 1983:307). Madeline Duntley's insightful article explores the role of fieldwork, ritual experience, and the final written analysis as significant and interrelated aspects of any understanding of ritual performance. Edith Turner also emphasizes the importance of ritual experience and shows that ritualized celebrations are events for play. Both authors argue that elaborately constructed theoretical frameworks may miss the most significant meanings embodied in ritual actions.

Ritualized celebrations enhance group solidarity, dispel conflict between groups, and validate and reinvent society and cultural beliefs. John M. Coggeshall examines festivals as ritualized public events that preserve and recreate ethnic and religious identity for German-American and Greek-American communities. Ethnic identity is constantly negotiated during liminal ritual time by ethnic members and outside visitors; a tension that illustrates the ongoing dialectic between the preservation of tradition and "Americanization" of these social groups. Gwen Kennedy Neville discusses how ritual serves to unify and perpetuate Southern kinship, Protestant congregation, and Southern community while celebrating a larger American identity and cultural ethos. She also argues for the consideration of regional influence on cultural forms as another significant level of social identity.

Rituals can be viewed as rites of passage and as social dramas; both kinds of events are powerful experiences that transform the participants into a new way of being. This transformative power allows ritual to serve as a mechanism for empowerment in a multicultural society. Jon Michael Spencer views the ritual of testimony in Black Holiness-Pentecostal worship as a rite of intensification that builds group solidarity and reinforces religious faith in an oppressive society. Patricia B. Lerch discusses the pow-wow of the Waccamaw people of North Carolina as a social drama that allows for the reinvention and manipulation of social identity through time.

The rituals associated with the life-cycle of an individual or family also reflect the larger social and cultural contexts in which they are embedded. Pamela R. Frese describes how the mortuary complex in Anglo-American culture reflects gendered identity on a number of levels: family status and kinship relationships, his/her standing in the larger community and/or nation, and beliefs in cosmological processes in general. Carlos G. Vélez-Ibáñez examines the interrelationship between U.S. Mexican family life-cycle rituals, civil-religious celebrations, and the sponsor's economic identity and well-being in an Anglo-dominated society. Finally, Karen Leonard explores the historical dimensions to the relationship of family heritage, festivals, and civil-religious celebrations for Punjabi-Mexicans. In addition, she illustrates how these rituals respond to national and international political forces while they perpetuate ethnic pluralism in a multicultural American society.

Two essays are particularly interested in how ritual validates class identity and how this affects the individual and his or her relationship with family and community. Rachel Mason's work with the fishing culture in Alaska is an important contribution to how drinking ritual functions within an occupational group to validate and perpetuate the individual, group, and community in response to changing economic conditions. Michaele Thurgood Haynes' analysis of the Coronation ritual of the upper class in San Antonio, Texas suggests that these ceremonies define and affirm identity on at least three levels: class, regional heritage, and family.

In the last essay, J. R. McLeod argues that the Presidential Inauguration in the United States is designed to validate American myths and to legitimize the President as the leader of a multicultural United States. He explains that this ritual operates by highlighting some elements of a pluralistic society while masking others as it functions to affirm group solidarity and a national identity.

Any one book can only touch on the richness of the beliefs and practices that help identify the many peoples and cultures of the United States. This book does illustrate that ritual celebrations are important ways in which some people in the United States validate and recreate aspects of their biological, social, and cultural identity. Many of the papers on ritual in this volume highlight the inequities embedded in this society in terms of gender, race, class, and cultural heritage. Rather than perpetuate these social and cultural injustices, we must move in our understanding of a diverse American heritage away from a consideration of "sub" cultures that are evaluated in terms of the "appropriate" cultural model of the "ideal" ethnic group. For this reason among others, it is important that the anthropological perspective on the distinction between "us" and "other" be incorporated into a multidisciplinary American studies. Many anthropologists also recognize that ritual is a real, lived experience that affects the biological, spiritual, and social world as it is understood by the ritual participants. We hope that the following essays will highlight the need to explore all dimensions of a ritual experience while providing new visions of American identity expressed through ritual celebrations.

BIBLIOGRAPHY

Abrahams, Roger D.
    1987 "An American Vocabulary of Celebrations." In *Time Out of Time: Essays on the Festival*. Alessandro Falassi (ed.) Albuquerque: University of New Mexico Press. Pp. 173-183.

Alba, Richard, D.
    1990 *Ethnic Identity: The Transformation of White America*. New Haven: Yale University Press.

Allen, Paula Gunn
    1986 *The Sacred Hoop: Recovering the Feminine in American Indian Tradition*. Boston: Beacon Press.

    1989 (ed.) *Spider Woman's Granddaughters: Traditional Tales and Contemporary Writing by Native American Women*. Boston: Beacon Press.

Anzaldúa, Gloria
    1987 *Borderlands La Frontera: The New Mestiza*. San Francisco: Spinsters/Aunt Lute.

Asante, Molefi Kete
    1987 *The Afrocentric Idea*. Philadelphia: Temple University Press.

    1990 *Kemet, Afrocentricity and Knowledge*. Trenton, NJ: Africa World Press.

Bauman, Richard (ed.)
    1992 *Folklore, Cultural Performances, and Popular Entertainments: A Communications-Centered Handbook*. Oxford University Press: New York.

Bell, Catherine
    1992 *Ritual Theory: Ritual Practice*. New York and Oxford: Oxford University Press.

Bruner, Edward M. (ed.)
1983 *Text, Play, and Story: The Construction and Reconstruction of Self and Society*. Washington, DC: The American Ethnological Society.

Cannadine, David, and Simon Price (eds.)
1987 *Rituals of Royalty: Power and Ceremonial in Traditional Society*. New York: Cambridge University Press.

Damon, Frederick H., and Roy Wagner (eds.)
1989 *Death Rituals and Life in the Societies of the Kula Ring*. De Kalb, IL: Northern Illinois University Press.

Deegan, Mary Jo (ed.)
1989 *American Ritual Dramas: Social Rules and Cultural Meanings*. Contributions in Sociology, no. 76. Westport, CT: Greenwood Press.

Falassi, Alessandro (ed.)
1987 *Time Out of Time: Essays on the Festival*. Albuquerque: University of New Mexico Press.

Faris, James C.
1990 *The Nightway: A History and a History of Documentation of a Navajo Ceremonial*. Albuquerque: University of New Mexico Press.

Fernandez, James
1986 *Persuasions and Performances: The Play of Tropes in Culture*. Bloomington: Indiana University Press.

Frese, Pamela R., and John M. Coggeshall (eds.)
1991 *Transcending Boundaries: Multidisciplinary Approaches to the Study of Gender*. New York: Bergin & Garvey.

Frese, Pamela R.
1991 "The Union of Nature and Culture: Gender Symbolism in the American Wedding Ritual." In *Transcending Boundaries: Multidisciplinary Approaches to the Study of Gender*. Pamela R. Frese and John M. Coggeshall (eds.) New York: Bergin & Garvey. Pp. 97-112.

Frisbie, Charlotte J. (ed.)
1989 [1980] *Southwestern Indian Ritual Drama*. Prospect Heights, IL: Waveland Press.

Geertz, Clifford
1983 *Local Knowledge: Further Essays in Interpretive Anthropology*. New York: Basic Books.

1986 "Making Experiences, Authoring Selves," In *The Anthropology of Experience*. Edward M. Bruner and Victor Turner (eds.) Urbana and Chicago: University of Chicago Press. Pp. 373-380.

Ginsburg, Faye and Anna Lowenhaupt Tsing
1990 *Uncertain Terms: Negotiating Gender in American Culture*. Boston: Beacon Press.

Grimes, Ronald L.
   1988 "Ritual Criticism and Reflexivity in Fieldwork." *Journal of Ritual Studies.*
   2(2):217-239.

   1990a *Ritual Criticism: Case Studies in Its Practice, Essays on Its Theory.*
   Studies in Comparative Religion. Frederick M. Denny (series ed.) Columbia:
   University of South Carolina Press.

   1990b "Victor Turner's Definition, Theory, and Sense of Ritual." In *Between
   Literature and Anthropology,* Kathleen M. Ashley (ed.) Bloomington: Indiana
   University Press.

Handelman, Don
   1990 *Models and Mirrors: Towards an Anthropology of Public Events.*
   Cambridge: Cambridge University Press.

Harison, Faye V. (ed.)
   1991 *Decolonizing Anthropology: Moving Further toward an Anthropology
   for Liberation.* Washington, DC: American Anthropological Association and
   Association of Black Anthropologists.

Humphrey, Theodore C., and Lin T. Humphrey (eds.)
   1988 *"We Gather Together": Food and Festival in American Life.* Ann Arbor
   and London: UMI Research Press.

Karp, Ivan, and Steven D. Lavine (eds.)
   1991 *Exhibiting Cultures: The Poetics and Politics of Museum Display.*
   Washington, DC: Smithsonian Institution Press.

Karp, Ivan, Christine Mullen Kreamer, and Steven D. Lavine (eds.)
   1992 *Museums and Communities: The Politics of Public Culture.* Washington,
   DC: Smithsonian Institution Press.

Kertzer, David I.
   1988 *Ritual, Politics, and Power.* New Haven: Yale University Press.

Kinser, Samuel
   1990 *Carnival, American Style: Mardi Gras at New Orleans and Mobile.*
   Chicago: University of Chicago Press.

Lewis, Gilbert
   1988 [1980] *Day of Shining Red: An Essay on Understanding Ritual.*
   Cambridge: Cambridge University Press.

Lincoln, Bruce
   1991 *Emerging from the Chrysalis: Studies in Rituals of Women's Initiation.*
   Oxford: Oxford University Press

Luedtke, Luther S. (ed.)
   1992 *The Society and Culture of the United States.* Chapel Hill: University of
   North Carolina Press.

Mahdi, Louise Carus, Steven Foster, and Meredith Little (eds.)
   1987 *Betwixt & Between: Patterns of Masculine and Feminine Initiation.* La
   Salle, IL: Open Court.

Marcus, George, and Michael Fisher
1986 *Anthropology as Cultural Critique: An Experimental Moment in the Human Sciences.* Chicago: University of Chicago Press.

McLeod, John
1991a "Ritual and Rhetoric in Presidential Politics." *Central Issues in Anthropology.* 9 (Spring).

1991b "The Cult of the Divine America: Ritual, Symbol, and Mystification in American Political Culture." *International Journal of Moral and Social Studies* 6(2):1-24.

Merelman, Richard M.
1991 *Partial Visions: Culture and Politics in Britain, Canada, and the United States.* Madison: University of Wisconsin Press.

Metcalf, Peter, and Richard Huntington
1992 [1979] *Celebrations of Death: The Anthropology of Mortuary Ritual.* Cambridge: Cambridge University Press.

Minh-ha, Trinh T.
1989 *Woman, Native, Other: Writing Postcoloniality and Feminism.* Bloomington and Indianapolis: Indiana University Press.

Morris, Brian
1987 *Anthropological Studies of Religion.* Cambridge: Cambridge University Press.

Mukerji, Chandra, and Michael Schudson (eds.)
1991 *Rethinking Popular Culture: Contemporary Perspectives in Cultural Studies.* Berkeley: University of California Press.

Napier, A. David
1992 *Foreign Bodies: Performance, Art, and Symbolic Anthropology.* Berkeley: University of California Press.

Neville, Gwen Kennedy
1987 *Kinship and Pilgrimage: Rituals of Reunion in American Protestant Culture.* Oxford: Oxford University Press.

Ohnuki-Tierney, Emiko
1983 "Monkey Performances: A Multiple Structure of Meaning and Reflexivity in Japanese Culture." In *Text, Play, and Story: The Construction and Reconstruction of Self and Society.* Edward M. Bruner (ed.) Washington, DC: The American Ethnological Society. Pp. 278-314.

1986 [1984] *Illness and Culture in Contemporary Japan: An Anthropological View.* Cambridge: Cambridge University Press.

1987 *The Monkey as Mirror: Symbolic Transformations in Japanese History and Ritual.* Princeton: Princeton University Press.

Prell, Riv-Ellen
1989 *Prayer and Community: The Havurah in American Judaism.* Detroit: Wayne State University Press.

Rose, Dan
    1989 *Patterns of American Culture: Ethnography and Estrangement.*
    Philadelphia: University of Pennsylvania Press.

Schechner, Richard
    1985 *Between Theater and Anthropology.* Phildelphia: University of
    Pennsylvania Press.

Schechner, Richard, and Willa Appel (eds.)
    1989 *By Means of Performance: Intercultural Studies of Theatre and Ritual.*
    Cambridge: Cambridge University Press.

Smith, Jonathan Z.
    1987 *To Take Place: Toward Theory in Ritual.* Chicago and London:
    University of Chicago Press.

Turner, Edith, with William Blodgett, Singleton Kahona, and Fideli Benwa
    1992 *Experiencing Ritual: A New Interpretation of African Healing.*
    Philadelphia: University of Pennsylvania Press.

Turner, Victor W., and Edward M. Bruner (eds.)
    1986 *The Anthropology of Experience.* Urbana and Chicago: University of
    Chicago Press.

Vélez-Ibáñez, Carlos G.
    1983 *Rituals of Marginality: Politics, Process, and Culture Change in Central
    Urban Mexico, 1969-1974.* Berkeley: University of California Press.

Wagner, Roy
    1986 *Symbols That Stand for Themselves.* Chicago and London: The
    University of Chicago Press.

CELEBRATIONS
OF IDENTITY

1

Observing Meaning: Ritual Criticism, Interpretation, and Anthropological Fieldwork

Madeline Duntley

"Observing meaning" requires a reappraisal of fieldwork approaches to ritual. This study will follow Clifford Geertz's call to do some creative interdisciplinary "fiddling around." It turns to the "humanities for explanatory analogies" which might well serve the social sciences (Geertz 1987:521). Insights from the humanities can prompt fieldworkers to reconsider ritual—to see it as a dynamic and complex "composition" in its own right, rather than merely a "window" on cultural life. Seeing how critics of art, theater, and literature grasp the subjectivity and indeterminacy of meaning in artistic compositions can spur fieldworkers to reexamine the sequence and stylistic structure of ritual as a locus of meaning. Efforts to study the aesthetics of ritual are already underway in the emerging school of ritual criticism (Grimes 1990). Ritual criticism, by challenging the fieldworker to assume the role of "ritual critic," enlarges the scope of one's opportunity to "observe meaning" in North American ritual.

RITUAL: A WINDOW OR COMPOSITION?

Fieldworkers generally describe ritual meaning in two ways. First, they find meaning embedded in the functional aspects of ritual: why the ritual is staged and what it is meant to accomplish, such as initiation, or life-transition passage. Second, they locate meaning in the order and unity ritual provides for participants: ritual creates social solidarity, forges ethnic identity, and engenders *communitas*.[1]

In focusing upon the functional and unifying aspects of ritual, many anthropologists tend to see ritual as a "window" on culture. Through this window, the fieldworker can observe the fusion of the symbolic and practical aspects of human life: the intersection and synthesis of a society's ethos and worldview (Bell

1992:27). For them, meaning is found when the fieldworker successfully cracks the code of a society's complex symbol system which is being enacted, displayed, or expressed in the ritual.

If ritual is a window on culture, then the fieldworker is relegated to using ritual as a tool, an instrument. While the ritual-as-window concept does provide focus for the fieldworker, it invites the observer's gaze to scan the view, the landscape outside the window. The fieldworker looks through and beyond the ritual to focus primarily on what is presumably more valuable than the ritual itself: knowledge about the social system or culture in which the ritual is produced. Within the theoretical framework of ritual-as-window, the fieldworker pinpoints meaning primarily in the intersection or relationship between the ritual actors and the greater society at large. To locate meaning in the functional aspects of a ritual is to assume that it is forged largely by the ritual participants even before they enact, dramatize, or idealize their relationship to a larger cultural or sacral presence.

Catherine Bell documents this tendency in her recent analysis of current theories of ritual. She shows how many theorists' "construction of meaning" in ritual depends upon "a model of ritual based [on] . . . two structural patterns—in which ritual is both activity and the fusion of thought and activity" (Bell, 1992:31). These two patterns then spiral into a third, wherein the dichotomy between a thinking theorist and acting ritualist is "simultaneously affirmed and resolved" (1992:31). Bell's commentary on Geertz's use of this third pattern highlights a common anthropological approach to meaning in ritual. In Geertz's model

> ritual participants act, whereas those observing them think. In ritual activity, conceptions and dispositions are fused for the participants, which yields meaning. Meaning for the outside theorist comes differently: insofar as he or she can perceive in ritual the true basis of its meaningfulness for the ritual actors . . . the theorist in turn can grasp its meaningfulness as a cultural phenomenon. Ritual activity can then become meaningful to the theorist. Thus, a . . . focus on ritual activity renders the rite a veritable window on the most important processes of cultural life (Bell 1992:28).

The participants themselves create meaning within the confines of the ritual, and it is accessible to participant observers. Fieldworkers who study ritual in this way affirm the communicative potential of ritual, even in cross-cultural examinations. They insist that ritual-as-window presents a clear, unobstructed view: that ritual is a cultural performance with distinct boundaries, easily observable by the trained fieldworker. With mirror-like realism, ritual reflects the values, concerns, and dynamics of a culture.

When fieldworkers neglect what Tom Driver calls ritual "technique" and sequential order, they fail to document the variety of meanings produced by the ritual (Driver 1991:144). Studying the sequence, boundaries, and stylistic character of a ritual reveals experiential and aesthetic meanings created, discovered, exchanged, passed, and taught from participant to participant, between participants and practitioners, amongst actors and audience, and between fieldworker and informants.[2] Even current ritual theory merely attempts to define the perimeters and parameters of ritual—either exploring what ritual is by examining what it is intended to do, or highlighting its recurring features such as formalized, repetitive behavior. Recently it has been suggested that the only characteristic all rituals share is that they are "activities . . . set off as distinct and privileged vis-à-vis other activities" (Bell 1992:92). This qualifier bypasses a ritual's format and sequence, and focuses instead upon the ritual actors as they relate to a society or a culture at large. Homing in on this process of "privileging" certain behaviors discounts the precise details and dynamics of a ritual's order, technique, mood, aesthetic, and style. Clearly, the close study of a ritual's format is not normally seen as the way to access and assess meaning in ritual.

RITUAL AS COMPOSITION

For the fieldworker to tap new reservoirs of meaning in ritual, it will be necessary to focus attention upon the way it is designed and composed, how the various elements in a particular ritual flow together, and how its components depend and build upon one another. And the fieldworker must do more than simply describe the sequences: he/she must translate and assess the stylistic elements of a ritual. This means that a fieldworker must now interact with rituals as if they were complex "compositions." The root word of composition is the Latin *componere*, "to put together." Just like other compositions in music, art, and literature, ritual compositions are a "congruence of forms." Ritual is created by a process of integration wherein different "forms are related in such a way as to constitute an organized whole" (Maquet 1986:119). Rituals are designed; their stylization and sequential action are often constructed to evoke aesthetic power, pleasure, and meaning. Rituals are complex compositions containing a variety of art forms such as dance, music, and other performative sequences. Many of the ritual actors use ritual objects and wear costumes which are treasured art forms both within and outside the ritual context. Claiming that ritual is a composite of various art forms is to ensure that it eludes easy classification and interpretation.

To conceive of ritual as a composition demands engagement from all parties involved. It highlights and intensifies the role and purpose of the fieldworker as both participant and observer. The fieldworker not only observes actions and reactions, but is called upon and expected to personally experience the composition. This, in turn, enlarges the boundaries of the ritual event. Is ritual-as-composition bounded within the staging or performance of the rite? Or do the boundaries of any given composition necessarily include the entire "performance sequence"? Richard Schechner's suggestion for widening and blurring the boundaries of theater can be creatively and fruitfully applied to ritual. Schechner bemoans the fact that scholars and critics pay "attention to the show" but not to the events preceding and following the performance. Why not analyze "the whole seven-part sequence of training, workshops, rehearsal, warm-ups, performance, cool-down, and aftermath?" (Schechner 1985:16).

Schechner also includes a much wider range of people as "participants." In order to judge the intensity of a performance it is necessary to examine the "experiences and actions of all participants, from the director to the child sleeping in the audience" (Schechner 1985:12). To entertain this thought in terms of ritual is to propose that fieldworkers seek information from ritual practitioners, the participants, the directors (who may or may not participate directly), and the spectators or audience. This suggests yet another variable in the assessment and location of meaning: while the roles of audience and ritual actor remain static, the persons assuming those roles often change each time a ritual is repeated. How might this shift of individual actors modify the meanings in ritual?

Schechner insists upon the uniqueness of each performance. Changing the personalities of both participants and spectators can alter the mood, intensity, and success of a composition's performance. A performance is tied directly to the "audience that hears them, the spectators who see them. The force of the performance is in the very specific relationship between performers and those-for-whom-the-performance-exists" (Schechner 1985:5). This dynamic between spectator and ritual participant is rarely examined by the fieldworker. Yet, Schechner's analysis of this relationship's impact upon dramatic performance suggests that the connection between performer and spectator may in fact be a central locus of meaning and emotion in ritual. Spectators are well aware of the quality and artistry of a performance, and can sense the precise moment when a performance "takes off": "A 'presence' is manifest, something has 'happened.' The performers have touched or moved the audience, and some kind of collaboration, collective special theatrical life, is born" (Schechner 1985:10). Many participant-observers can recall being swept up in the intensity of a ritual performance. In fact, the mood induced by a well-performed ritual is often called "communitas." Schechner chooses instead to locate spectator emotion within the aesthetic-critical spectrum, calling it an enthusiastic appreciation of a "good" performance.

Perhaps ritual, like other compositions in art, dance, and music, does not constitute a single message sent intact to receivers. Jacques Maquet, a self-proclaimed trailblazer in the anthropology of art, points out that any complex composition is a poor vehicle for embodying a single, communicative message. Compositions not only employ various forms and symbols, but they also rely upon beholders or spectators for assignments of meaning. This suggests that compositions are not only rife with polysemic signifiers, but that a vital component of their "meaning" is attributable to the audience or spectators. And yet each individual exposed to the composition has his/her own "symbolic understanding" which is uniquely informed by "past experiences." These experiences are then used by the beholder to both "endow and attribute meanings" to the composition (Maquet 1986:156).

Each ritual is a one-time event, with varying dynamic, associational, and aesthetic meanings, all affecting the audience and participants differently. Just as each staging or viewing of a composition is a unique experience, no two performances of the "same" ritual will ever be identical. This calls into question the "scientific" nature and replicability of fieldwork observation. Can the fieldworker really view the "same" ritual more than once? To say that one can observe the same ritual twice is to imply that ritual is a standardized text, existing independently of the performers and audience, capable of being read and re-read time and time again.

RITUAL, IDIOM, AND MEANING

It may be helpful at this juncture to explore the possibilities attendant upon thinking of ritual not only as a composition, but as a contextually specific "idiom." John Hospers utilizes the analogy of idiom to elucidate the essential nature of poetry as a composition. Poetry, like idiom, contains many shades of meaning. To understand the meanings of an idiom one must be "acquainted with the cluster of affective associations which gather around every word—the emotions they normally evoke, the images to which they give rise" (Hospers 1946:125). One might attempt to translate an idiom's meaning, but not without radically altering its specific form and content; its meaning can never be completely interpreted or isolated: "Poetic meaning is untranslatable; that is to say, this precise effect can be conveyed in no other way. It must remain just as it was presented or be destroyed" (Hospers 1946:131, 134). Form and format of ritual must be carefully studied, because its peculiar construction may be evocative of various kinds of meanings. To exclude any part or portion of the ritual action is to ignore the creative combination of the composition which might produce its power and efficacy, and perhaps engender a great deal of aesthetic and experiential meaning for participants, practitioners, and spectators alike.

The composer Felix Mendelssohn, addressed the primacy and integrity of a musical composition's form:

> What any music I like expresses for me is not thought *too indefinite* to clothe in words, but *too definite*. . . . If you asked me what I thought on the occasion in question, I say, the song, itself precisely as it stands. And if . . . I had in mind . . . definite words, I would not utter them to a soul, because words do not mean for

one person what they do for another; because the song alone can
say to one, can awake in him, the same feeling it can in another—
feelings, however, not to be expressed in the same words (Gurney
1880:357; emphasis in original).

Ritual compositions exist in specific forms because the meanings they evoke
cannot be produced precisely in any other way. Perhaps the amalgamated form
of ritual is the perfect vehicle for the evocation of meanings, and the source of
ritual's attraction and enduring practice. If the various meanings engendered
within a ritual could be manifested in a more effective and economical way, then
why would people continue to engage in ritual?

Mark Roskill has noted that "the central task of interpretation is usually
taken to be the proposing of meaning, symbolism, or signification" (Roskill
1989:11). This raises the question: how do fieldworkers see their roles as ritual
interpreters? Is interpretation a definitive, descriptive, scientific summation and
analysis of a cultural performance? Or would an "interpreter" be better conceived
of as a translator of a cultural form which must, ultimately, speak for itself? A
fieldworker's discussion of meaning in ritual is at best a one-dimensional
description in another language of the affective emotion, aesthetic power, and
effective relations produced by the complex composition of ritual.

RITUAL CRITICISM AND FIELDWORK

A new trend in ritual studies which incorporates insights from the humanities
into fieldwork practices is "ritual criticism." Ritual criticism is the brainchild of
Ronald L. Grimes, and it is a methodological stance reorienting the way fieldworkers study ritual:

The practice of ritual criticism depends on the basic humanistic
premise that rites, though they may be revealed by the gods are
also constructed by human beings and therefore imperfect. . . .
However sacred, rites are not beyond the ken of mortals. Therefore,
they are subject to ongoing assessment. They can be judged
wanting. They can be improved upon. They can fail (Grimes
1990:9).

The development of ritual criticism was partially inspired by the need for new
ritual theories to address and study the creative and compositional aspects of ritual.

Scholars in a variety of fields have devoted monographs to the creative and
spontaneous nature of ritual, and have documented the process of meaning-in-the-
making. Historian Mona Ozouf records the process by which French
Revolutionary festivals were designed, planned, and staged. Ultimately, these

rituals failed because they were constructed by the elite for the populace. The celebrations did not engender the populist spontaneity and loyalty necessary for the survival and perpetuity of a festival (Ozouf 1988:126-216). Sam Gill's study of Navajo prayer shows how a ritual composition's meaning cannot be established before the performance of the ritual, but is created within the context of the ritual itself. For the Navajo, prayer is a creative performance, not merely rote or standardized words (Gill 1987:89ff). Barbara Myerhoff's fieldwork with elderly Jews in *Number Our Days* describes a variety of created rituals including the "graduation-siyum"—a ritual combining elements of an Eastern European shtetl education rite with an American high school graduation ceremony. To succeed, such a ritual must be carefully crafted, melding the two traditions so well that "the seams do not show" (Myerhoff 1978:103).

Self-consciously "created ritual" is also the subject of a plethora of popular handbooks. Guides, texts, workshops, and seminars on constructing and performing rituals are being produced by sacred and secular groups as diverse as neo-pagans, wicca, men's movements, feminist groups, New Age, and liturgical renewal programs.[3] In North America today, fieldworkers can easily observe a ritual in the making. They have the opportunity to document the choices and changes made by ritual practitioners and participants before, during, and after the performance of a ritual. The planning and generative stages of many new or emergent rituals can shock a fieldworker ill-equipped with the theoretical mechanisms necessary to work on such ritual events. Recently, a student of mine doing participant observation of a neo-pagan consecration ritual was struck by the practitioner's insistence that she take part in the actual planning and execution of the ritual itself! What ritual theory could guide her in interpreting this ritual? How could she possibly look out the ritual-as-window and enjoy the view, if she was at the same time spackling the frame and settling the window in place on the wall?

Just as scholars and fieldworkers are becoming increasingly sensitized to the changing, evolving, and compositional character of ritual, they too must become accustomed to perceiving meaning in ritual as highly individualized and constantly developing. Meaning is necessarily both subjective and subjunctive. Most anthropologists are leery of looking for multiple meanings in ritual, and for good reason. To concede that meaning is highly subjective makes it extremely elusive to fieldworkers.[4] To suggest that meaning in ritual may be as various as the number of participants in the ritual is to open up all sorts of methodological difficulties. If all informants describe the meaning of a ritual differently, how many interviews are required in order to understand the insider's view? How can one interpret meaning in ritual if no generalizations are possible? Do multiple meanings make ritual virtually meaningless by opening the door to mere subjectivism?

THE FIELDWORKER AS RITUAL CRITIC

Ritual criticism dares to cast the fieldworker in the role of critic. The participant observer should not be denied access to the aesthetic assessments, choices, and experiences that the ritual composers and participants themselves readily employ and exercise. Criticism is a fruitful stance for a fieldworker faced with a situation where meaning is splintered and ambiguous. A critic assesses, weighs, considers, addresses, and calculates amidst a plurality of possible meanings, intentions, and evaluations. Traditionally, most social scientists avoid taking on the role of a "critic" and prefer the identity of an interpreter. Critics are generally perceived to be unscientific, emotional, and manipulative. Many ethnographers might well agree with the philosopher Arnold Isenberg that critics are to be feared because they do not simply lead us to "see things . . . that we had not seen before" but may just as easily mislead us to see things "that are simply not there to be seen" (Isenberg 1973:300).

Critics are also commonly thought to be judgmental. The word critic implies one who is apt to assume a value-laden attitude or posture toward ritual, or worse, employ personal preferences and partialities in ritual analysis (Grimes 1990:15). "Critic" also suggests critique or subjective interpretation. David Best points out that subjective assessments, especially in art criticism, are perceived to be particularly suspect and useless because there are "characteristically such wide and even rationally irreconcilable differences of critical opinion about the same work of art" (Best 1985:115).

While fewer ethnographers look toward objectivity as an attainable or even a desirable goal, some anthropologists continue to defend and maintain the reliability and replicability of their social scientific methods. The detached, but informed and empathetic stance continues to be celebrated in beginning texts in cultural anthropology which enjoin students to "seek out the insider's viewpoint," allowing and inviting the "informant . . . [to] teach them the culture" (Spradley and McCurdy (eds.) 1987:14).

Richard Schechner scoffs at this presumably objective method. The anthropologist may aspire to "see with a native eye" and "feel with a native heart" but this is actually nothing more than "sugar-coat[ed] arrogance" (Schechner 1985:13). Should an anthropologist deem to determine what a native eye sees or feels? After all, what is a native or insider's eye? Is "insider" really a collective entity, a bounded cultural group? Can one ever assume that all insiders' eyes see the same thing? Do all native hearts beat as one? Can one presume that all ritual participants feel, experience, and assign an identical, singular meaning to a particular ritual event?

SUBJECTIVITY, METHODOLOGY, AND MEANING

In the past, fieldworkers took great pains to avoid injecting any overtly personal assessment and involvement into their published accounts of ritual. They learn instead how to collect and record the cultural experiences of others.

This detached ethnographic persona is becoming obsolete as anthropologists examine reflexively their role as fieldworkers. When the social analyst's own "multiple identities" are addressed and incorporated into the fieldwork equation, ambiguity and indeterminacy in other cultures becomes easier to accept. The researcher suddenly finds him/herself engaged in the task of what Renato Rosaldo calls "decentering objectivism." Anthropologists' personal experiences in the field increasingly "render obsolete the view of the utterly detached observer who looks down from on high" (Rosaldo 1989:194, 224).

This reflexive exercise is particularly relevant to "indigenes"—fieldworkers who study their own culture or ethnic group. For them, methodologies grounded in the insider/outsider dichotomy provide little theoretical direction. Nita Kumar, an "Indian doing research on India," found her own identity so crucial to her fieldwork experience among the Banaras that her monograph bears the title *Fieldwork Memoirs*. Her search for a suitable "technique, a theory, a clear-cut method" led her to embrace what she calls a "holistic project" which was simultaneously a "voyage of self-discovery" and an exhilarating exposé of the "many worlds and the shifting positions of Self/Other" (Kumar 1992:11, 17, 19). Cindy Wong, a Hong Kong native studying Vietnamese Chinese in Los Angeles, confesses similar fieldwork dilemmas and discoveries. Despite cultural and generational differences, neither she nor her subjects "looked upon one another as 'others.' Not only does her work shatter the stereotype of the "homogeneous" cultural group, but it highlights "the richness of the ethnographic experience if it is approached with a sense of reciprocity" (Wong 1989:184-185).[5]

When ethnographers explore the relational and autobiographical dimension of their fieldwork, they often describe their interactions with informants as subjective, political, and personal. Yet these same ethnographers are less apt to view their own field contact with ritual activity as highly personal—an act just as engaged, committed, and absorbing as face-to-face encounters. This means that while ethnographers increasingly personalize "the other," they still objectify their own involvement in "the other's ritual." Perhaps there needs to be a methodological shift toward what Judith Okely tentatively terms "embodied knowledge."[6] Although Okely uses the phrase primarily to refer to skills such as milking cows and plowing fields, it seems that a fieldworker's embodied knowledge might range outside mere functional labor. Fieldworkers need to elicit, confront, and relay their own aesthetic, experiential, and profound personal engagements with the various rituals they perform during the course of field research.

Some fieldworkers have documented the process of "crossing the line" of detached ritual participation. Bruce Grindal witnesses, or rather, encounters, death divination among the Sisala of Ghana. His subjective involvement in this ritual is so extraordinary that he admits his fieldwork findings are not open to "empirical verification or replication under experimentally controlled conditions" (Grindal 1983:76). His only recourse is to attest with "intuitive certainty" that his fieldwork is reliable (1983:77). Grindal's remarkable account fails to follow the "canons of anthropological thought." In the end he sacrifices conventional method in order to articulate the experience. Grindal lets his description and analysis of the divination stand on its own as an exceptional documentary:

> I felt my body become rigid. My jaws tightened and at the base of my skull I felt a jolt as though my head had been snapped off my spinal column. . . . Strands of fibrous light played upon the head, fingers, and toes of the dead man. The corpse, shaken by spasms, then rose to its feet, spinning and dancing in a frenzy. As I watched, convulsions in the pit of my stomach tied not only my eyes but also my whole being into this vortex of power. . . . Then a most wonderful thing happened. . . . The corpse picked up the drumsticks and began to play (Grindal 1983:68).

The reader, no less than Grindal, stands "trembling in the aftermath" of this riveting encounter. Witnessing the dancing corpse profoundly "wounded and sickened [his] soul" and it remains "semihidden" in his consciousness for fourteen years (Grindal 1983:76-77). Grindal concludes that the death divination is nothing less than an "experience of great passion and mystery," words metaphysically commonplace, yet seemingly out of place in many anthropological fieldwork articles!

Fieldwork like Grindal's, though uninfluenced by the directions and intentions of ritual criticism, nevertheless is performed in a similar vein. Ultimately, Grindal learns that the ritual must stand for itself. What he experiences eludes description. His own procedure escapes classification. Yet, the entire encounter is replete with meaning and consequence.

One can condemn Grindal for his unscientific foray into the Sisala supernatural, or celebrate his methodological courage. Either way, his account is one of a special genre or species of fieldwork accounts, and it is echoed by other participant observer narratives like Maya Deren's dazzling portrayal of the "white darkness" of her own spirit possession (Deren 1970:247ff), of T.M. Luhrmann's fascinating fieldwork immersion in *Persuasions of the Witch's Craft* (1989), and Karen McCarthy Brown's self-revelation through initiation in *Mama Lola: A Vodou Priestess in Brooklyn* (1991).

Anthropologists need not discard their methods and modes of inquiry in favor of the critical quest for subjective and aesthetic meaning in ritual. Ritual criticism challenges the fieldworker to experiment with new methods, and to explore ways in which individual experience and encounter with ritual may enhance and enlighten fieldwork data. New models for fieldwork which integrate and recognize the experiential power and meaning within a ritual composition will at the very least stimulate cross-disciplinary exchange, and may in the end significantly widen the scope of many existing fieldwork projects engaged in "observing meaning" in ritual.

NOTES

1. Even studies which value the transformative nature of ritual often center meaning in ritual's ability to effect personal and/or social transition, metamorphosis, and change. The works of Clifford Geertz, Arnold Van Gennep, and Victor Turner are obvious examples here.

2. For a discussion of the pedagogical nature of ritual as it relates to the transmission of meaning, see Theodore W. Jennings (1982).

3. Some representative titles are Barbara G. Walker's *Women's Rituals* (1990) and Starhawk's *Spiral Dance* (1979), both featuring rituals inspired by Goddess and wicca spirituality. A good example of created rites of passage can be found in *Betwixt and Between: Patterns of Masculine and Feminine Initiation* (Mahdi et al., 1987) and in *Engineers of the Imagination,* a volume describing rituals designed by the Welfare State International, edited by Tony Coult and Baz Kershaw (1983).

4. The emergent fields of sociology/anthropology of art and aesthetic anthropology attempt to integrate so-called subjective analytical approaches like phenomenology and aesthetics into social scientific methodology. Consult Janet Wolff's *Aesthetics and the Sociology of Art* (1983), Jacques Maquet's *The Aesthetic Experience: An Anthropologist Looks at the Visual Arts* (1986), and John Forrest's *Lord I'm Coming Home: Everyday Aesthetics in Tidewater North Carolina* (1988).

5. The social scientific literature on reflexivity varies in approach and perspective. For a discussion of the postmodern "poetics and politics" of ethnography, see the essays in James Clifford and George E. Marcus's, *Writing Culture* (1986). Several articles in Richard G. Fox's collection, *Recapturing Anthropology: Working in the Present* (1991) offer a critique of the postmodern position, as well as address the reflexive dimensions of working in one's own culture here in the United States. Another more "scientific" perspective on indigene fieldwork is *Arab Women in the Field: Studying Your Own Society,* Soraya Altorki and Camillia Fawzi El-Solh, eds. (1988).

6. Judith Okely and Helen Callaway have edited *Anthropology & Autobiography,* (1992) the result of a 1989 Association of Social Anthropologist's Meeting on the same topic. See Okely's essay on participatory experience and embodied knowledge, pp. 1-28.

BIBLIOGRAPHY

Altorki, Soraya, and Camillia Fawzi El-Solh (eds.)
    1988 *Arab Women in the Field: Studying Your Own Society.* Syracuse, NY: Syracuse University Press.

Bell, Catherine
    1992 *Ritual Theory, Ritual Practice.* New York: Oxford University Press.

Best, David
    1985 *Feeling and Reason in the Arts.* London: Allen & Unwin.

Brown, Karen McCarthy
    1991 *Mama Lola: A Vodou Priestess in Brooklyn.* Berkeley: University of
    California Press.

Clifford, James, and George E. Marcus (eds.)
    1986 *Writing Culture.* Berkeley: University of California Press.

Coult, Tony, and Baz Kershaw (eds.)
    1983 *Engineers of the Imagination.* London: Methuen.

Deren, Maya
    1970 *Divine Horsemen: Voodoo Gods of Haiti.* New York: Chelsea House.

Driver, Tom
    1991 *The Magic of Ritual.* San Francisco: Harper San Francisco.

Forrest, John
    1988 *Lord I'm Coming Home: Everyday Aesthetics in Tidewater North
    Carolina.* Ithaca: Corness University Press.

Fox, Richard G. (ed.)
    1991 *Recapturing Anthropology: Working in the Present.* Santa Fe: School of
    American Research.

Geertz, Clifford
    1987 "Interpretive Anthropology."In *Perspectives in Cultural Anthropology.*
    Herbert Applebaum (ed.) Albany, NY: SUNY Press. Pp. 520-526.

Gill, Sam
    1987 *Native American Religious Action: A Performance Approach to Religion.*
    Columbia: University of South Carolina Press.

Grindal, Bruce T.
    1983 "Into the Heart of the Sisala Experience: Witnessing Death Divination."
    Journal of Anthropological Research 39(1):60-80.

Grimes, Ronald L.
    1990 *Ritual Criticism: Case Studies in Its Practice, Essays on Its Theory.*
    Columbia, SC: University of South Carolina Press.

Gurney, Edward
    1880 *The Power of Sound.* London: Smith, Elder.

Jennings, Theodore W.
    1982 "On Ritual Knowledge."*Journal of Religion* 62(2):111-127.

Hospers, John
    1946 *Meaning and Truth in the Arts.* Chapel Hill: University of North Carolina
    Press.

Isenberg, Arnold
1973 *Aesthetics and the Theory of Criticism.* Chicago: University of Chicago Press.

Kumar, Nita
1992 *Friends, Brothers, and Informants: Fieldwork Memoirs of Banaras.* Berkeley: University of California Press.

Luhrmann, T. M.
1989 *Persuasions of the Witch's Craft.* Cambridge: Harvard University Press.

Mahdi, Louise Carus, et al.
1987 *Betwixt and Between: Patterns of Masculine and Feminine Initiation.* La Salle, IL: Open Court.

Maquet, Jacques
1986 *The Aesthetic Experience: An Anthropologist Looks at the Visual Arts.* New Haven, CT: Yale University Press.

Myerhoff, Barbara
1978 *Number Our Days.* New York: Simon & Schuster.

Okely, Judith, and Helen Callaway (eds.)
1992 *Anthropology & Autobiography.* London: Routledge.

Ozouf, Mona
1988 *Festivals and the French Revolution.* Alan Sheridan (trans.) Cambridge: Harvard University Press.

Rosaldo, Renato
1989 *Culture and Truth: The Remaking of Social Analysis.* Boston: Beacon Press.

Roskill, Mark
1989 *The Interpretation of Pictures.* Amherst: University of Massachusetts Press.

Schechner, Richard
1985 *Between Theatre and Anthropology.* Philadelphia: University of Pennsylvania Press.

Spradley, James P., and David W. McCurdy (eds.)
1987 *Conformity and Conflict: Readings in Cultural Anthropology.* Boston: Little, Brown & Co.

Starhawk
1979 *Spiral Dance.* San Francisco: Harper San Francisco.

Walker, Barbara G.
1990 *Women's Rituals.* San Francisco: Harper & Row.

Wolff, Janet
1983 *Aesthetics and the Sociology of Art.* London: George Allen & Unwin.

Wong, Cindy
1989 "Doing Fieldwork on Chinese Vietnamese in America." *Amerasia* 15(2):179-185.

2

American Eskimos Celebrate the Whale: Structural Dichotomies and Spirit Identities Among the Inupiat of Alaska

Edith Turner

The Inupiat Eskimos of northern Alaska are consciously subsistence-oriented. Even under present conditions they appear to have an unbreakable grip on subsistence hunting. Such a way of life in the far north has brought about a division of labor, the men catching animals and the women processing them. In the yearly whale festival the villagers find themselves repeating and actually accentuating their female/male divisions. Also many other patterned oppositions may be observed in the festival which in an earlier anthropological era would have been analyzed according to structuralist theory. Now in the 1990s, I argue, following Inupiaq thought, that the principle of honoring the whale overrides any analysis based on structural dichotomies. I also discover in the highly visible patterning and elaboration in the festival a *play* effect, brought into existence by what the Inupiat call the spirit of the whale. A close-up description of the proceedings is necessary to convey what is going on, and for the close-up, the wider picture is also needed.

In 1867 Alaska became part of the United States, and it has become a major vacation area for nature-loving White Americans. But what of the peoples inhabiting these lands? Their numbers are growing, but not as fast as the Whites immigrate, and thus their power lessens. Life has changed greatly for the Inupiat, not from tourism, but from government attempts at assimilation. However their way of life has persisted. They are still subsistence hunters, particularly in Point Hope where I completed a year's fieldwork from August 1987 to August 1988, also making yearly visits afterwards.

There are two high spots in the year. These are the whaling hunt in April and May, and the whaling festival in June, celebrated to honor the whales the hunters have caught.

The whaling festival lasts for three days and shows a progression from minor to major in key and a growth of excitement each day. The first day the boats are

enshrined, on the second day the frozen *muktuk* (fat with skin) of the whale's
flipper is given out, and on the third the people eat cooked whale and join in an
exuberant blanket toss. The tone is one of pleasure and a dominating "Inupiat"
character which emerges in a strong emphasis on the right kind of food preparation, the right kind of display and presentation of meat, the right clothes and
trimmings, along with various quietly circulated but centrally valued stories of
the whale hunt itself. The festival takes off as a phenomenon in its own right,
and as such has become a defensive weapon against the powers of assimilation
which emanate from the local school and state government.

INUPIAT PAST AND PRESENT

To place this festival in its context I will briefly sketch the history and
present conditions of the Inupiat in their village life. The village is located 140
miles north of the Arctic circle on the northwest tip of Alaska, on the end of a
twelve-mile-long gravel spit that points into the ocean towards Russia.   The
village is ancient, at least 2,600 years old, thus it vies for the honor of being the
oldest continuously settled center in the North American continent.
The past was cruel to the Inupiat. They suffered a long period of contact in
which commercial whaling devastated their population (from several thousand
people down to 179), and another period of missionizing which devastated their
culture. Point Hopers were taught by both influences, whalers and missions, to
fear their shamans, and indeed they began to do so. But they did not give up the
healing work that shamans used to perform. Here the response was to power
their healing with what is now known as "Eskimo spirituality," a mixture of
Christianity and shamanism.
Contact with Whites and the coming of the missions thus constituted a
threshold of change, a *limen*, in their history. However, as far as the practical
aspects of their lives were concerned, the daily work of sea and land hunting went
on much as usual on the long spit of gravel, with the addition of firearms and
supplies of store goods, which they now feel are necessities. The basic bilateral
kinship system remains, retaining adoption, namesake relationships, and clan
links, as well as divorce, with concomitant benefits in social cohesion owing to
the proliferation of links between half-siblings.
In the 1970s, after the finding of Arctic oil, further changes began, but there
were also some interesting continuities as we shall see later. The major impact
brought about by new money from oil (Rogers (ed.) 1970)—a certain small percentage of which came the way of the Inupiat whose land it was—consisted of
new housing, a big school, a clinic, and the formation of a village business corporation to invest the money allocated to Natives from the sale of oil land at $3
per acre. Crooked Whites soon battened onto the money allocated to Point
Hope, under the guise of lawyers' help and "fine investment opportunities"
which were nothing but scams, with the result that now this corporation is in

Chapter 11, neighboring on bankruptcy. An air pervades the village that is a mixture of prosperity and economic collapse. Ups and downs of mood are prevalent. The people's land and means of subsistence are continually threatened by the changing provisions of Alaska state law. Little by little they are being forced to relinquish any self-determination they managed to win (Berger 1985). Thus the setting of my essay is that of a minority community under pressure, an old modernized community but with a long memory.

At the time of writing (1992) the population has risen to about 700, of whom about thirty are White, the rest being Inupiat. I work mainly with the women, trying to absorb their way of life and join in their subsistence work. At every turn I am faced with a "natural" division of labor between the sexes, because in this hunting milieu the success and efficiency of the women's work of processing the men's catches means survival for the tribe.

THE WOMAN AND THE WHALE

Women are the bonding force that keep the culture together, and it is that culture at least as much as political pressure that is proving resistant to White hegemony. Women are particularly important during the whaling hunt. "The woman catches the whale," is the great maxim of Point Hope whaling. That is to say, without a wife there is no way a whaling captain can catch a whale. In practical terms, she recruits most of the crew, seeking among relatives for the best harpooner, the best paddlers, and the best cooks among the women. She is vital to the immense task of cutting up and storing the whalemeat. In the past she was known as the main dynamic factor in actually *bringing* the whale—it was her attraction, her shamanic sexuality, that brought the largest beast of all to the hunters. Even now, before the whaling season there is a quiet rite at the full moon. The wife takes her special bowl containing fresh water and lifts it to the moon. She calls to the moon for a whale to come. Then she hears a drop falling into her bowl. It is a tiny whale, sent from the moon in answer to her call. Now a whale will come. This was told me by two captain's wives in 1988. One early account tells how the woman was seen returning from this rite with a whale's tail emerging from her mouth—she was a shaman. The whale came to the village through her, visibly, in this vision.

Next, in the early spring the whaling captain's wife has to clean her ice cellar, a hole deep in the permafrost, and make it ready to refrigerate the new whale meat. I myself helped my neighbor to clean her ice cellar, a malodorous job, but we had to do it, for cleanliness is required by the whale. The whale is a spirit and can hear and smell everything. (Indeed I have seen its eardrum, a sensitive membrane six inches in diameter, so much better endowed than ours. Even we can hear for miles over the quiet ice.) Her house too has to be clean for the whale to come to it, and goodness must reign there. The skin she sews to cover the whaleboat has to be bleached white in sea water, for the whale loves whiteness and cleanliness. It will come and give itself willingly to those whom it judges to be worthy.

It was the woman who could bring the open water, who could open the long frozen sea ice so that a whale could swim through. She used to go down to the ice[1] with her drum and her small son. Then she found a crack in the ice, of which there were many owing to ice movement. She squatted over the crack with her son, one leg on each side of the crack, then she played her drum, and sang her own shaman song—such songs had great power. After the rite she saw the crack widen and widen, and eventually it became open water, two hundred yards wide, a mile wide, and the whale came through. Then, when the whale was sighted from the edge of the ice, she would lie down with her feet toward the water while the captain made a gesture at her with his harpoon, just touching her with it. She now walked away, and as she did so the whale was drawn irresistably after her—and towards the waiting hunters. Her title in fact was "whaling captain," *umialik*.

Once back in the house she was quiet while her husband was out on the water. And this still applies. She does few of her active tasks, remaining in a kind of trance of generous passivity, as Tom Lowenstein (n.d.) calls it, maintaining her existence in synchrony—even identity—with the whale's own "generous passivity" during the time that her husband's perfect white whaleboat steered alongside it. On May 1, 1988, the wife of a certain successful whaling captain was in the laundromat while her husband was whale hunting. Somehow she knew she must move very slowly and quietly while sorting the clothes for the wash. She *knew* this was the time. Yet it was a surprise when the news of the catch was brought to her. At a certain level the woman *is* the whale, the key to nourishment and food for a hunting people. This is concretized by Inupiat artists who frequently carve the face of a woman with a whale's tail emerging from her mouth.

When the whale is caught, the whaling captain sends to his wife the whale's flipper, the first meat cut off. In the old days they used to lower it down to her through the skylight of the sod house—an unusual means of entry, for the skylight was never used as a door save for flying shamans and spirits. But we have already noted the spirit nature of the whale. Indeed, the whale's head, the home of its spirit, is returned to the water after the body has been cut up, and thus the spirit will be able to reincarnate and come back to them in a new body.

The woman is the human link in the cosmological cycle (see also Fienup-Riordan 1983:189-235). As we have seen, "The woman catches the whale." The man says modestly enough that the whale comes to him because it likes him. The woman *is* the whale, *is* the link. The cycle goes: wild whale, the attraction of the woman, the whale's willing death, the immortality of its spirit, its reincarnation the following year, and so on around to the woman. Yet the woman does not strike at the whale. Her role in the butchering is to take the internal organs, the organs of blood, from the whale's belly and bring them under domestic processing. She takes them in the midnight twilight, privately, with her women assistants. She *is* the human connection in the cosmic cycle. The actual power of connectedness that Eskimo culture is all about finally focuses on her—that connectedness between the whaling captain, the woman, and the whale, a connectedness seen in the polysynthetic style of the language as Edna Ahgeak Maclean terms it (1980:v), also seen in the active kinship system widened by means of adoption, divorce, extra pseudokinship terms, and the concept of reincarnation, also in skin sewing, and in dancing, in healing, and the bonding of old to young through the imparting of knowledge and history.

THE WHALING FESTIVAL

In June the hunt is over and the meat is cut up and taken to the ice cellars. Now comes the whaling festival, sometimes called "the blanket toss" (*nalukataq*; see Zumwalt's able analysis published in 1987; the film *Festival of the Whale* 1976). A flurry of competitive stitching begins among the women to make new parkas and mukluk boots in honor of the occasion. Whale flesh is set fermenting in barrels. The wet meat starts to sizzle and give off sweet-sour champagne-like aromas. This food, *mikigaq*, represents another major skill of Inupiat women. Mikigaq is meat halfway between raw and cooked, and that quality is in keeping with the character of the first day of the festival, when the whale boats are dragged halfway up the beach. Together with the whipped caribou fat mixed with berries known as "Eskimo ice cream"—a frothy production—the ferment of mikigaq initiates the excitement of the festival, the blanket tossing, the throwing of candy, the spout of the whale.

All is ready and the relatives arrive by plane on the Sunday. The village attends a church service, with the accent on thanksgiving.

Early next morning, on the first day, some of the villagers visit the cemetery out towards the point to pay their respects to the dead, thus joining the past with the present, an act of braiding the past and the present of the community together.

The festival itself is an event for the clans. The two clans each have its own festival ground, called *qalgi*, situated outside the village, one on each side.

The Day of Fermented Meat

The first day is the feast of fermented meat. Here the captains' wives and their women relatives take over most of the action. Here we see a celebratory aspect of the division of labor taking form in the processing and distribution of food. Two of the three days of the festival demonstrate and celebrate this division of labor.

The men of the successful whaling crew bring their boat halfway up the beach and lift it off the sled, then take the sled and up-end it to make a stand on which to place the bow of the boat (see photograph 1). The stern is placed on boxes to raise the whole boat up level. The boat is now enshrined on pedestals. The men place the paddles upright in the triumph position of the hunt. They bring a flagpole bearing the stars and stripes, and lash it to the front of the boat. In 1988 I could see what made this particular spot on the tundra so important. At the very bow itself there lay on the gravel the skull of a whale, the part of the body in which the spirit of the whale is felt to reside. The foot of the flagpole passed through the front and back holes of this peculiar skull. The people saw this as honoring the whale. The boat now looked gallant, with paddles upright, the flag active in the wind, the boat itself raised on high, the whole linked to the spirit chamber of the skull below—the men had achieved a kind of apotheosis of the boat. The enshrinement united boat and equipment and whale together along with the past, present, and future acts of those particular crewmen—the future because the whale was pleased by the festival and would come again to them the following year.

In front of the boat the men laid boards, on which the captain's wife and her women relatives placed wooden barrels of mikiyaq fermented meat. This was the day for mikiyaq, ripened now by its five-day processing, an ephemeral food that would keep no longer than five days. Doughnuts, coffee in large thermoses, Koolaid, and cupcakes were also ready. The whaling captain's wife took her place in the center and made a short prayer of gratitude for their whale. The preacher prayed. Then a swirl of people came forward from each side and seated themselves in two half moons in front of the boat, visitors to the left and locals to the right. At once the crew women commenced to feed the people, starting with the fermented meat, serving it with their hands (see Zumwalt 1987:266). They distributed the meat with gestures halfway between care and abandon, commencing with the elders, then their own crew, then the helpers, then the entire clan and visitors. The guests opened up plastic bags to receive the meat. Someone lent me a plastic bag too. Soon we were all taking mouthfuls from our plastic bags and licking our fingers appreciatively. A round of doughnuts followed, then quickly coffee and Koolaid. The ritual feast was soon over.

The Day of Frozen Meat

The second day was the day of the flippers. It celebrated a different type of formality. It took place at the festival ground itself, an area of stony flower-covered tundra set with gigantic whale jawbones making an entrance at one end and with bone markers forming a square inside. The men arrived with their Honda ATVs pulling up the four boats of the successful crews. The boats were now all the way up from the shore. The men lined them up, not on pedestals this time but tilted over lengthways on their sides, placed end to end, with paddles erected at the bow of each boat. These boats were set up as shelters from the wind in front of which the whaling captains could sit, places representing those most

1. Day One: Crewmen draw their boat halfway up to the festival ground and set it upon the skull of a bowhead whale. Photograph by Bill Hess.

corresponding to the captains' place on the sea. I could see a theme of correspondence throughout the whaling festival—all was very close to the actual sea event of the catching of the whale, but the festival was not that event, it was its likeness on land—a symbol, of course, a major one (Zumwalt 1987:272). But as we shall see there were many odd things about it as a symbol. The word "*qagruk*," the people's word for the festival, means literally, "arrow," as if it were something that flies off above everything on its own, once projected. A related word, *qagga*, means "outside," "away."[2] Just outside the entrance of the *qalgi* grounds, marked by the whale jawbone arches set as an entranceway, the whaling equipment was enshrined for all to see, albeit casually enshrined. In higgledy-piggledy piles lay grub boxes, big orange floats, ropes, sheaves of long-handled knives and choppers and hooks for the cutting process, and the harpoons themselves with the barrels attached, now empty of bomb and barb. Under those things could be seen several bloody newly-cut jawbones, each more than ten feet long, one from each newly caught whale. These in turn had been heaped on top of other jawbones from previous seasons, so that the place constituted a history of Point Hope's whaling for years back,[3] with the present uppermost. Very close to all the now sacralized equipment were parked a large number of Honda ATVs belonging to the participants.

Men on Hondas now approached, drawing behind them sleds with huge frozen slabs of the best meat of all, the raw frozen muktuk fat and skin of the whale flipper, the tail itself (that which merges the shaman woman and the whale), which they unloaded onto plywood sheets in the center of the festival ground. It was the men who cut this meat into slices. They were reproducing the original scene of the butchering of the whale, where the men cut up the muktuk meat and the women the internal organs. Those organs would be served next day. Now young women were arriving with large metal bowls containing Eskimo ice cream, made from berries whipped up with caribou fat and flavored with seal oil. Everything today was frozen, not fermented nor cooked. Pilot bread (cracker) was ready to serve with the "ice cream," which seemed to me more of a savory dip than a dessert.

The captains moved forward and occupied their fur-covered seats in the boat-shelters. Each boat sheltered its own crew. In each sat the captain, harpooner, older crewmen, and one or two honored men guests. No women or children occupied the boat shelters at this stage.

Then came the distribution of the flipper. One of the captains had caught his first whale that season and it was his privilege to start the distribution (see photograph 2). This was formal. He called a name, and the recipient came forward—there was no rushing about. Individual names were called, and these were Inupiat names where possible. The individual then walked forward to the whaling captain, took the muktuk flipper gift from his hand, licked the muktuk, and walked back to her place with it. It seemed that at this point, the point of greatest distribution, when everyone without exception was to receive some muktuk, there took place a reversal of this general inclusiveness from the general to the

2. Day Two: Day of the flippers. The whaling captain calls the name of one of his helpers, who will approach and receive a slice of raw whale flipper. Photograph by Bill Hess.

particular. First, that small piece of specialty whale possessed the value of the whole whale. Then each special person was part of the whole village, confirmed and consolidated in her special Inupiaq place. The individual had to take an active step to qualify for this slotting into the collective pattern. There had to be a response by an act of will to this call. The call was from the generosity of the whale. The eating was a communion with the spirituality of the whale, and at the same time an acceptance of assigned membership.

To whom did the captain first present the muktuk? To the *women healers.* And why to them? Tracing the meaning of healing in Inupiat eyes it is very clear that this gift was recognized as the highest gift of the Inupiat, deriving from the now "unmentionable" past of shamanism. The festival dared to recognize healing because it was of obvious benefit to all—now that it had become Christianized and beyond the taboos of the Whites.[4]

Then came the blanket toss. It was the duty of the captain who had caught his first whale to offer the skin from his own boat to make the blanket. Therefore the men took the sealskin hull off his boat and spread it out on the ground. They cut through the hard dry skin and re-sewed it to make it into a square. It was certainly a man's job to cut that iron-hard hide. The sewing was done with an awl, not a needle which was the instrument of the women. The act of making holes with the awl and poking a point of thick sinew thread through the hole provoked various sexual jokes. "Ever heard of a *sperm* whale?" They shook with laughter. They sewed the two pieces together into one blanket twelve feet square. Then they fitted rope handles all around the sides.

Now the people were gathering to the center of the *qalgi* ground. The stronger ones came forward and grasped the rope handles, while at the back the drummers seated before their boats commenced the tossing songs. Soon there was an entire square of people beginning to tug on the rope handles making the blanket rise and fall, rise and fall. Now there was a jostle and the whaling captain climbed onto the blanket and went into the middle. Everyone called out, "One! Two! Three!"—then they gave an enormous tug and he went flying into the air stiff-legged—he was not actually jumping but was lifted by the propulsion of forty pairs of hands (see photograph 3). There was laughter and a scream of joy at his ascent. He rose high up aloft in his brilliant blue captain's parka, levitated and dancing upon the blue sky with his legs, a big man, supremely happy. Then the Whump! of the fall. He was still on his feet, head up in triumph. His wife went onto the blanket next, carrying a large paper bag full of candy for her to scatter. This was because she was the mother of a little boy. When up high, her bounty would be thrown out. It reminded me of the whale's spout. There were so many links—woman to whale to maleness. They tossed her, and as she rose she contrived to tear open the bag and fling the contents everywhere. There was a rush of elders—now was their chance, for only the elders were allowed to grab this flying candy. I myself, being an elder, rushed for candy too, and lost many a chance for a treat. In desperation I finally sat down on three wrapped pieces—and even then old Lydia tried to grab them from under

3. The blanket toss. Photograph by Bill Hess.

me. We were roaring with laughter. I did get my three pieces. Meanwhile it was the healer's turn on the blanket, then young men turning somersaults, then all and sundry including me, and I disgraced myself by falling over.

The Day of Cooked Meat

The last day was the cooking feast. It can be seen how as the days of the festival progressed, the scale of group adherence grew wider and wider, until by the final dance at the end of the third day the whole village was united. The cooking feast was marked by a division of women and men spatially, the women at their outdoor cooking stoves and the men celebrating in front of their tilted-up canoes. Again general liberality was the mood.

The women took their full whaling-camp equipment to the festival ground, particularly the stoves which had once stood inside the tents down on the ice. Now the stoves were set up on the land with their chimneys anchored by wire. The whaling captains' wives got busy cooking whale internal organs and meat, all kinds of game, and doughnuts (see photograph 4). The girls were soon taking bowls containing hundreds of cooked meat portions, along with doughnuts and coffee to the crowd. We stuffed ourselves that afternoon until we could eat no more.

The blanket toss continued, and the festival finally ended with an all-village Inupiat dance in the school gymnasium (see photograph 5). It was notable how the members of erstwhile hostile factions sat together amicably in the drumming row. Here food was presented, not on a clan basis, but to everybody.

Late in the night the equipment at the grounds was retrieved and the portable John taken away. All was quiet in the low sunlight of the tundra save the rustling of garbage around the tall bones.

A STRUCTURAL ANALYSIS OF THE FESTIVAL?

As an experiment I will recapitulate the event in terms that emphasize structural markers.

After the *spring* whaling in the *sea* is over the boats are pulled up in *summer* onto the *land*, the festival ground. The paddles, once used in the sea *below*, are set *up above*. *Men* occupy the *center* of the ground with their boats which it had been essential to keep *level* on the sea; now they are *upturned*. *Women* occupy the *periphery*. *Raw* whale parts are served by the *men, calling individuals to them*. *Cooked* and *fermented* whale parts are served by *women, approaching the crowds* to do it. The boat *skin*, sewn by *women* when *wet*, is taken off the boat *frame* which was made by *men*. The skin, now *dry*, is sewn by *men* to make the blanket. The skin of the blanket was formerly designed to keep the hunters *safe*,

4. Day Three: Day of the cooking. A whaling captain's wife cooks meat for the crowd. Photograph by Bill Hess.

5. The elders drum and sing for the dancers. Photograph by Bill Hess.

down on the surface of the *sea*, now it is used to provide a spice of *danger*, tossing people *up* in the *air*.

Note the oppositions:

spring/summer
sea/land
below/above
men/women
center/periphery
level/upturned
raw/cooked and fermented
individuals/crowd
frame/skin
dry/wet
safety/danger
sea/air
down/up

It looks as if the division of labor had been celebrated in every aspect of the symbolism of this festival, as if a crystallization of binary discriminations had gone to the extreme.

I tried to discuss these oppositions with my Inupiat consultants, Ernest Frankson, my friend Jim and his wife, and Annie. But there were no takers. The list of oppositions, especially "women and men," and "sea and land," didn't seem to matter to them. But when I repeated what I had learned from them about honoring the whale, they warmed to me.

So, essentially, the structuralist theory did not suit the Inupiat. Nor did an interpretation of the festival as an act of opposition to the Whites as such, though nationalist Inupiat knew they needed to resist the encroachments of the Whites and guard their culture so that the whale would continue to be honored— a rather different way of looking at it.

It could be argued that I did not consult with the people about their own kinship structures, that is, who was "high" or "low" in the local hierarchy. Would not the elders be happy to term themselves "high," would not the men claim they stood for the right hand and the women for the weaker left? That would not work either, because no subsistence member in Point Hope is in authority. For example, in the skin-sewing group that was organized to stitch the boat hull, in no way does even the oldest woman put herself in authority over the others, nor do any of them. As regards male and female, the ubiquitous adage, "the woman catches the whale," and the obvious equality of a woman like my friend Annie, did not seem to uphold the "women are the weaker" theory.

Honoring the whale, then—what is entailed in that? Are we able to map out a theory which the Inupiat themselves might recognize? And further, should we stop at "Inupiat theory"? Is there some theory of our own that might be inspired enough to bridge the gap between the two cultures—like the shaman crossing his precarious bridge?

First, for matters that the Inupiat would recognize at once, such as the values that are sought before and during the festival. Which issues most engaged the participants? First and foremost, *giving*, the ability to feed the village until it was absolutely satiated. Then sewing a fine parka, and the particular quality of the *mikiyaq* and doughnuts; for the men, the unboasted fact of having brought in whales, due not to them but to the spiritual intent of the whale and the excellence of their wives. Then their daring at the blanket toss, and afterwards the exactness and address of their dancing. The quality of each particular whale as food and the skill in the processing came to the fore again and again. And behind all that, the story of the catching of each animal—such a story goes around the village and is quietly savored.

But the whaling festival took off in a curious way that seemed to go beyond these concerns. Those curious binary distinctions noted above were actually there, to be seen on the ground, and were interesting however much the Inupiat appeared to discount them.

Let us start by calling the phenomenon "structuralism as play," not of law. Perhaps "the game of form." Structure as law, as Victor Turner said, may become pathological and even break open into cruelty. As art it is joyous, freely elaborating, exuberant, the apparent opposite of itself. This kind of elaboration is germane to the genre of play, in fact, originates in it. The whaling and the festival show it. Both are to do with superabundance, with the Rabelaisian whale on a Gargantuan scale. The same fascination with superabundance and with pattern is seen in other cultures: in the baroque in Western art and in Mexican Churriguaresque, in the shaman's curlicues carved in ancient Ipiutaq spiral motifs and in the crowns of the old shaman kings of Korea, in Apache sand paintings, Huichol wool paintings, and Aztec codices, in the *veve* arabesque floor designs of Voodoo and the *riscado* floor sketches of Brazilian Umbanda, in African circumcision masks, and in all the extraordinary extravaganzas of oriental art. So much is complex exuberant jollification. One might indeed capture this "structure," so-called, for "communitas" and get it drunk or mad, like Bottom or Malvolio.

Thus I was indeed able to regard the Qagruq as a festival that throws up binary discriminations indiscriminately, as many festivals do. Let us start, like the Inupiat, from the original spirit of the whale. The meaning that flows from the whale, then, spins off elaborations of structural significance, scintillating, refracting, rearranging, or inverting sometimes, developing something corresponding to verbal and grammatical and logical form, creating neat kaleidoscopic paired effects of not only binary but sextuple, multiple mirrorings. These are focused and fall into place where only the rough outlines are found in everyday society and nature. The whole village sees its women on one side, and the men on the other, where these are so often mingled in everyday life. It sees the elders gathered and feeds them first, while the young serve them: old and young. The difference between sea and dry land is of the very essence in this festival, it is a matter here of the very flowery ground beneath one's feet, not just good to think in the mind, but experienced in the body. Why would you need to *talk* about it all? You show your joy by simply rushing to Qagruq, you are *doing* the whale and its coming. And the matters of "high/low," the upright paddles, the blanket toss—these are in keeping with the culmination of the year. These are ephemeral phenomena coming into existence and fading away again, part of the special character of celebration but not ruling principles, absorbed in the spirituality of the whale and the connectedness of all things, expressed in healing, the language, the kinship system. As for the nature/culture distinction, it appears that the Inupiat celebrate exactly the opposite of any such distinction, they celebrate something like Lucien Levy-Bruhl's law of mystical participation by which all things, natural, human, and especially in this case those things carved out of ivory, things created, have a spirit. There is no culture/nature distinction. This is a fundamental matter and takes us out of the realm of psychology and logical laws to the realm of the spirit and even play. It takes us, furthermore, out of the realm of metaphor because Qagruq is not held in order to *represent* the whale, but to actually honor it. We have to get to the nitty-gritty. Victor Turner approached the essence of celebrations by showing us the nature of a liminal ritual—in which anything can happen, when participants indulge in the oddity of extremes and contrasts and pairings and reflexive discriminations that are fun for fun's sake, anything but "structural." They are *loved*, not *feared*, not ordered from above but indulged in from below, positively relished; explored and elaborated, not immutably ordered and dreaded. Each year the mikiyaq could be different. The ferment is alive, the whole festival bubbles up like a long-expected geyser from the depths. It *transpires*, to use Ron Grimes' phrase about true ritual.

One can't avoid the mikiyaq, slobbery, carnal, delicious; getting it out of the barrel is like a hand exploring sex, it is black and odorous, flavored with a bouquet that is something between champagne and fish. The flags are gallant in the stiff breeze, each designating a whale. (The big forward dipping movement of the hand that everyone in the village has been making also signifies the whale.) The boats are raised painstakingly on Day One, literally enshrined with their paddles erect, revered in the liminal halfway place. The boats are not yet fully advanced to the festival grounds, but are hailed at this stage with the mikiyaq food, by women whose hands rummage in deep bloody buckets. Then on Day Two the boats are taken to the place of the jawbones, four square, in pairs, framing the sky. All the tundra is now patterned with sky-marking upright motifs—flags; boats on their sides in a hedge barrier (not a pressure ridge of ice this time); paddles upright, whale bones upright, stove chimneys upright and wired into position, there for outdoor cooking, not indoors, not in the village, not on the ice nor the ocean. On Day Two there is raw frozen fat with its skin, the best of the muktuk. On Day Three the women cook heart, stomach, intestines, and kidneys, blobby objects in a big mass, soft "women's" organs, feeding everybody. Then there is the making of the blanket out of sealskin, dry this time, not wet as it was when originally fitted on the boat; punctured with awls and fastened together with thongs, not sewn wet with cunning halfway sewing in two adjacent rows for waterproofness. Now, firmness for the blanket is essential, male firmness and strength. Next it is the time of the men and captains, the drummers, and the leapers tossed by the hands of the inner core of the village, the tossers. And this is fun, not on the Chukchee Sea but on the tundra, land. There, the waves tossed, now there are human-made waves. The leapers are happy, intelligent, with that bit of daring in a danger that they have created, not under the rule of necessity.

We see an increase of domesticity at the festival, but none of it is ordinary domesticity. The cooking scene is a replica of ice-camp life, the nomadic hunter's world, not the world of the house. The women use the same stove and pipe as down on the ice, except that the pipe is anchored with wire, just as the tent was anchored with rope to enormous chunks of ice; the same pots and pans, the same Coleman stoves, and doughnuts made in the same way.

The whaling feast is the elaborate distillation of connectedness. Sea matters have been brought *to* the land, the whale is literally incorporated *into* the people. All those particular elements of the festival—the personalities newly highlighted by the calling of names, the kaleidoscopic ornamentation of parkas, the odd regularities of custom—are brought together and finally united in the last all-village dance where all partake of the whale.

Is this a legitimate way to describe it? The fact that the people do not think in such literary terms is a difficulty. Is there a legitimate style, a people's style? Would such a style resemble the productions of the Commission on History, Language, and Culture at the North Slope Borough, Barrow, which consist of literal transcriptions of Inupiat stories, a kind of folklore? Is the private world of the anthropologists[5] an illegitimate enterprise, with its structuralism, processualism, postmodernism, critical anthropology, political correctness, deconstructionism, radical empiricism, interculturalism, terms which seem estranged from the big crowd, the events, and the laughter? I have only looked at what I could see and become carried away by it. The people themselves are totally enthusiastic about their festival—that we have in common.

Still, we anthropologists have eaten the apple of Eden and like it, and will go on eating it.

Where the views do converge is in the maintenance of the culture itself. The people themselves choose whom to honor at the festival. They honor the healers, and the elders, those who are most Inupiat. The festival anchors the culture, and the culture anchors the Inupiat and ensures their persistence.

I do not term this "analysis," nor just "meaning," but the reporting of fact and experience at a different level. At Qagruq the whale comes; it comes to the whole village through the agency of the women and men. It comes to the land. That is why the people are tossed on the boat skin, leaping higher than anything else on land, because the whale has come. *It*, the whale, is leaping. It organizes and reorganizes everything, it particularizes, distinguishes, focuses, gives coherence like the holograph made by a laser beam. It breaks out in dancing. As the Inupiat say, if they respond and dance, the animals come to them. Then the circle of the cosmos moves, it circulates. Adding this spirit element is like adding the square root of minus one to certain mathematical problems: everything becomes plain and the equation works out.

NOTES

My thanks are due to my sponsors, the Wenner-Gren Foundation for Anthropological Research and the University of Virginia, and also to James and Mary McConnell. I am particularly grateful to Dorcus Rock, Rosella Stone, Ernest Frankson, Dina Frankson, Molly Oktollik, and Rex and Piquk Tuzroyluk, who were my guides and educators in their different ways. I thank Theodore Mala, Rosita Worl, Lori Krumm, Karlene Leeper, Ann Riordan, and others, who assisted the research plan at various stages. The people of Point Hope gave me unstinting help and affection which I remember with gratitude.

1. Personal communication from an Inupiaq woman consultant, a fervent member of the Assembly of God.
2. As in the Messenger Feast where arrows are fired by the hosts over the heads of the messenger guests, projecting hostility *away* from them.
3. Mollie Oktollik could name the source of each jawbone and the year the animal was caught.
4. Maniilaq, the Eskimo health and cultural organization of the Northern Alaska Native Association, NANA, at Kotzebue, claimed that of all the genres of Inupiat culture, indigenous healing most fully represented that culture.
5. I quote James Provenzano's article, "Two Views of Ethnicity": The structural functionalist position of many social scientists puts them:

> at odds with advocates seeking to alter the life situation of ethnic minority groups in America. . . . As ethnic groups combine to concern themselves with the development of ethnic consciousness as an adjunct to organization it becomes ever more necessary that social scientists make every effort to comprehend and incorporate the use of ideology by particular groups into the analytic tools devised to deal with these observed phenomena (1976: 386).

> Social scientists whether Durkheimian, Marxist, or some other stripe, are being ignored by ethnic minorities not because we are racists or bigots, but because we are irrelevant to their problems (1976:400).

BIBLIOGRAPHY

Berger, Thomas R.
   1985 *Village Journey: The Report of the Alaska Native Review Commission.*
   New York: Hill and Wang.

Festival of the Whale
   1976 Videotape. KUAC Productions, Anchorage.

Fienup-Riordan, Ann
   1983 *The Nelson Island Eskimo: Social Structure and Ritual Distribution.*
   Anchorage: Alaska Pacific University Press.

Lowenstein, Tom
   n.d. *Ancient Land: Sacred Whale.*   mimeograph.

Maclean, Edna Ahgeak
   1980 *Abridged Inupiaq and English Dictionary.*   Fairbanks: Alaska Native
   Language Center, University of Alaska.

Provenzano, James
   1976 "Two Views of Ethnicity."   In *Ethnicity in the Americas.*   Francis Henry
   (ed.)   Hague: Mouton.   Pp. 305-404.

Rogers, George W. (ed.)
   1970 "Change in Alaska: The 1960s and After."   In *People, Petroleum, and
   Politics.*   20th Alaska Science Conference, 1969, University of Alaska. College,
   Alaska: University of Alaska Press.   Pp. 3-14.

Zumwalt, Rosemary Levy
   1987 "The Return of the Whale: Nalukataq, the Point Hope Whale Festival."   In
   Time Out of Time, Essays on the Festival.   Allesandro Falassi (ed.) Albuquerque:
   University of New Mexico Press.   Pp. 261-275.

3

Sauerkraut and Souvlakia: Ethnic Festivals as Performances of Identity

John M. Coggeshall

To outsiders, ethnic festivals all look alike. Rows of booths offer savory foods to families enjoying an afternoon meal under brightly colored awnings. Groups of young teens, dressed in unusual costumes, dance in strange steps to music unfamiliar to audiences, who applaud enthusiastically for the performers. By the end of a long weekend for the organizers, bills have been paid and booths dismantled. A good time has been had by all, and functionally oriented researchers observe that both ethnic identity and sponsors' coffers have been enriched as a result.

The generic festival I have just described could have been hosted by virtually any Euro-American ethnic group in the United States, and it rather generally depicts two specific events I have studied: those of a German-American and a Greek-American group. Although quite similar in some ways, these festivals also differ. It is through a comparison and contrast that we can see how, and in what ways, these festivals express the ethnic identity of their hosts. In effect, a festival is a drama which must be interpreted carefully in order to discover its meanings. This paper describes two such performances and examines the ways in which ethnic groups utilize festivals to present, enhance, and protect their cultural identity.

Much of the anthropological work on social phenomena as drama has been initiated by Victor Turner (although see Goffman 1967, for example). These performances may take several forms, from religious rituals to even theater in modern societies (Turner 1986:42). In theater as in other performances, one finds linked together sacred and secular, dance, song, architectural symbolism, ritualized feasting and drinking, and the enacting of mythic or heroic plots drawn from oral tradition (1986:42). Ethnic festivals, of course, contain precisely these same elements, and thus may be as socially powerful as other, more sacred or more formal, social performances.

But there is a significant difference between the somber formality of a Roman Catholic Good Friday Mass and the jovial informality of an ethnic festival. Don Handelman clarifies the distinctions, proposing a category of public events he terms "events that present the lived-in world" (Handelman 1990:42). Celebrations such as parades and festivals, while not as solemn as religious rituals, are still highly effective conveyors of social meaning. A festival, for example

> holds up a mirror to social order, selectively reflecting versions of the latter. . . . Such events . . . assert the determinacy of the significance they close and enclose; and so they are given over wholly to the making of expressive meanings through interpretation (Handelman 1990:48).

More precisely, festivals express a group's identity as the community offers to an often enthusiastically appreciative audience various elements of its culture in a patently obvious manner. In other words, groups consciously select from a number of identifiers those which they feel most, or best, typify themselves. Ethnic foods, folk dances, and traditional music all openly display elements of a group's identity familiar both to insiders and outsiders (see Kalcik 1984:38). Food, in fact, serves as "an ideal vehicle for symbolic elaboration" because of its flexibility (Van Esterik 1982:207-208). By means of these symbols, both observers and participants obtain a sample of what the group itself defines as intrinsic to its identity.

These symbolic elements reveal an identity by their deliberate presentation during the festival. Groups, Turner (1982:14) noted, use performances to celebrate themselves. Such social dramas increase group excitement, which in turn creates a sense of enhanced attention to the meanings of the symbols displayed at the ceremony (MacAloon 1984:9-10). Thus, through the use of symbols, festivals become "powerful vehicles for the expression of the group priorities" (Esman 1982:199). As symbols are collectively shared by the group, they provide a feeling of unity "so essential to a sense of belonging and community" (Scourby 1984:64). In effect, groups directly advertise and strengthen themselves through the presentation of symbols during ethnic festivals.

Groups also advertise and reinforce themselves in more subtle ways as well. As Turner (1982:11) reminds us, one must examine the meaning behind the form, the "inner significance of the object" (1982:11). Ethnic traits presented at festivals not only demarcate groups, but their juxtapositioning with alternate traits increases the power of their symbolic messages. The contrast between "our" traditions and "their" traditions imbues ethnic characteristics with an additional dimension of symbolic meaning (Van Esterik 1982:220; see also Rauche 1988:214). These symbols gain in significance as identifiers as they are compared, either deliberately or unintentionally, to the attributes of outsiders.

However, certain traits become even more symbolically important as ethnic identifiers because they occur specifically within the specialized time of a festival (Kapferer 1979:13). Such symbols have a positional meaning; that is, they draw some of their eloquence from the context in which they occur (Turner 1982:21). Thus polka dancing or beer drinking, for example, as behaviors in themselves, are not necessarily ethnic. But, within the boundaries of a festival, these activities become imbued with new and highly significant meanings for both insiders and outsiders; in effect, they now help to define an identity.

Besides the deliberate presentation and/or manipulation of symbols to express an identity, groups may also keep certain aspects of themselves private. In other words, groups offer a facade of cultural elements which they consciously choose to present to others as an expression of their own identity, and which others interpret contextually in a variety of ways. Equally important, however, are those symbols of identity which emically are considered definitive (or embarrassing—see Errington 1987:655), but which are nevertheless kept hidden from the prying view of outside. . The screen of ethnic traits presented at a festival represents a "safe" or "correct" view of a group's identity. The fact that the group considers some symbols too valuable to present in public also helps define the group.

Ultimately, festivals as rituals not only present or manipulate symbols but they also change their participants as well. By rearranging space, time, and cultural symbols, festivals create a liminal period (Turner 1969:94-111), a subjunctive mood separate from the indicative mood of normal social activity (Turner 1986:41-42). Persons entering this time are transformed by the power of the ritualized removal (Turner 1985:16), even if only temporarily (Kapferer 1979:14). Thus, ethnic festivals not only define the identities of their participants, but they also reaffirm them as well. It is indeed possible to "be Greek for a weekend" on several levels.

Complicating the interpretation of the presentation and performance of ethnic identity at a festival is the varied sophistication of the audience. At typical festivals, the observers consist of both insiders and outsiders, who may read an entirely different interpretation into aspects of the event. This means that symbols unveiled during these performances speak on several levels: some will be obvious to both members and non-members; some will be apparent to insiders but not to outsiders; some will be understood by visitors but overlooked by locals; and some symbols will remain hidden from view entirely. Ethnic festivals, to successfully convey a group's sense of identity, must speak to all constituencies in a wide variety of ways.

The systematic analysis of a festival, then, involves a "thick description" of such an event (Geertz 1973:7-10). The ethnographer must consider the presence or absence of cultural symbols, the power of the performance context to transform those symbols into meaningful elements, the multivocality of those symbols for varied audiences, and the diversity of the audiences interpreting the per-

formance. These general observations will be applied to a discussion of the ethnic festivals of two Euro-American groups.

OVERVIEW

The Germans arrived in the Midwest primarily in the nineteenth century and
have assimilated but have not completely acculturated (see Coggeshall
forthcoming). In Southwestern Illinois, they remain primarily residents of small
farming communities and represent several different religious traditions,
primarily Roman Catholic and Lutheran (various synods). To this day, the
landscape of southwestern Illinois still displays an ethnic character, expressed by
place names such as New Baden and Germantown, the host community.

In contrast, the Greeks arrived in upstate South Carolina relatively recently,
and so retain a great deal more vivid recollections of the "Old Country" (Scourby
1984:51-53, citing Boyd 1948; see also Saloutos 1964:386). Residents of a
large urban center along an industrializing interstate corridor, the Greeks of
Greenville do not reside in an ethnic neighborhood. Nevertheless they all share
the common bonds of their language, heritage, and religion.

Information for this article has been gathered through various means. I
attended the Spassfest at Germantown, Illinois, during the summer of 1985, and
have collected additional data on similar festivals during fieldwork throughout the
mid-1980s (Coggeshall 1988, 1992). For the past three Septembers I have attended the Greek festivals in Greenville, and have collected additional data
through interviews with participants and community residents.

SPASSFEST IN GERMANTOWN

Spassfest has been held for the past twenty-three years in Germantown, a rural community about forty miles due east of St. Louis, Missouri. The weekend
festival takes place on several baseball diamonds at the edge of town, within easy
view of a state highway. Carnival rides and game booths adjoin two huge beer
tents from which beer is sold on both Saturday and Sunday. Despite the fact that
the festival is sponsored by the Roman Catholic parish of St. Boniface (virtually
synonymous with the entire town), nearly everyone drinks beer, mostly brands
provided from area breweries.

To the west of the ever-popular beer tents lie an equally-large bingo awning
and a permanent pavilion with picnic tables, where food is sold. The male
volunteers from the parish cook and serve bratwurst, knockwurst, German potato
salad (served warm, with a vinegar-based dressing), applesauce, and sauerkraut.
Large families of three and four generations gather to dine and drink together in
the shade and to enjoy the nearby entertainment.

In front of the larger beer tent is a stage upon which the main bands perform, with room for public dancing between the tent and bandstand. The band plays a medley of songs, among which are typical German ones, such as polkas or schottisches. Other songs, although sung in English, continue folksong traditions from generations past. Even some of the band names themselves sound German: one could not mistake the "Germantown Boomkessel Band," for example, for a country-western group.

Senior citizens, families, and friends enjoy the German *Gemutlichkeit*, while children of all ages attempt the games of chance and challenge the rides. Several men parade their ethnicity for the entire crowd: one wears an authentic costume brought by a relative from Austria (he claimed), while another wears non-functional black suspenders bearing "Spassfest" written in red spangles. The smells of bratwurst and beer mingle with the sounds of laughter and the bingo-caller's drone under a cloud-studded blue August sky. For the weekend at least, the community becomes an enthusiastically real "German town."

To both residents and visitors alike, Germantown's Spassfest is obviously a German festival. From the caricatured figures on the brochure to the festival emblem (in the shape of a beer stein), certain symbols of ethnicity are openly presented during this performance. Beer, bratwurst, and sauerkraut, for example, are emically and etically definite German foods. Polkas and other songs reflect an obvious heritage, too. Finally, the exaggerated costumes of the musicians and several parishioners announce to all the festival's ethnic sponsor.

While these elements are obvious to both Germans and non-Germans alike, Germans interpret some of these same traits on a deeper level as well. Food, beer, and dancing formed in the past an integral part of German social activities, and today, German-Americans still define these as essential for an enjoyable gathering with family and friends. Thus it is no coincidence that beer drinking and polka music would be found at Spassfest; they would still be found at every local German-American private party, especially wedding receptions. Likewise, the presence of extended families means little to outsiders, but to the rural Roman Catholic Germans, large families reflect their own views of social solidarity and continuity. Finally, the neatness of the town and the orderliness of the festival grounds proclaim for Germans a deep-seated pride in their community.

Other items presented at Spassfest, though, are emically insignificant. However, to outsiders, they speak volumes about German ethnic identity. The residents of St. Boniface's parish, for example, no longer consider religion as a defining characteristic. However, the apparently inconsequential announcement about Sunday Masses on the brochure proclaims to outsiders what is to them a definitive component of the identity of the town and its people. More subtle still is language, or, more accurately, dialect. The German language has not served as an ethnic marker for several decades, and so to insiders this aspect of their identity has been lost. However, most residents, particularly the older ones, still use a distinct dialect, readily recognizable as "Dutchy" to non-

Germans (Coggeshall 1988). Merely by speaking, then, Germantown's residents express an identity as German-Americans.

Perhaps the most indirect etic interpretation of a symbol stems from the outsiders' perceptions of the entire community. To residents, Germantown simply looks normal (albeit clean). Outsiders, of course, already associate fastidiousness with a German identity, and thus the orderliness of Germantown only emphasizes and exaggerates this trait. As one non-resident commented, Germantown appeared to be so neat that even grass seemed forbidden to grow between the cracks of the sidewalks. Emically normal perceptions may become etically ethnic characteristics.

Not all signifiers of ethnic identity, however, are presented during this festival. The community recognizes some as significant and yet chooses to keep these private and hidden. For example, the Germans define themselves as a group in part through stereotypes, both of themselves and of neighboring groups. Thrift and conservatism are seen as positive emic values, while frugality and stodginess are their contrasts (as expressed by non-Germans). While Germans view these positive traits as intrinsically self-definitive, they nevertheless do not consciously display these values at their festivals.

"BE A GREEK FOR A WEEKEND"

In many ways the grounds of St. George's Greek Orthodox church resemble a stage, and this is not coincidental. Located within the space created by the church, the Hellenic Center, the dining area, and a row of food booths, the Greek festival links food, dance, culture, and religion into a deliberate whole. Audiences consist of parishioners and visitors, all of whom participate in the dances and consume the food. Held to benefit the church's building fund, the three-day festival ends on Sunday evening, to the disappointment of baklava-stuffed outsiders and to the relief of exhausted volunteers.

The festival offers numerous introductions to, or refreshers of, Greek culture. For example, along one wall in the parish center's gymnasium are exhibits of Greek costumes and artifacts from the Old Country, as well as small booths selling locally made crafts. Along the opposite wall winds the food line, offering Greek dishes and assorted drinks: iced tea (served pre-sweetened with every Southern afternoon or evening meal) and beer or wine for a small price. Along the back wall lies the focus of the festival for many people: the dessert table, packed with numerous types of delicious, home-made sweets.

On the bottom floor of the parish center, other activities take place. Here the community offers Greek-language instruction to parish children. In one unlocked classroom, primary-level flash cards and brightly colored posters explain the Greek alphabet and terms for colors. In two other rooms, videos depicting modern Greece and classical Greek art and architecture are shown to visiting audiences. A larger room has a small gallery of paintings of Greece, a long table of imported Greek foods from a local supermarket, a display of jewelry and clothes (all for sale); and a small presentation area for hourly cooking demonstrations. Audiences also get to consume the results.

Offered continuously throughout the weekend are tours of St. George's church, partly to explain an unfamiliar Christian doctrine to Protestant neighbors, but also to deliberately connect Greek culture and religion. The curious enter and sit in the pews, while on the altar "stage" one of the parish priests explains Orthodox theology and its reflection in the church's architecture. Afterwards, the visitors (mostly Southern Baptists and Methodists) ask questions.

In the large enclosed space created between the booths and buildings, a non-local band plays traditional and modern Greek songs. Introduced by an emcee every two hours, costumed folk dancers (parish children) entertain within a wide audience circle. The announcer explains the origin and context of the dance and then one of three groups (divided by age) performs. Afterwards, the emcee invites onlookers to participate, and several parishioners join in, serving as unofficial dance instructors for novices. Enclosed by space and surrounded by ethnicity, parishioners and visitors find it easy and enjoyable to "be Greek for a weekend."

Like the German-American festival, the Greek festival presents obvious aspects of ethnic identity to both insiders and outsiders. Assailing the ears and nostrils for blocks around, the sounds of Greek music and the smells of Greek food proclaim the festival for all. As one enters the gates of the parish grounds, one sees young dancers performing in traditional Greek costumes. Church tours deliberately open another aspect of Greek identity to public scrutiny. Inside the Hellenic Center, festival goers may see Greek crafts, Greek scenes (painted and projected), more Greek foods, and even Greek words and names. Outsiders hear Greek spoken to one generation of festival participants and English to another. For the weekend, a small corner of a Southern city becomes transformed into another country, while parishioners get to reinvigorate their self-identity through the experience.

Besides these overt symbols of ethnicity, the Greek-Americans interpret others with a significance known primarily to themselves. Church tours, for example, not only offer a glimpse into Byzantine theology and design but, more implicitly, define religion as an integral component of Greek identity (see Chock 1981:55; Scourby 1984:77). Moreover, the Greek foods and dancing both appear frequently at social activities such as rites of passage, and so function as symbols of hospitality which a Greek-American would normally offer to any visitor (see Scourby 1984:75). In fact, according to the parish priest, St. George's festival actually represents a symbolic Greek home, demonstrating the unity of belief and fellowship found there traditionally.

Besides emic perceptions not perceived etically, though, the festival also presents outsider conceptions of identity overlooked by insiders. For example, the Greek terms in the center's classrooms are ignored as commonplace by

parishioners, but outsiders read them as additional evidence of an exotic difference. Likewise, many younger parishioners speak Greek to older relatives out of
respect, often switching back to English without being aware of deliberately acting "ethnic." Outsiders, of course, immediately recognize the foreign speech and
view it as another obvious indicator of ethnicity.

While both Greeks and non-Greeks interpret the symbols presented at the
festival on various levels and to various ends, there are some aspects of Greek
identity which even the group members keep hidden from outside view. Greeks,
for example, view themselves as hard-working, self-sacrificing immigrants, having struggled to gain successful careers despite often overwhelming odds.
Likewise, they view themselves as crafty business people, making a lucrative
living from their enterprise and labor (see Chock 1981:48-49). While Greek-
Americans view these as intrinsic qualities, they also recognize that to deliberately construct their parish festival to exaggerate these traits would trivialize
the effort they cheerfully volunteer, and might antagonize the neighbors they
have invited as friends. Thus, these characteristics remain known but unex-
pressed.

COMPARISONS AND CONTRASTS

Spassfest in Germantown and the Greek festival in Greenville reinforce and
reflect the ethnic identities of their host groups in a variety of ways. Merely a
glance at the festival programs of both reveals a number of traits which the
groups proclaim, and visitors expect, as obvious markers of identity. Other
symbols require more careful interpretation, by both insiders and outsiders.
Some characteristics remain unique to only one group, while others remain hidden from view entirely. Like scenes and props in a play, these elements, or their
absence, provide a dynamic context in which both group members and non-
members can express, experience, and examine ethnicity.

Both outsiders and insiders define the Greeks and Germans by several obvious
features. The caricatured dancers on both programs, for example, suggest to
parishioners and visitors alike that dance and music form an integral component
of ethnic identity. These then become even more enhanced by the wearing of
"traditional" costumes. Audiences at both festivals, too, expect to find typical
foods, such as sauerkraut or souvlakia. By common agreement between insiders
and outsiders, food, dance, and music are regarded as characteristically ethnic, and
thus both the Germans and Greeks openly display these attributes at their respective festivals. Through this presentation, the host groups gain an enhanced
sense of identity as well.

In fact, both groups exhibit certain traits because outsiders expect these as
definitively "ethnic." For example, a German festival without beer, bratwurst,
and sauerkraut, or a Greek festival without baklava, lamb, and souvlakia, could
never be authentic in the eyes or the minds of outsiders. Ethnic groups, through

their festivals, react as much to etic expectations as they do to emic definitions (see also Esman 1982 and Rauche 1988). Both internal and external perceptions delimit the experiencing of ethnic identity.

Other symbols, though, express an identity on both a superficial and a deeper level. For example, food and dance not only proclaim an obvious identity, but also demonstrate the warmth and fellowship that both groups wish to offer their visitors as sincere signs of hospitality. Large families for the Catholic Germans reflect their belief in the importance of community solidarity, while church tours for the Greeks underscore their emphasis on religious faith. These characteristics might also be perceived as distinctively ethnic by outsiders, of course, but insiders read these same traits with a more profound interpretation as well.

Some elements remain insignificant for insiders but are viewed as ethnic by outsiders. The German dialect, for example, sounds normal to locals but to visitors marks the users as definitely ethnic. Likewise, community of origin (e.g., Germantown), especially when coupled with a distinctive accent, signals a German identity for the speaker as perceived by non-locals. For the Greeks of Greenville, wine or beer represent ordinary family beverages; for their Bible-Belt fundamentalist Christian guests, however, the use of alcohol at church functions, especially on Sunday, undeniably reveals an ethnic heritage. Similarly, the presence of Greek lettering and words in the parish hall classrooms eloquently speak of an identity as well. While outsiders in Illinois and in South Carolina observe different ethnic actors at different festivals, the interpretation of their performances remains the same: some emically normal behaviors become etically ethnic.

While the elements shared by both ethnic festivals are informative, equally of interest are those elements not in common. The Germans, relatively early arrivals in Illinois, have by now assimilated, and thus feel no need to display family heirlooms harking back to a nineteenth century country long since forgotten. To the more recently arrived Greeks, however, such articles retain nostalgic memories for first-generation newcomers, and thus prominently appear at the Greek festival. German dances such as polkas still possess a certain ethnic flavor, but have at least in part entered the American popular mainstream. Thus the Germans would not emphasize dances at their festival as much as the Greeks, whose steps and sounds demonstrate more of an Old World flair, particularly to a Southern audience.

Perhaps the most striking contrast between the two festivals is the differential importance placed on religion. To the Greek-Americans, their Orthodox Christian faith forms a significant component of their identity, and thus they proudly display and explain their "unorthodox" beliefs to their primarily Protestant visitors. In contrast, German-Americans do not consider their religious beliefs as overtly indicative of their identity due to a variety of factors (e.g., diversity of original immigrant beliefs and degree of assimilation). Thus the Germantown residents feel no need to offer tours of a "normal" building or belief. Cultural elements deliberately omitted from a performance reflect a perception of group identity just as readily as those which are formally presented for review.

One aspect of ethnic identity that remains virtually hidden from outside inspection is the value system of each group, expressed through stereotypes. For example, the Germans define themselves as thrifty, hard-working, and conservative; attributes which they believe have created productive and stable communities. Greeks view themselves as hard-working, self-sacrificing business people; making a successful living through their own intelligence and enterprise. However, neither group consciously chooses to present these values for public scrutiny. Both groups, too, recognize the etic stereotypes leveled against them, but they do not elect to retaliate in public by opening a Pandora's box of potentially destructive viewpoints.

By exposing these delicate concepts to the damaging sunlight of social interaction where their validity can be tested, it is possible that Germans and Greeks might find their perceptions of themselves and of others ridiculed or even contradicted. The stereotypes of a group, like the value system of a culture, form a core of beliefs from which behaviors emanate in turn, drawing their meaning and purpose from the values within. To have these stereotypes challenged then directly threatens a group's very self-concept. Thus it is no coincidence that both Germans and Greeks retain their right to the privacy of many of their values, in order to protect their identity.

On the other hand, festivals might still be interpreted as expressing these stereotypes, but in a very subtle way. The neat, orderly festival grounds at Spassfest, for example, might be seen to mirror the neatness of German-American communities and likewise the stereotypical orderliness of residents' lives. The many craft boutiques at the Greek-American festival might reflect the mercantile interest of that group. However, for these values to become apparent through a festival, one needs to know the emic perceptions of the groups in question first, in order to "see" the stereotypes displayed through real behaviors. In fact, ethnic festivals require more than a superficial "thin description" of symbols alone; they also require a thorough "thick description" of the cultural context in which the festivals occur (see Geertz 1973).

Why ethnic expressions such as food and dance are overtly presented (even emphasized), and others such as language or values are ignored or downplayed, perhaps demonstrates a general definition of hyphenated Euro-Americans in American culture. Comparative studies of other ethnic festivals might find in common an emphasis on food, music, and dance (see, for example, Rauche 1988 and Esman 1982). Thus, it may be possible to read ritualized Euro-American ethnic festivals as macro-symbols of "ethnicity" in general American culture.

In fact, the idea of festivals themselves underscores the fundamental (idealistic) value in American society of the non-threatening melting pot. It might be argued that Euro-American ethnic festivals remain politically acceptable because of the degree of cultural freedom allowed in the United States. On the other hand, the festivals could be offering an American audience only those elements which they consider to be non-threatening to the social *status quo*; foods and dances carry no hidden political agenda. Festivals provide a safe place to "experiment with crossing these [cultural] boundaries" (Kalcik 1984:60) without, perhaps, questioning the consequences of those boundaries. The possibility of linguistic and religious diversity, even though ostensibly legally guaranteed in the United States, may in actuality challenge the American melting pot ideal, and thus would be downplayed at ethnic festivals. In short, the argument may be: superficial cultural differences (e.g., food) are acceptable, but one should not challenge the indivisibility of American society by suggesting a more fundamental cultural plurality.

This possibility can be tested by examining the ethnic festivals of groups most likely to threaten the position of the privileged classes. While both African- and Native-American groups host various regional festivals (e.g., South Carolina's Gullah Festival), it may be argued that such presentations offer only carefully-controlled characteristics deemed politically acceptable to largely White, middle-class audiences. It may be impossible for these groups to present demands for religious equality, displays of past or present injustices, or skits ridiculing Euro-Americans. For most Americans, the safe confines of a festival permit the superficial acceptance of cultural diversity defined as curious foods or entertaining dances. White American society may find it too disturbing to accept true cultural equality, which subsequently might require a painful redistribution of political and economic power.

CONCLUSION

Ethnic festivals, then, are much more than presentations of bundles of traits offered for public consumption. They can, and should, be interpreted as a reaffirmation of identity through performance; to be viewed on a multitude of conscious and subconscious levels and by an audience with varied degrees of sophistication. Thus, for an accurate understanding, one needs an etic awareness of the actors' actions, costumes, props, and lines as well as an emic perception of what those same elements mean to the actors themselves. This detailed libretto of interpretation allows for a better comprehension of and appreciation for the power of the performance. An audience equipped with this program can then relax and enjoy the show.

BIBLIOGRAPHY

Boyd, Rosamonde
    1948 *The Social Adjustment of the Greeks in Spartanburg, South Carolina.*
    Spartanburg, SC.: William Printing Co.

Chock, Phyllis
    1981 "The Greek American Small Businessman: A Cultural Analysis." *Journal of Anthropological Research* 37:46-60.

Coggeshall, John M.
    1988 "One of Those Intangibles: The Manifestation of Ethnic Identity in Southwestern Illinois." *Journal of American Folklore* 99:177-207.

    Like Salt and Sugar: German-American Ethnicity in Southwestern Illinois. New York: AMS Press (forthcoming).

Errington, Frederik
    1987 "Reflexivity Deflected: The Festival of Nations as an American Cultural Performance." *American Ethnologist* 14:654-667.

Esman, Marjorie
    1982 "Festivals, Change, and Unity: The Celebration of Ethnic Identity Among Louisiana's Cajuns." *Anthropological Quarterly* 55:199-210.

Geertz, Clifford
    1973 "Thick Description: Toward an Interpretive Theory of Culture." In *The Interpretation of Cultures*. New York: Basic Books. Pp. 3-30.

Goffman, Erving
    1967 *Interaction Ritual: Essays in Face-to-Face Behavior*. Chicago: Aldine.

Handelman, Don
    1990 *Models and Mirrors: Towards an Anthropology of Public Events*. Cambridge: Cambridge University Press.

Kalcik, Susan
    1984 "Ethnic Foodways in America: Symbol and the Performance of Identity." In *Ethnic and Regional Foodways in the United States: The Performance of Group Identity*. L.K. Brown and K. Mussell (eds). Knoxville: University of Tennessee Press. Pp. 37-65.

Kapferer, Bruce
    1979 "Introduction: Ritual Process and the Transformation of Context." *Social Analysis* 1:3-19.

MacAloon, John J.
    1984 "Introduction: Cultural Performances, Culture Theory." In *Rite, Drama, Festival, Spectacle*. J. MacAloon (ed.) Philadelphia: Institute for the Study of Human Issues. Pp. 1-15.

Rauche, Anthony
    1988 "*Festa Italiana* in Hartford, Connecticut: The Pastries, the Pizza, and the People who 'Parla Italiano.'" In *We Gather Together: Food and Festival in American Life*. T. Humphrey and L. Humphrey (eds.) Ann Arbor: UMI Research Press. Pp. 205-217.

Saloutos, Theodore
    1964 *The Greeks in the United States*. Cambridge: Harvard University Press.

Scourby, Alice
    1984 *The Greek Americans*. Boston: Twayne Publishers.

Turner, Victor
    1969 *The Ritual Process: Structure and Anti-Structure*. Chicago: Aldine.

    1982 "Introduction." In *Celebration: Studies in Festivity and Ritual*. V. Turner (ed.) Washington, DC: Smithsonian Institution Press. Pp. 11-30.

    1985 "Process, System, and Symbol: A New Anthropological Synthesis." In *On The Edge of the Bush: Anthropology as Experience*. E. Turner (ed.) Tucson: University of Arizona Press. Pp. 151-173.

    1986 "Dewey, Dilthey, and Drama: An Essay in the Anthropology of Experience." In *The Anthropology of Experience*. V. Turner and E. Bruner (eds.) Urbana: University of Illinois Press. Pp. 33-44.

Van Esterik, Penny
    1982 "Celebrating Ethnicity: Ethnic Flavor in an Urban Festival." *Ethnic Groups* 4:207-228.

4

Individual and Community in a Protestant Symbolic World: Presbyterian Belief, Ritual, and Experience in the American South

Gwen Kennedy Neville

The individual as solitary pilgrim leaving home to seek one's fortune is a powerful image in the symbolic representation of Protestant life and thought. This is Max Weber's individual Protestant, acting out the ethic of capitalism, achievement, and personal image that is congruent with the modernized, Protestantized world of the late-twentieth-century United States. Weber would say that it is one of the significant images, played out in Protestant experience, that has helped to create this particular capitalist world. This image of the separate, accountable individual is taught in the Protestant pulpit and the Sunday school, but also it is prominent in the symbolic representation within the curriculum of the American public school. Philosophically rooted in both Calvinistic Protestantism and in the Enlightenment individualism that influenced John Dewey and, earlier, the framers of the Constitution, the ideology of the individual is pervasive in American thought. And so it is not surprising that this grand value placed on the separateness of the person and the freedom of each one to leave, travel, acquire, accomplish, and excel is one that remains basic to the working out of capitalism and capitalistic experience (see Weber 1958 [1905]).

The image of the community is a competing image in Protestant thought, especially strong in the teachings and ethics of the Calvinistic tradition—a tradition that has had an important, shaping influence on American Protestant worldview. The Christian community is represented as an affiliated network of "the Elect," bound together by their collective salvation, a group to which the individual belongs and to which he or she has certain obligations. Both of these images—that of individual and that of community—and the cultural imperatives they embody are strong motifs in American Protestant belief. And yet they appear on first analysis to be diametrically opposed to one another—to be two prescriptions which are impossible to fulfill at the same time. It is, in fact, impossible to at once leave home and stay at home. Being an individual places certain limits on being a member of a community.

In this chapter I attempt to explore the relation between these two apparently contradictory demands as they are found stated and enacted within one American Protestant group, the Presbyterians in the Southern United States. My goal is to illuminate some of the ways in which theology is performed in ritual expression and in the social arrangements of lived experience. Through performances of belief, conflicting demands are resolved and made doable and bearable in the complex mobile society of "modern" America. In order to explore these connections I focus on one particular group within American Protestantism, the "Presbyterians." In the region we know as the American South the Protestant denominations have in the past often been lumped together for purposes of analysis, both in religious studies writings and in the writings of anthropologists; I suggest that it is through separating these into sub-sets and small units that we gain full appreciation of the diversity of Protestant life in this one region alone. The same diversity might also be discovered through using this approach to religious life within Protestantism in other regions of the United States.

My interest in the American South as a cultural region and in the Presbyterians within this region reaches back to my earliest anthropological fieldwork in 1970, when I undertook a study of the Presbyterian summer community of Montreat, North Carolina, as research for my doctoral dissertation. At Montreat I discovered a periodic assembly of kin and co-believers whose ordinary lives were lived out in individuated, nuclear families, following the classic Protestant imperative to leave home and become individuals and to stand alone before God. In their sacred time, however, these individuated pilgrims reassembled into vast kin groups and formed religious communal groups that led me to use the label "ethnic community" for these White, Anglo-Saxon Protestants (Neville 1978). Over the years I explored further the intriguing set of reunions that became gradually visible among not only the Presbyterians but also Methodists and Baptists in North Carolina, Georgia, Tennessee, and Texas. I came to see the reunions as a pilgrimage complex through which Protestant symbolic worlds could be enacted, and in which a tradition could become stated that presented an inversion of Catholic worlds and traditions (Neville 1987). Over the years I have looked at these questions through the lens of social function and social structure combined with symbolic analysis. I attempt here to focus on elements of social process and on the cognitive and cultural maps that act to frame and to motivate the behavioral processes one observes as ritual and ceremonial life. I explore the relation of beliefs about individual and community to the enactment of these beliefs in ritual and their connections to historical and present experience.

I have suggested in earlier work that in the symbolic world of the Southern Presbyterians the constructs of individual and community live side by side in the idea of the Covenant. The notion of Covenant People is a doctrine that forms an umbrella under which the Presbyterian individual exists with integrity while at the same time being a member of several overlapping symbolic and social entities—the family, the congregation, and the civic order, or town.[1]

SOUTHERN PRESBYTERIANS

The Southern Presbyterians are a Calvinistic Protestant denomination in the American South. Between 1861 and 1985, a separate denominational church existed, known as the Presbyterian Church in the United States. The Presbyterians of the colonial times were closely tied to the Church of Scotland; these historically related theological and ecclesiastical traditions have continued their sense of connectedness over time. They share a common ancestry in the Scottish Reformation; they are also related structurally, doctrinally, and historically to the Presbyterians of Ulster and to the English Presbyterians.

Presbyterians of Scotland, North Ireland, and England sent out embryo communities in the seventeenth and eighteenth centuries to become a part of the culture of colonial North America. It is this common ancestry going back to John Calvin, John Knox, and to the Westminster Confession, and an accompanying kin-based "ethnicity," that sets apart the Southern Presbyterians from their Baptist and other Calvinistic neighbors and which makes them more similar to New England Puritans than to Southern evangelicals (Neville 1978). They are also separated from the Baptists doctrinally and in church polity. The distinctive features of Presbyterian church government setting them apart from Southern Baptists are seen in a series of representative bodies including session, presbytery, synod, and General Assembly. The distinctive feature of doctrine is expressed in the practice of infant baptism, in contrast to Baptist adult baptism.

In their social-economic organization, the Southern Presbyterians have historically been the owners of small and mid-sized farms and of small business in towns. Early settlers formed communities in scattered open-country neighborhoods, linked together by a church and cemetery at the crossroads (for an expansion of this model, see Arensberg and Kimball 1965). This settlement pattern was especially typical of eighteenth-century and early nineteenth-century North Carolina, Virginia, and east Tennessee. As townsfolk, early Presbyterians were classical Weberian capitalists and professionals—merchants, physicians, lawyers, judges, and teachers. Their belief in individual reading and interpretation of Scripture led them to form early frontier schools in the ministers' homes and later to found denominational colleges for the training of ministers and the education of the laity.

Presbyterians ascribe theologically to the notion of the individual vocation, or "calling" as Weber predicted. The theology also includes the idea of the Christian community in which individuals are linked through overlapping memberships to a set of communal obligations. The individual is not only a solitary person but an individual who enters the world and travels in it as part of "a peo-

ple"—a people who as a group have been called. This is the notion of the
Covenant, resulting in a special kind of collective that allows for individuation.

The Covenant is a contract made by God with a chosen people, and here the
Presbyterian language echoes the language of the Old Testament shared with the
Jewish tradition, who also see themselves as a "Covenant People." In this contract God spoke to Moses and to Abraham not only as individuals, but to these
men as part of an entire nation who were then to respond to God through the
joint working out of their history in faithful obedience. The idea of obedience
here is never an idea of individual obedience, of good works or of expiation, but
of faithful following of God's commands as a people, and therefore living in this
world in "grace" and of being the Elect as an interconnected set of families and
communities rather than as isolated individuals alone. The figure of Jesus appears as a fulfillment of God's promise of a Messiah, and the Christian community is the New Testament version of the idea of the Covenant people.

The working out of the idea of the Covenant people in actual social expression, in historical patterns of individuals and groupings, is an intriguing one.
There are at least three theological entities that correspond to three very real social entities to which individual Presbyterians belong and in which they may act
at the same time both as individuals and as members of a community. These
theological entities are represented by the idea of the family of faith, expressed
visibly in the extended kin group tracing ancestry to a common ancestor; the
idea of the communion of saints, or the priesthood of believers which takes on
visible form in the congregation; and the idea of the City of God, or the
Kingdom of God on earth, which is the symbolic representation of the local
community of civic order in the town. Each idea or theme is seen performed in
recurrent ritual expressions and in social order. I will comment briefly on these
metaphors and their social use and on the rituals in which they are expressed.

CULTURAL EXPRESSIONS

The first of the symbolic units of membership to which I have pointed is that
of the family of faith. The individual in the Presbyterian tradition is born into a
family that is larger than the American classic "nuclear family" of mother, father, and siblings so often described and studied by sociologists for the Anglo-
Saxon middle and upper middle classes. The person here is born into a family
consisting of all the descendants of one common ancestor (or, technically, into
two such families on the principle of bilateral kindreds; that is, one's mother's
and one's father's families). One is aware of one's aunts, uncles, and cousins
through the annual reunion, but also through constant reminders in cards for
birthdays and holidays, and through gatherings for Thanksgiving, Christmas,
weddings, and funerals. The Southern family has been depicted well in works of
literature, and the South has come to be associated with extended kin groups,
which I have described in my own study of reunions and homecomings. I have

suggested that the extended ancestor-focused family is actually an example of a classic cognatic descent group and that the annual reappearance of this group as a "family reunion" constitutes one aspect of an elaborate system of Protestant pilgrimage (Neville 1987).

The large summertime reunion of this descent group is a processual metaphor for the family of faith. Here the construct takes on full expression through the powerful symbols of space, time, food, and personal relationships, stating the centrality of kinship and descent in Presbyterian life. I have labeled these vast reunions "kin-religious gatherings" and "folk liturgies." They are at once kin-based and religious because of the way in which the reunion draws together and makes visible an idea of family and at the same time makes visible an idea of religious communal life that is impossible to fulfill on a day-to-day basis in a modern society. The family of faith is the family welded together in the Covenant; the family gathered together under the trees for the summertime reunion is the family forged through a return pilgrimage to honor one's ancestors and one's home place of origin in a world of nucleation and fragmentation. The food that is presented on long tables—ham, fried chicken, potato salad—is food for an outdoor communion, an inversion of the Eucharist in which all the family is united through the commensal celebration (see Neville 1987 for a further elaboration of this process of inversion and symbolization).

Other ritual processes also symbolize and materialize the abstract idea of family of faith. The words of the baptism ceremony, for example, refer to the child as a "child of the Covenant," as an "inheritor of the kingdom"; the infant is given a name at this time and is welcomed into the "household of God." One's personal identity is developed within the cognitive world of belonging to a family within the family of God, conceptualized by a network of families joined together by multiple ties. One is nurtured within the extended group of relatives with the understanding that an expected part of the life plan is to grow up and leave. The journey outward will include stopovers with numerous relatives, and there will be rhythmical returns for holidays, reunions, birthdays, and summertime. Often the first destination on the journey is a denominational college (Davidson, St. Andrew's, Agnes Scott, etc.), where at least some of one's friends will be children and grandchildren of the friends of one's parents and grandparents. The ideal is the goal of completing the web of life by marrying within the denominational fold and passing along the faith to a new generation. My ethnographic study of this life cycle indicates that it is not only possible but also probable that the Southern Presbyterian person will develop individually with a keen sense of theological and social membership in a "greater family" and to find within the web of Presbyterian families a suitable marriage partner. The alterations of leaving and returning are woven together into a cultural pattern that includes and accommodates the conflicting demands and personal and group obligations. The Covenant theology, which holds that one's salvation is fixed for all time not by one's own actions but by the actions of God, creates a certain freedom from conflicting demands and makes the failure to resolve conflict bearable and manageable for the apparently isolated individual.

In commenting on the strong ties between Covenant theology and the family-ancestor tradition in Presbyterian thought and practice, one prominent church-man noted the following: "Since we are a part of the 'saved' community through birth into it, the ancestor/parent actually becomes an instrument in the process of salvation itself—something like a 'priesthood of all parents' to go along with that of 'all believers.' In affirming the values of family and kin the Covenant theologian is, in fact, affirming his or her own theological identity—as well as a family one" (Hall 1987).

A second symbolic unit of membership for the individual in Covenant theology is the *priesthood of believers* of the *communion of the saints*. The congregation is the local residential entity through which one receives and lives out salvation as a member of the Elect. There is a slot, a position—an "ascribed status," if you will—that is designated for each person who joins or is born into the church, and it cannot be lost or forfeited. This membership offers to the person the ultimate degree of freedom to act, move, work, and achieve, to become a capitalist or a professional as an expression of one's "calling." The mover has only to affiliate with another Presbyterian congregation in order to continue his or her residency, so that the denomination itself becomes an enlarged version of the local congregation to which the individual belongs. In the language of belonging, one might say "I am a Presbyterian" in the same way one says "I am a Maxwell" or "I belong to the Westminster Presbyterian Church" as one would say "I belong to the Maxwell family."

All of the important life-crisis rituals are celebrated in the presence of the congregation rather than in front of the minister and family alone—baptism of infants or of new members, the "joining of the church" by successive cohorts of adolescents, the marriage ceremony, and the funeral. Little social dramas have been played out in every congregation over questions of whether to allow weddings of non-members in the sanctuary of the church, whether to allow burial of non-members in the old country church cemeteries, and over the propriety of holding funerals in funeral homes rather than in the church itself. The living and the dead congregations are united in the presence of the cemetery adjacent to the early colonial churches in the Southeastern United States.

The ceremony enacting symbols of congregational membership is the Church homecoming. On the annual day of the church homecoming or church anniversary, the scattered "sons and daughters of the congregation" return for worship, dinner on the grounds, and visits to the graves of the ancestors, who in this case are also founders of the congregation. In the town and urban congregations, the ancestors in the civic cemetery are honored on special days that commemorate congregational history and recall the founders, and members who move into new towns and cities are assimilated into the fabric of kin and congregation woven partially through the intercongregational ties of kinship and history of other transcongregational movers. The mobile society is made more stable through the existence of a safety net of nonchanging membership in this extension of the family of faith into the life of the congregation.

A third symbolic entity of which the individual in Covenant theology is a member is the entity of the civic, expressed in the idea of the *City of God*, or the Kingdom of God. This civic metaphor is congruent with the idea of the town in the history and experience of the Scots and Scots-Irish Presbyterians, that of the town as an envisioned civic order that expresses Protestant ideology. In the preindustrial South the town was the spatial result of the Enlightenment rationality of planning. Squares, streets, and civic boundaries were strategically placed for purposes of government, legal record-keeping, and commerce. The early county seat town was a hub of Southern community life, connecting a trade network of farms and villages into an administrative coordinating nexus. A second wave of towns came to the South with the railroad. Land speculators drew off straight lines parallel or perpendicular to the railroads and named these "Main Street," "First Street," and so on. In the early nineteenth-century Southern United States, the town became as important to the Protestant way of life as had the farm and church neighborhood in the century before. Most of the cities in the South, with the exception of early colonial port cities, grew out of commercial towns, becoming commercial cities with their own form of civic order and industrial pride.

The City of God in Presbyterian thought was never a heavenly city. It was and is a metaphor for the ideal kingdom of God established in *this* world through careful, orderly planning, and the prevailing of the Elect community in the creation of a rational, nonchaotic, theological-political domain. In this envisioned city, God is the mayor; the ideals of justice, mercy, and truth prevail; and the government is rational and representative. The government outlined in the U.S. Constitution is, in fact, clearly reminiscent of the Calvinistic ideal structure found in the planned theocracy of Geneva and in the polity of the Presbyterian churches today.

The town as an idea provides an order, the *civitas*, in which each person is a citizen, an individual with a separate identity holding certain rights and privileges of citizenship. The citizen is a member of the civitas but has the freedom to move or to explore outward without losing citizenship. This enables citizens of a national state to move about freely within the nation's boundaries or to use their passports to travel abroad. "I am an American" or "I am a Texan" expresses a basis of national or regional affiliation, just as "I am a Philadelphian" or "I am a New Yorker" does for a city or town. In Scotland one expresses this same local affiliation by the statement "I belong to Edinburgh" or "I belong to Selkirk." Theologically the citizenship idea of "I am a citizen of God's Kingdom" becomes "I belong to the church," "I am a Christian," or "I am a Presbyterian." I explore this idea more elaborately in the study of civic ritual in a Scottish town (Neville 1989; Neville n.d.).

The idea of the town as a religious entity, in the style of Calvin's theocracy, is enacted in one place each summer for the Southern Presbyterians, and that is in the established summer colony of Montreat, North Carolina. This gathering of old families in cottages augments a conference center and is incorporated as a town by the State of North Carolina. When I first visited Montreat in the late 1960s it was wholly owned by the Presbyterian Church in the United States (Southern Presbyterians) and served as a tightly controlled meeting spot for summertime chataqua-style gatherings of like-minded people. By the time of my dissertation fieldwork in 1970, the community had been incorporated and could no longer exclude those who had not purchased a "gate-ticket" to enter the narrow road leading into the religious grounds. Today Montreat continues to be a magnet summer community for thousands of Presbyterians who live scattered over the South and to provide one example of a civic order merged with a theological entity prescribing the lived order of the People of God in a city on earth. It can only exist temporarily, however, for the great majority of the residents, the summer people. It is impossible in our mobile social order to live through the year in such a communal environment while at the same time meeting the requirements of individuality. And so, again, we find an instance of the establishment of a ritual gathering through which the person's conflicting cultural demands can be temporarily satisfied.

The idea of membership in the Covenant community provides one with the necessary passport to move about through the terrain of one's own and other religious domains. One is empowered to become a business person or a professional, to labor in any arena of the world's enterprise, to fulfill one's individual "calling" without relinquishing one's citizenship in the Kingdom of God. Such is the nature of permanent residency, citizenship status. It provides the portfolio of documents that allows safe passage through the labyrinth of economic opportunity and cushions the blows of disaster.

PATTERNS AND MEANINGS

In summary, certain patterns can be identified within Presbyterian symbol, ritual, and experience that sheds light on the puzzle of resolving cultural contradictions implicit in the two ideas of the lonely pilgrim and of the Christian community. I list a few of these patterns that have begun to emerge as I toy with this piece of the puzzle:

1. Southern Presbyterian tradition stands apart from the traditions of other mainstream Protestant denominations in the South—especially those of the majority Baptists and Methodists. This apartness is signified and symbolized in the configuration of Calvinistic teaching known as Covenant theology.

2. Covenant theology constructs a cognitive map in which the individual does not face the world alone as the isolated, solitary capitalist described by Weber, but as a member at birth in three overlapping symbolic and social entities—the family of faith, the ancestor-focused kin group; the priesthood of believers, the local congregation and the transcongregational denomination; and in

the City of God, the civic order of the town. The individual is allowed wide latitude of educational and career choice and of geographic mobility as a result of this fixed membership of the Elect, which depends not on the person's good works and right living, but on the prior choice of God.

3. The Chosen People idea frames a cultural identity and a "sense of peoplehood" in which the emphasis is on the life in this world, not in a world beyond. The concept of "Covenant life" refers not to the life of a person, but to the life of a people, an interconnected network supporting one another through the life cycle. Having been already saved by the grace of God, the individual is free from having to earn or prove one's salvation by good works or capitalistic enterprise while at the same time being provided important social support for achieving the very goals and rewards that capitalism has to dispense.

These patterns and other patterns based on other ethnographic data—too extensive to include here—testify to the intricate connections among aspects of Protestant life, experience, symbol, ritual, and belief. This is the cultural complex Max Weber (1958 [1905]) referred to as "meaning-in-action." Emile Durkheim puzzled over these same problems in search for connecting cultural imperatives toward individuation with social collective identities and their symbolic forms (Durkheim 1947 [1912]). The style of analysis I explore here was pioneered for the study of symbolic life in America by W. Lloyd Warner in the Yankee City series (1961) and has been carried on by some of his followers. The tradition of Victor Turner and Edith Turner adds additional momentum to this established beginning (Turner 1969, 1974; Turner and Turner 1978) but has focused primarily on non-Western and then on non-American religious worlds. Combining the approaches of both Durkheim and Weber, the recent studies in the American South by James Peacock and Ruel W. Tyson, Jr. (1990) and the collection of essays by their students and students of Patterson (Tyson, Jr., Peacock, and Patterson (eds.) 1988) provide a good example of the use of models from a perspective combining interests in the connection of Protestant belief and behavior. As a final example, I point to the project on Catholics in the Southern United States headed by Jon Anderson and tentatively entitled *Bible Belt Catholics: Place, Space, and Memory in the American South* (Anderson, McDonough, and Neville n.d.). The approach I advocate is one in which a search for *meaning* is grounded in a search for the *performance of meaning* in ceremonies, gatherings, regularized and routinized events, and other instances of human community life.

The analysis of belief systems within Protestant theology in convergence with their expression in performed culturally visible events has the potential of shedding new light on an understanding of the interconnections of belief and behavior within anthropological theory generally. Often the theology of Protestant groups in America, Europe, and elsewhere has been the exclusive analytical territory of theologians and church historians, while the analysis of cultural performance and of ritual has been exclusive property of the anthropologists. I suggest that it is only through combining the study of belief in Christianity with ritual performance in Christianity that we will arrive at some of the insights and understandings that we have hoped to attain for religions that are "Other" and for religions that are more closely a part of "Ourselves."

As a part of the endeavor suggested above, it is also important, I suggest, to separate religious groups in the United States for analytical purposes by region as well as by denomination. It is the awareness that "Southern Presbyterians" are distinct from all American Presbyterians that triggered my own interest in these studies many years ago. The region of "the South" has historically been one that has its own distinctive cultural, economic, and social features and remains distinct despite the influx of newcomers and the emergence of the Sun Belt in recent years. Finally, in addition to separating regions for analytical purposes, it is also important to separate the Protestant denominations within the American regions, realizing that the Southern Baptists and Southern Methodists are different from Southern Presbyterians. Both these exercises of separate analysis will produce a diverse and complex picture of religion and of ritual celebrations of identity that is much needed in the analysis of American life.

NOTES

I wish to thank all those who have assisted me in these studies over the years. An earlier version of this paper was delivered in a session organized by M. Jean Heriot for the 1987 AAA meeting in Chicago entitled "Mainstream American Religion: Protestant Belief Systems and Lifeways."

1. Field work on which this paper is based has spanned the years 1970 to the present and has focused on Presbyterian culture, while also including materials for comparison on Methodists and Baptists in the Southern United States. I have studied family reunions, annual homecomings, cemetery association days, camp meetings, and denominational conference centers. This paper calls on additional materials from Presbyterian history, congregational life, and religious doctrine. For more information on Presbyterian history, see Earnest Trice Thompson (1963). For an example of these doctrines stated for religious education purposes, see Shirley Guthrie (1967). The "Southern Presbyterian Church" was officially The Presbyterian Church in the United States from 1861 until 1985. It is now merged with the Northern branch of the denomination, becoming the Presbyterian Church in the United States of America.

BIBLIOGRAPHY

Anderson, Jon, Gary McDonough, and Gwen Kennedy Neville
    n.d. *Bible Belt Catholics: Place, Time, and Memory in the American South.* forthcoming.

Arensberg, Conrad M., and Solon Kimball
    1965 *Culture and Community.* New York: Harcourt Brace.

Durkheim, Emile
1947 [1912] *The Elementary Forms of Religious Life*. New York: Free Press.

Guthrie, Shirley
1967 *Christian Doctrine*. Richmond: John Knox.

Hall, Hartley.
1987 Personal Communication.

Neville, Gwen Kennedy
1978 "Kinfolks and the Covenant: Ethnic Community Among Southern Presbyterians." In *The New Ethnicity: Perspectives from Ethnology*. John Bennet (ed.) Annual Proceedings of the American Ethnological Society. Chicago: West Publishing.

1987 *Kinship and Pilgrimage: Rituals of Reunion in American Protestant Culture*. New York and London: Oxford University Press.

1989 "The Sacred and the Civic: Representations of Death in the Town Ceremony of Border Scotland." *Anthropological Quarterly* 62(4):163-173.

n.d. *The Mother Town: Symbol, Ritual, and Experience in the Borders of Scotland*. forthcoming.

Peacock, James, and Ruel W. Tyson, Jr.
1990 *Pilgrims of Paradox*. Washington: Smithsonian Institution Press.

Thompson, Earnest Trice
1963 *A History of the Southern Presbyterians*. Vols. I and II Richmond: John Knox Press.

Turner, Victor
1969 *The Ritual Process*. Chicago: Aldine.

1974 *Dramas, Fields, and Metaphors: Symbolic Action in Human Society*. Ithaca, NY: Cornell University Press.

Turner, Victor and Edith Turner
1978 *Image and Pilgrimage in Christian Culture: Anthropological Perspectives*. New York: Columbia University Press.

Tyson, Ruel W., Jr., James Peacock, and Daniel W. Patterson (eds.)
1988 *Diversities of Gifts: Field Studies in Southern Religion*. Urbana and Chicago: University of Illinois Press.

Warner, W. Lloyd
1961 *The Family of God: A Symbolic Study of Christian Life in America*. New Haven: Yale University Press.

Weber, Max
1958 [1905] *The Protestant Ethic and the Spirit of Capitalism*. New York: Charles Scribner's Sons.

5

The Ritual of Testifying in the Black Church

Jon Michael Spencer

RITUAL OF INTENSIFICATION

The testimony service in the Black church, particularly in the Black Holiness and Pentecostal churches, has traditionally functioned to prepare the Black religious community to endure the hardships of the world by replenishing individuals' spiritual resources and by shaping and rejuvenating the worshipers' common consciousness. It is a ritual (and rite) of intensification insofar as this rebirth occurs each week when Black churchgoers gather to "have church." Testimony service, the first major section of the worship service, allows the worshipers through singing, testifying, and shouting (dancing) to sing, speak, and enact the positive involvement of God in their lives during the past week, thereby strengthening their faith and unity for the new week.

The testimony service is not only a ritual of intensification but also a ritual of transition, for it carries the *cultus* into the "service of the word" (preaching) and the "closing service" (altar call, healing, benediction). Functioning in this transitional capacity, the testimony service actually transforms the *congregation* of the structured world of experience and intradependence into the cultus of the antistructural realm of worship and extradependence (dependence on God). *Intradependence*, according to social scientist Bruce Reed, refers to the disposition of self-autonomous individuals functioning in the world with their confirmation, protection, and sustenance in their own hands. By the end of the week, individuals are nearly drained of the spiritual resources that help sustain them, at which timely point there is a natural return to the realm of extradependence (Reed 1978:15, 32, 34, 35). Extradependence—the dependence on God as the extra-human source for confirmation, protection, and sustenance—enables individuals to tolerate and begin to eliminate inner disorientation, weakness, and pain. The worshiping community, once reintensified, can then break up into its individual selves as it reenters the structural world of intradependence (Reed 1978:74, 78-79). This oscillation between intradependence and extradependence is so natural for religious human beings that philosopher Martin Buber refers to it as the "two primary metacosmical movements of the world." The movement to extradependence is "reversal to connection," "the recognition of the Centre and the act of turning again to it." The movement to intradependence is the individual's "expansion into its own being." It is in *reversal* that *expansion* is "born again with new wings." Says Buber: "He who truly goes out to meet the world goes out also to God" (Buber 1937:95, 100, 116).

When the testimony service functions ideally, even those worshipers seeking escape rather than healing are inhaled into a healthy extradependence, where they can begin to eliminate inner disorientation and pain. When the service of the word (preaching) and the closing service (altar call, healing, benediction) fulfill the "reversal to connection" which has been begun by the testimony service, then those worshipers appropriately inhaled into extradependence via the testimony service can also be exhaled out of extradependence therapeutically transformed. This "expansion into one's own being" is thus, as theologian Robert Williams phrases it: "the more enduring experience of sensing that we are being upheld and cradled by strength that is not of our making, something, as Howard Thurman would say, that gives to life a quality of integrity and meaning which we could never generate" (Williams 1987:171).

The testimony service functions ideally when there is an honest sacrificial sharing of personal stories with the church community. As in any dialectic between an individual and the community, it takes courage to share personal stories. This is especially true since there is a certain degree of verbal and kinetic evaluation of each story by listeners. Nonetheless, by each person sacrificing his or her personal story in the form of testimony, many stories are gained in return, stories with which each worshiper can compare and nourish his or her own, whether one actually testifies or not.

Testifying is also beneficial to the larger unchurched community. When rejuvenated churchgoers carry the stories shared during the testimony service back into the community—along with reminiscences of the singing, preaching, and healing—those who are infrequent in their church attendance are able to glean some of the benefit of what went on during worship. They are able to experience worship second hand. In other words, those who are infrequent in their church attendance, but dependent on the attendance of relatives or friends, are carried spiritually by those women and men who regularly attend church and are cyclically rejuvenated by the worship.

THE STRUCTURE OF TESTIMONY

The testimony service, usually preceded by the song service, is generally the climactic segment of the devotional service which includes opening song, scripture, and prayer (occasionally proceeded by prayer requests). Typically there are one or two "devotional leaders" (two men *or* two women) who lead the testimony service. The devotional leader may open the service by saying something like: "The testimony service is open to testify as to the glory of God. Let's have church saints." The testimony service lasts between approximately fifteen and sixty minutes. In very large churches a time limit may be placed on testifying—one minute, for example, although most worshipers tend to go over time. Occasionally someone testifying will "ride on the back" of the hymn raised by the previous speaker, repeating its words so the other worshipers can make the thematic connection. Whereas the worshipers usually stand one at a time to testify, in some churches all who wish to speak stand and await a cue from the devotional leader. In one particular church the worshipers know that at a given time the choir will sing and following the chronological testifying of each of its members to the background of the music, any of the worshipers who have not yet spoken may stand and "testify in one voice." The completed testimony service does not flow dubiously into the "service of the word" via some spontaneous activity that shifts the course of events. The devotional leader usually says something such as: "This ends our testimony service and we now turn the service over to our pastor."

The means by which the testimony service functions to intensify individual faith and the social and spiritual bond of worshipers are multifold. First, testifying is a response to the biblical command for the redeemed (Psalms 107:2) to make known the doings of the Lord (Psalms 105:1). By making known God's doings, others going through trying experiences are encouraged to endure. Testimony also comprises the sharing of problems and petitioning of special prayer from the worshipers. Confessional testifying, where one confesses neglect to respond to the calling of the Spirit to speak with or pray for that distressed person during the week, may follow such petition. On the other hand, a particularly talented singer may use testifying as a practical and creative means of employing his or her gift for the exhortation and edification of the congregation. Or, if one of the ministers misses the gathering and greeting part of the service, he might "check in" with a testimony.

Singing plays a crucial part in the process of congregational synchronization in all of these instances. It is the congregation's channel of entrance into the antistructural realm of testifying—that is, the spiritual realm of God's doings, problem solving, faith building, and communal confessing. For instance, if a testimony indicates that a person is mourning the loss of a loved one, any one of the worshipers may raise a hymn of consolation. In one such case, the pastor of the Pentecostal church led the repeated singing of this chorus:

> Jesus will fix it for you
> He knows just what to do;
> Whenever you pray let him have his way,
> Jesus will fix it for you.

As a "watchman on the wall" (Isiah 62:6), the minister is supposed to know when and what kind of hymn to interject in order to help provide for the need of certain individuals while simultaneously intensifying the communal bond.

The dynamics at work in this ritual of intensification would be described by Buber as an "I-Thou" relation: "Community is the being no longer side by side (and, one might add, above or below) but *with* one another of a multitude of persons. And this multitude, though it moves towards one goal, yet experiences everywhere a turning to, a dynamic facing of, the others, a flowing from *I* to *Thou*" (cited in Turner 1969:127). When many selves *feel* their persons singing, thereby becoming physically aware of their own person, it is not to the obliteration of the relation *I-Thou*. It is is not an *I* feeling *I* without that *I* also being *with Thou*. Even though the hymns selected as communal entrance into individual testifying tend to be textually *I*-centered, the singing congregation transmuted into the testifying of the individual creates such a strong relation that it is best described as an *essential We*. Anthropologist Victor Turner explains this with reference to Buber:

> Buber does not restrict community to dyadic relationships [*I* and *Thou*]. He also speaks of an 'essential *We*,' by which he means 'a community of several independent persons, who have a self and self-responsibility. . . . The *We* includes the *Thou*. Only men who are capable of truly saying *Thou to* one another can truly say *We with* one another' (Buber cited in Turner 1969:137 [emphasis in original]).

This *essential We* is what Turner terms "communitas"—that heightened form of community relation that best occurs in the antistructural realm of extradependence. This communitas, which "transgresses or dissolves the norms that govern structured and institutionalized relationships and is accompanied by experiences of unprecedented potency," is often momentarily superseded by "spontaneous communitas," which is "a phase, a moment, not a permanent condition." "Spontaneous communitas," according to Turner, "has something 'magical' about it. Subjectively there is in it the feeling of endless power" (Turner 1969:128, 139-40). When these potent spiritual moments latent in antistructure are revealed, the *essential We* (communitas) spontaneously becomes what I will call an *ultimate We* (spontaneous communitas). Buber himself admits that there is such a state beyond *I* and *Thou*, wherein the *I* is swallowed up by the *Thou*, which is no longer *Thou*, but "that which alone is." "That which alone is" is what Buber describes as the Self, delivered from all being conditioned by *I*, merged in God such that the saying of *Thou* ceases for lack of twofold being (Buber 1937: 83-84).

THE ISOCHRONISM OF SINGING-TESTIFYING

Opening one's testifying with singing is part of a long-standing tradition in the Black church. The singing-testifying isochronism (an isochronism being a single event comprised of two or more parts) is a practice in postbellum Black Protestant and Holiness churches that found its way into Pentecostalism when it commenced in 1906 at the famous Azusa Street revival in Los Angeles. Sounding nearly identical to the contemporary accounts to be examined shortly, a 1907 report of "a colored brother" testifying at the Azusa Street revival is proof of the persistence of the tradition:

> A colored brother arose and sang the verses of a hymn, the people joining in the chorus: 'The Blood, the Blood, is all my plea; Hallelujah, it cleanseth me.' He then said: 'Hallelujah! I am so glad I can testify that the blood cleanseth me. Oh, the sweetness! My heart is full of love for Jesus. I am so glad I can take up the cross and work with Him now and follow Him. Oh, I know I am leaning on the Almighty's arms' ("The Pentecostal Assembly" 1907:2).

The reason testifying typically begins with and is thematically built upon hymns is partly because the meter and rhyme of hymns make them more memorizable than scripture. As a key source of lay theology, hymns further function to distinguish the language of testifying from that of secular talk.

The use of a hymn in the singing-testifying isochronism is not merely for stylistic or aesthetic purposes. The selected hymn is a piece that alights upon the life of the speaker and addresses God's doings during the period of intradependence. Sometimes a single hymn remains with an individual one week after another as a means of comfort and healing during a particularly trying period in life. In such an instance the person testifying will often say before singing the hymn, "The Lord put this song in my heart" or "I was led to sing this song" or, following its singing, "Bless your name Lord, that song was really deep down in my heart." Some hymns have a long emotional history. A person may remember that a particular hymn was the favorite that a mother or grandmother used to sing when testifying or that a father or grandfather liked to sing when lining the hymn. Perhaps little attention is paid to these hymns while one is growing up until some blessing or crisis causes them to take on special meaning.

Unless a hymn is original or the person testifying specifies, "*I*'ve got a song ringing in my soul and *I* want to try singing it to the Lord," the congregation joins in the singing as a means of entering into the testifying. Typically the person testifying will lead a round or two of a chorus. Usually beginning in an unmetered way, a hymn picks up tempo and rhythmic regularity as the congregation joins in and begins to clap and the musicians begin to play. The singing continues until the one who raised the hymn, frequently the one who is singing the loudest, stops to testify. If the individual gets caught up in the song, the singing may continue incessantly. "A few times I can remember starting a song and never getting around to testifying," one woman attested (cited in Dargan 1982:79). If testifying is not to follow the singing, then the one who raised the hymn will simply take a seat after saying something like, "I thank God for that song."

Since testifying, which is spoken, tends to open with singing, then the testimony service is comprised of a balance between speaking and singing. Singing smoothly connects one act of testifying (speaking) to the next and often prompts the spoken parts to be more or less musical. This balance and underlying musicality results in greater fluidity between acts of testifying. Also, because music is itself able to evoke emotional associations, the music of a hymn is able to speak to both the former testimony and the ensuing one, thereby providing emotional transition between "stories." Bennetta Jules-Rosette, in her study of an independent Apostolic church in Africa, terms this the "coherence factor": "The 'coherence factor' that seems to be consistently realized is that singing, whenever it takes place, follows speech without an appreciable gap in time. This factor does not determine what will be sung or the length of time allowed for singing. In this way, the ceremony is maintained as a continual flow of sound of which the components are negotiable" (Jules-Rosette 1975:132). In the testimony service the continual flow between musical and spoken sound— the "coherence factor"—enables the stories to comprise one disconnected narrative.

Cadential Rite in Testifying

The rite of entering into the ritual of testifying commences with singing, which is followed by salutation that "gives honor to" the Lord, the clergypersons, on down to the members and friends. The rite of "entering out," the theologically substantive part, is comprised of a three-part formula.

1. The first segment of the cadential rite is, in its simplest form, "I'm saved, sanctified, and filled with the Holy Ghost." This basic formula is variously embellished as "I'm saved, sanctified, and have the baptism of the Holy Ghost," or "I'm saved, sanctified, Holy Ghost filled, and fire-baptized," or "I'm saved, sanctified, baptized, and filled with the Holy Ghost and fire." One woman, perhaps not yet Spirit-baptized, really individualized the saying with "I'm saved, I'm sanctified, and I'm satisfied." Another started off by saying "I'm saved from sin." Pre-formula words also personalize the saying: "I thank God this morning that I can say without a doubt that I'm saved, sanctified, and have the Holy Ghost fire deep down in my soul." There was a time when Holiness and Pentecostal worshipers regularly recited an extended version of the formula: "I'm

saved, I'm sanctified, I have the baptism of the Holy Ghost and fire, have the walking-halelujah, fire burning in the flesh, joy unspeakable."

2. Inner spiritual experiences tend to overflow outward to participate in the empiric meanings and applications they generate. Here, the threefold formula (saved, sanctified, and Spirit-baptized) is immediately followed by a statement of intention and application—an *antecedent* and *consequent*. The intention (the *antecedent*) is stated as, "I got a mind to live right." After leading the congregation in the repeated singing of "I'm gonna serve the Lord," a worshiper began testifying that "having a made-up mind" (intention) is for the purpose of service: "I thank God for that little song of praise, 'I'm Going to Serve the Lord.' My heart is fixed and my mind made up, and it makes it easy for you to serve the Lord. You cannot serve unless you have a fixed heart and a made-up mind." It is feasible that this segment of the cadential rite was derived from one of the hymns Holiness and Pentecostal worshipers sometimes sing:

> I've got a mind to live right (2X)
> I've got a mind to live right every day.
> I tell Jesus, give me a mind to live right
> I've got a mind to live right every day.

Following the singing of two more verses (in which the words "do" and "talk" replaced "live"), one woman testified: "I thank God this morning for that little praise, for that's my testimony—I have a mind to talk right and I have a mind to do right. Truly I thank God for that this morning."

The *consequent* is a statement of will, for example, "I feel like going on." The antecedent and consequent may be stated together as: "I got a made-up mind to go through with the Lord." Some worshipers allude that "going on" and "going through" with the Lord are life-denying passages: "I made up my mind years ago that I'm determined today to *run my life* as never before." Whereas the statement of determination naturally implies intention, to state one's intention without confirming one's determination seems to be an incomplete formula. Though saved, sanctified, and Spirit-baptized, one must have both the *mind* (intention) to "live right" and the *will* (determination) to "run on" in order to truly "fight the good fight of faith."

3. After announcing one's salvation, sanctification, and Spirit-baptism, plus one's mind and will to "live right" and to "run on," what follows in the cadential rite is petition for prayer. Usually this is stated as "I desire your prayers," or "Pray my strength in the Lord," or "Pray much for me." The most potent cadential petition incorporates the element of mutuality, which helps maintain the heightened experience of communitas:

> I'm saved, I'm sanctified,
> Holy Ghost filled and fire-baptized;

Pray for me,
I'll be praying for you.

The following example casts the cadential petition in the context of the complete rite:

I'm yet saved and I'm sanctified
Holy Ghost filled and fire-baptized.
I have a deep determination in my soul
To press my way on up to meet the soon-coming king.
I desire your prayers
To pray my strength in the Lord.

Movement into Testifying

Singing is the channel by which worshipers are brought into the experience of testifying. If a testimony is to be mournful then a mournful hymn best addresses the speaker's remorse and coherently brings the congregation into the position of being able to empathize with the experience of the speaker. If a testimony is to be celebrative (as most are) then the hymn raised is appropriately jubilant. Although singing transmutes the worshipers into the narrative experience of the speaker, it is equally important in bringing the speaker to the point of readiness to sacrifice his or her testimony with the group. One worshiper explained it this way: "Some songs automatically break down walls and barriers. I don't know if you've ever experienced being burdened or tied up in knots so that you don't even know what to say. Certain songs can open you up, so that by the time you've finished that song, you're down at the altar and you're ready to talk" (cited in Dargan 1982:78).

The following singing-testifying isochronisms illustrate how singing brings the *I* and the *Thou* smoothly into the "essential We" of testifying. The first example was led by the musician of a small storefront Pentecostal church. Following a verse sung solo to his own guitar accompaniment, the worshipers joined in the chorus:

Hold to his hand, God's unchanging hand (2X)
Build your hopes on things eternal;
Hold to God's unchanging hand.

After another verse and two choruses, he began testifying:

Praise God—hold to God's unchanging hand. Praise God—That's
part of my testimony this morning, saints. Praise God—I've made
up my mind to hold on to God's unchanging hand. Praise God—

> Sometimes the road gets hard—Praise God—and it seems like there's just no end to anything—Praise God. But I just gotta continue to hold on to God's unchanging hand; realizing—Praise God—as long as we—Praise God—keep our hand in the master's hand—Praise God—after a while—Praise God—everything will be alright—Praise God.

While some testifying makes only brief reference to the introductory hymn, the coherence of the singing-testifying isochronism is most evident when, as the next example illustrates, the testifying is built around the hymnic theme.

> I'm blessed, better than blessed, praise the Lord (2X)
> When I'm tossed round at sea, O the Lord watches me;
> I'm blessed, I'm blessed, O praise the Lord.

Succeeding a second verse (and introductory salutation), the speaker storied:

> I praise God for that song, 'I'm Blessed, Better than Blessed'. . . . I praise the Lord because that song was ringing in my heart. Yesterday afternoon we went to a nursing home, and we went around and sung Christmas carols—some of the girls and I from the job—and I tell you, it really touched my heart because I looked around and saw how blessed I really am. And I'm here to praise God, because I don't care how young you are or how old you are, you can still be in that condition. And I'm here to praise God because we are blessed, better than blessed! And if we just look around and see how blessed we really are, we can really give God the praise; because God deserves all the praise that we've been giving Him this morning. I praise God because I feel good on the inside. I praise God for being saved, sanctified, and have the Holy Ghost and a mind to live right. I desire your prayers.

One way of gauging the effectiveness of the singing-testifying isochronism in generating communitas is when another worshiper is moved to "ride on the back" of the singing-testifying of the speaker. "I thank God for that song," a worshiper responded in this instance, "that I too can look around and say that the Lord has been good to me."

Some testifying is more on the order of exhortation than testimony. Quite consistent with the nature of the position of devotional leader, it is often that person who gives an exhorting testimony and is creative in using it to lead the worshipers into brief potent religious experiences, such as shouting or speaking in tongues. The speaker may occasionally exhort first and then drive the message home with a hymn. In the ensuing instance, however, the devotional leader opened with singing that began slowly in a free style, with the organist "tuning in" a sustained accompaniment:

> Just another day that the Lord has kept me (2X)
> He has kept me from all evil with my mind stayed on Jesus
> Just another day that the Lord has kept me.

Against the backdrop of softly sustained chords, the devotional leader then exhorted: "You know, we might think it's for something good that we've done that the Lord has kept us. But I can say by His grace it is He that has kept us, and not we ourselves. I'd like somebody to just help me sing that song." In the same drawn-out style the devotional leader had the congregation join her in singing verses one and two. Having led the group to this depth of antistructure, she increased the tempo to a double time (twice as fast), and the second verse was thrice sung to the accompaniment of the drums, tambourines, and clapping. Shouting ensued and the *essential We* "spontaneously" burst into ultimacy—the *ultimate We*.

THE MEANING OF SHOUTING

Testifying about victory over worldly travail frequently functions as spiritual, mental, and physical transmutation into the most trenchant form of ritual celebration in the Black church—shouting. *Shouting* refers interchangeably to praising the Lord with a loud voice and to holy dancing. In this case, shouting is "dancing the music" or "acting the music." Insofar as shouting is stylized celebration in the testimonial ritual of intensification, "dancing the music" is ritual dance. Variously referred to as "getting happy," "getting religion," or "having church," shouting is, the people say, "like 'fire shut up in my bones'" (Jeremiah 20:9). It is, they say, "joy unspeakable and full of glory" (1 Peter 1:8).

The classical Pentecostal view of shouting involves an "anointing" from the Holy Ghost, but shouting in obedience to the ordinance to praise the Lord with dance (Psalms 150:4) is no more the result of an "anointing" than clapping in compliance to the command for the people to clap their hands (Psalms 47:1). "Sometimes I just feel like praising Him in the dance," said one woman. "But when the anointing does come on me to dance—when it comes on me this way I go for days! This really doesn't happen very often, it's like a special occasion" (cited in Dargan 1982:79). Unless the "watchman on the wall" stops the music in order to check for "dancing in the flesh" (carnal response to the music), there is no plenary means to check for "dancing in the Spirit" (spiritual response to the Spirit).

When the "fire of the Holy Ghost" does descend on worshipers, there is sure to be dancing. Some will dance in the pews while others will move into the aisle. Those who identify with the musicians may be drawn toward the instruments where they can better bathe in the music. Some will sojourn to their favorite corner (their closet), while others will gravitate toward the sacred center before the altar. This inner center is the principal place of visibility and authority where testimony is led, scripture read, prayer rendered, healing delivered, solos sung, tongues spoken, and conversion is ritually consummated. If shouting is, as James Cone suggests, a renewal of the initial conversion crisis, such that conversion and shouting are "different moments in a single experience" (Cone 1986:26), then perhaps gravitation toward the sacred center is a form of "creative regression." As such, shouting is not a dysfunctional attempt at escapism, that is, an individual attempting to escape reality by obliterating her or his estranged past. Rather, the past remains but is transformed.

Music is a means of drawing worshipers into the realm of ritual dance, wherein the dancers can envisage themselves worshiping God with their entire persons. *Singing the music* also strengthens the communal bond, but *dancing the music* is more representative than song of what it means to be saved, sanctified, and Spirit-baptized. Neither sung music nor its accompaniment can adequately represent the high places of spiritual intensity like dancing can. What is finally being communicated to God and about the worshiping cultus' interaction with God is not that which is sung but that which is ritualized in shouting. This is evidenced in the fact that shouting is usually twice as trenchant and thrice as lengthy as its introductory singing-testifying isochronism. Sociologist E. Franklin Frazier alludes to this when he says: "singing is accompanied by 'shouting' or holy dancing which permits the maximum of free religious expression on the part of the participants." In Holiness and Pentecostal churches, says Frazier, shouting is the "chief religious activity" (Frazier 1974[1964]:59, 61).

It will be illustrated below that shouting is a point of transmutation from the singing-testifying isochronism into even greater ultimacy, the ultimacy of being "slain in the Spirit." First, it is important to show that one's reception not only of the initial ability to shout (at conversion for instance) but of a personalized style of shouting is a rite of passage. In the medium of testifying, one woman announced the occasion and led in its ritual celebration:

> He gave me the dance last Sunday—Priase God. I didn't even
> know it till I went home—Praise God. When I was dancing in my
> feet something said, 'look down'—Hallelujah. I was so excited—
> Hallelujah Jesus. I didn't even realize He gave me the dance—
> Praise God. Hallelujah Jesus! (3X) Hallelujah! (2X). . . . I didn't
> even realize when I got home—Praise God—that He gave me the
> dance in my feet—Praise God . . . I always wanted to dance for the
> Lord—Hallelujah.

Spontaneously the young woman began demonstrating for the worshipers the dance that the Lord had given her, to which the organist (who had been sustaining chords in the background) and the instrumentalists responded with the appropriate "shout" music. The worshipers clapped, stomped, and beat their tambourines.

The greater ultimacy to which shouting often leads is that of being "slain in the Spirit." This is different from what is known as "agonizing in the spirit." When one is "agonizing in the spirit" (travailing or making strong supplication and prayer to the Lord) and the Spirit is making intercessory groanings, it is believed that the flesh is trying to bring itself under submission to the Spirit. When one is "slain in the Spirit" it believed that God's Spirit has taken dominance over the human spirit (trance) and that one is literally overwhelmed (collapse): *dance—> trance—> collapse*. As worshipers lay "slain," it is said that they are experiencing the euphoric afterglow of the anointing—God is refilling them, giving them visions, or bringing them internal peace. Being "slain in the Spirit" is to "enter out" of a powerful spiritual experience with divine imperative. It is to revitalize the worshiping community with even greater effusing power than if one had "entered out" by one's own accord. It is, in the language of John 7:38, the flowing out of one's belly living rivers of water.

The isochronism of singing-testifying in Holiness and Pentecostal worship often leads to the isochronism *dance—> trance—> collapse*. Through singing, testifying, shouting, and being "slain," Black worshipers have long sung, spoken, and enacted the positive and therapeutic involvement of God in their lives, thereby intensifying their individual faith and their community strength as they endure the ways of the world.

BIBLIOGRAPHY

Buber, Martin
1937 *I and Thou.* Ronald Gregor Smith (trans) Edinburgh: T. & T. Clark.

Cone, James H.
1986 *Speaking the Truth: Ecumenism, Liberation, and Black Theology.* Grand Rapids, MI: Eerdmans.

Dargan, William T.
1982 "Congregational Gospel Songs in a Black Holiness Church: A Musical and Textual Analysis." Ph.D. dissertation, Wesleyan University.

Frazier, E. Franklin
1974 [1964] *The Negro Church in America.* New York: Schocken.

Jules-Rosette, Bennetta
1975 *African Apostles: Ritual and Conversion in the Church of John Maranke.* Ithaca, NY: Cornell University Press.

"The Pentecostal Assembly"
1907 *The Apostolic Faith.* 1(1) (April): 2.

Reed, Bruce
1978 *The Dynamics of Religion: Process and Movement in Christian Churches*. London: Darton, Longman and Todd.

Turner, Victor
1969 *The Ritual Process: Structure and Antistructure*. Ithaca, NY: Cornell University Press.

Williams, Robert C.
1987 "Worship and Anti-Structure in Thurman's Vision of the Sacred." *Journal of the Interdenominational Theological Center* 14(1 & 2):161-174.

6

Powwows, Parades and Social Drama Among the Waccamaw Sioux

Patricia B. Lerch

This chapter describes the relationships among powwows, parades, and social drama among the Waccamaw people of southeastern North Carolina. The powwow and parade celebrate the Indian heritage of the community. Relatives, friends, and neighbors join in the festivities and tourists watch the dancing and the parade. As a cultural experience, powwows and parades are carefully crafted performances, expressions, or representations of the Waccamaw's history and present reality as they wish to present it. Structuring the event—defining the limits, organizing the activities, inviting speakers, and registering participants—provides order and gives meaning to this community festival. The Waccamaw powwow is patterned and modeled after pan-Indian powwows. But as the organizers define it, they also define themselves through it, and so the powwow becomes an expression of their social identity.

Today, Native American powwows are common events in the United States. In the state of North Carolina, these public celebrations of Indian traditions and identity have drawn tourists and visitors into Indian communities for twenty or more years. What is a powwow? A powwow is first of all a gathering of people of Indian ancestry to celebrate that ancestry. The gatherings take place at a powwow ground or any area reserved for this event. The images include feathered warbonnets and beads. The sounds include drum beats and yelps. These images and sounds are common to pan-Indian tribal events. The supratribal or pan-Indian character of the powwow has led anthropologists and others to disparage its acceptance among traditional Native American cultures because they fear it may replace culture-specific traditions. Others view it as the only Indian pattern visible in the life of many highly acculturated tribes (Howard 1955; Paredes 1965; Rynkiewich 1980; Siegel 1983; Thomas 1965). The powwow celebrations of the Waccamaw Sioux provide an opportunity to consider how ritual and performance define their identity in contemporary American culture.

Visitors to North Carolina are often unaware of the state's Indian population. The federally recognized Eastern Band of Cherokee, located in the western part of the state, are better known than the state-recognized tribes which make up the majority of the Indian population (Lerch 1992a). The Waccamaw Sioux tribe is one of the latter group. The 1,300 people on the tribal roll live in two rural communities in the southeastern part of the state. Their ancestors first appear in the historic records at the beginning of the nineteenth century and it is likely that they are descendants of the Siouan-speaking tribes that once lived along the coastal plain (Lerch 1992a). Their only connection with the western Siouan speakers is through their adoption in the twentieth century of the pan-Indian powwow, with its Plains Indian regalia.

The Waccamaw remained fairly obscure and little known outside of their region until after 1970, when they organized their first annual powwow. However, "being known as Indian," or recognition in both a formal and an informal sense, has always been important to the Waccamaw (Lerch 1992b). Public funding for Indian schools concerned Waccamaw leaders from 1910 to 1964. Federal recognition occupied their leaders once from 1949 to 1950 and again in 1982 when they initiated efforts to submit a federal acknowledgment petition to the Bureau of Indian Affairs. Thus, "being known as an Indian" has significance personally and legally for the Waccamaw (Lerch 1991). Since its inception, the powwow has publicized the presence of the Waccamaw to their neighbors and very effectively advertised their community over the years. It has focused attention on their Indian ancestry in a dramatic and public way.

In the first part of this chapter, social drama analysis puts into perspective the historical events leading up to the first annual powwow in the Waccamaw community and explains why the Waccamaw began powwows in their community. In the latter part of the chapter, the parade and performances of the 1991 powwow are described in detail. Preserving the flow of events in my description is critical to the powwow experience and I present enough description so that the reader begins to see and hear what most visitors see and hear in order that the dramatic performance aspect of the powwow as social drama becomes evident.

Social drama analysis focuses on the study of culture in a framework of continuous change, of adjustments to conflict and tension that always characterize social life. Victor Turner says that social dramas "are units of aharmonic and disharmonic process, arising in conflict situations" (Turner 1974:37). The fieldworker may observe one or all of the four major phases of a social drama: breach, crisis, redressive action, and reintegration. A breach is a break in the normal routine caused by a break in some regular way of conducting social life. A breach is followed by a crisis phase which reveals the veiled lines of tension in social relationships. Tension is there all along but it is dormant or suppressed. After the breach, tensions surface in individuals as fears or anxieties. Individual anxiety stems from the "liminal" characteristics of crisis as this is a time before things have been worked out between the groups. The third phase is the redressive phase when the sense of crisis is forestalled by "leading or structurally representative members of the disturbed social system" (Turner 1974:39). The events of this phase are particularly important. Turner offers this advice to a fieldworker studying social change:

> study carefully what happens in phase three, the would-be redressive phase of social dramas, and ask whether the redressive machinery is capable of handling crises so as to restore, more or less, the status quo ante, or at least to restore peace among contending groups. Then ask, if so, how precisely? And if not, why not? (Turner 1974:41)

The redressive phase deserves careful study because it also shares the liminal features of crisis. He continues by saying:

> For the society, group, community, association, or what-ever may be the social unit, is here at its most 'self-conscious' and may attain the clarity of someone fighting in a corner for his life. Redress, too, has its liminal features, its being 'betwixt and between,' and, as such, furnishes a distanced replication and critique of the events leading up to and composing the 'crisis' (Turner 1974:41).

The Turners broaden Van Gennep's concept of liminality to include "not only transition but also potentiality, not only 'going to be' but also 'what may be'" (Turner and Turner 1978:3). This broader interpretation allows a more expansive or creative redefinition of social relations, one less bounded by prescribed social definitions of status.

The last phase is "reintegration of the disturbed social group or of the social recognition and legitimization of irreparable schism between the contesting parties" (Turner 1974:41).

While fieldworkers may observe all four phases of a social drama as it actually unfolds in the life of a community, I did not have this opportunity. I first met the Waccamaw in 1981 and I did not attend my first powwow until 1982—years after the social drama that led to the adoption of the powwow had ended. The original powwow represents one of several actions taken by Indian leaders during the redressive phase described above. The social drama that led to the adoption of the powwow began during the civil rights era of the 1960s, when African-Americans led minorities in scaling the walls of segregation. Once these walls crumbled, social relations could be redefined. These redefined social relations initiated a whole new set of breach/crisis events that are redressed by the contemporary powwow. The 1991 powwow, a phenomena of the reintegration phase, is different from these earlier powwows and can be viewed as an on-going social drama in its own right.

THE FIRST WACCAMAW POWWOW AS SOCIAL DRAMA

The Breach

In 1964 the Civil Rights Act was passed and in its aftermath, the public schools of North Carolina dismantled their segregated school system. The Columbus County School Board alerted parents of their intention to comply with this act in a notice dated March 3, 1965. It read: "In Compliance with the 'Civil Rights Act of 1964,' every child in the Columbus County School System shall have the right to attend a school freely selected without regard to race or color, effective with the 1965-1966 school year."[1] Parents were told to let their school principal know what school they chose to enroll their children in by April 16, 1965.

The Crisis

This news was greeted by many Waccamaw with dismay and fear. The Waccamaw Indian School's future was in jeopardy. One member of the class of 1967 remembers those days:

> I had mixed feelings. Some of the first feelings I had was we do not want to go [to the integrated school] and be with other groups because they know nothing about us and we know nothing about them. But then after reading some of the materials that had been presented about things that would be offered [at the new school], I had a change of view.

This graduate's statement expresses the fears of her parents and neighbors who were concerned about the upcoming change. The Waccamaw Indian School symbolized the Indian battle for recognition (Lerch 1988, 1992a). Generations of parents had presented petitions through their school committees to secure public funding for Indian schools and the recognition that this brought to them. Many people experienced discrimination first hand in the surrounding towns and sought to isolate their children as much as possible from its humiliating effects. Families feared the loss of a sense of community that their schools represented, a loss of their traditions, and a loss of their identity. The parents of the graduate quoted above were afraid that their children would not be treated fairly, offered the same opportunities in school as others, or would drop out of school. In their community, with few telephones or cars, if a child stayed out of school, the parents were visited by teachers or alerted by neighbors. This closeness, it was feared, would be lost.

The fears expressed by parents were well-founded. How would the Indian identity of children be reinforced if they went to integrated schools? Of the

12,043 students in the county schools in 1965, 56 percent were White, 41 percent were Black, and only 3 percent were Indian.[2] As a tiny minority, what would prevent the school officials from classifying them as "colored" or "Negro" as they had consistently done in the past? How would the parents be represented on the school committees of these integrated school? Would their committeemen be as effective in making their concerns heard as in the past? The Board administered the schools through a series of school committees representing the local schools. This system was established in July 1885.[3]

The Waccamaw schools were a powerful force for the socialization of Indian identity. The children who attended the schools were Indians. The teachers who taught at the schools were Indians, although not always Waccamaw. The school committeemen were leading men from the Indian families of the community. Education was filtered through the lens of Indian culture and values. Since discrimination and prejudice faced *all* non-Whites in the surrounding towns and cities, the Indian schools did their best to deflect the worst blows by teaching their students not only how to read, write, and compute, but also how to evaluate and defend their self-identity as Indian. The closing of the school preceded several redressive actions. These actions included the formation in 1970 of the North Carolina Commission of Indian Affairs, the adoption of the powwow, the securing of five acres of tribal land, and the incorporation of the Waccamaw Siouan Development Association.

Redressive Action

At the 1991 Waccamaw powwow, the remarks of the Commissioner reflected upon the efforts of Indian leaders in 1970 to form the North Carolina Commission of Indian Affairs (Lerch 1992a). The Waccamaw leader Chief Freeman, father of Chief Pricilla Jacobs, was actively involved. He met with Indian leaders from North Carolina to work out the details of the newly forming Commission. The Commission offered the opportunity to formalize already existing ties among the Indian communities. For example, the Lumbee Indians, the largest of the state-recognized tribes in North Carolina, provided the teachers and the preachers that worked in the Waccamaw communities from 1930 through 1964.

I see the formation of the North Carolina Commission of Indian Affairs as a redressive mechanism. School desegregation threatened the smaller Indians communities with social extinction. The Cherokee had federal recognition and with the Lumbee, who received state recognition in 1953 and a type of federal recognition in 1956, were less threatened but they could still participate if they so chose (Lerch 1992a). A formal organization within the state government that served the economic and social needs of Indian people could strengthen Indian communities. The Commission provided a way for Indian communities to become legally recognized by the state. Soon after its formation in 1971, the

Waccamaw, the Coharie, and three urban Indian associations received state recognition. The Commission strengthened Indian communities by offering information and assistance with grantsmanship, leadership skills, and economic development. Supratribal or pan-Indian organizations, such as the Commission, have played an important role in the recent political resurgence of Native Americans across the United States (Cornell 1988).

The powwow is another redressive mechanism. Through the efforts of the current tribal Chief, Pricilla Jacobs, the Waccamaw held the first powwow in 1970. Reflecting back on those days, Chief Jacobs describes them with a mixture of nostalgia and sadness. She recalls her reasons for initiating the powwow:

> We needed that here to try to revive our Indian culture. This was a way of doing it—letting other people see. Mostly we had always had a problem with recognition as Indians anyway. Most people [non-Indians] didn't know anything about Indians—[just] a group of people out here in the woods that nobody knows much about, never even thought about too much. It was our intention to bring [Indian] people together for fellowship, to see what each other was doing [other tribes], to share our arts and crafts with one another, [to share] the progress. At that time, all the Indian tribes were doing the same thing, we were all getting started in it at the same time, trying to revive our culture. That was the purpose of the powwow at that time.

Her remarks suggest the "communitas" that she and others experienced during those early powwows (1970-1976) when they were more like "family reunions" than they are today:

> Back then [1970-1976], we didn't have to worry about paying someone to come do drums or do dancing—it was mostly a sharing thing then, we were sharing with each other, and it was real good then. The purpose somewhere down the line got from the culture and tradition to a money-making festival. That's the way I see it.

The sadness she describes is normal. Communitas is an experience and cannot be sustained. It is a characteristic of liminality and "anti-structure." Communitas is a fleeting realization that despite individuality there can be oneness. Turner recognized this feature of communitas:

> We thus encounter the paradox that the experience of communitas becomes the memory of communitas, with the result that communitas itself in striving to replicate itself historically develops a social structure, in which initially free and innovative

> relationships between individuals are converted into norm-
> governed relationships between social personae (Turner 1982a:47).

The later powwows might try to recapture something of the earlier ones but for
those who were there, the experience becomes a memory.

Two other redressive mechanisms moved the Waccamaw out of crisis.
Shortly after the first powwow, community leaders approached one of the large
paper companies to ask for a donation of five acres of land that would serve as a
center of community life. They were successful in securing this gift in part because their own economic role in the forestry industry earned them a reputation
as hard-working and industrious people. They publicized their efforts, making it
clear that they were an Indian community, by holding a small powwow complete with regalia when the land was donated in a public ceremony. A small
group of leaders, including Chief Freeman and his daughter, Chief Jacobs, proceeded in 1976 to file with the state of North Carolina for the incorporation of
the Waccamaw Siouan Development Association (WSDA). The Articles of
Incorporation state that: "the corporation will itself undertake demonstration
and ongoing projects to serve the health, education, general and economic welfare needs of the Waccamaw Siouan Indians, in particular." The WSDA eventually matured into a fully developed governing body with an elected tribal
board. Powwow planning and preparation became the responsibility of the staff
of the WSDA where once it had been that of the Chief's family.

Reintegration Phase

The social drama triggered by the 1964 Civil Rights Act initiated a realign-
ment of social relationships. Indians and African-Americans attended schools
with Whites for the first time in the history of North Carolina. The Waccamaw
Indian schools closed and the leadership role held by the school committeemen
diminished in importance. The WSDA's executive director and tribal board assumed more and more responsibility for community projects. The Chief's role in
tribal affairs after 1975 was reduced to ceremony. Outside of the community,
the state provided legal definition and leadership for the state-recognized Indian
communities. Non-Indian neighbors came into the Waccamaw community to
watch Indian dancing and watch the parade. Some even attended as participants
marching in the integrated high school band or delivering speeches as invited
politicians. I suspect that many of these changes model the social drama process
with its reoccurring phases of breach, crisis, redress, and reintegration. Over the
years, the powwow proved to be a flexible and durable institution and reflects
the changing needs of the community.

As an ongoing process of reintegration, powwows gradually have changed
over the years. From 1982 until 1991 the basic pattern of Indian dancing, parades, and pageants has been altered to accommodate baseball games,

weightlifting contests, gospel choirs, talent shows, and disco dances. From time to time, powwow planners have debated the merits of including one or another of these events. My observations lead me to conclude that powwows are focused on certain core features such as Indian dancing, parades, Indian food (home-cooked meals especially enjoyed by the elderly and their families), and the Indian princess pageant, and as a ritual, draws large crowds. Powwows reflect the needs of the Indian community in the era of redefined social relationships. The nostalgia with which those early powwows are remembered reflect a memory of communitas resulting from redressive measures to end a crisis in the community. As Turner points out, the "self-conscious" nature of redressive mechanisms reflects the degree to which the community felt cornered, fighting for its life. Communitas is a transitory experience and there is always the possibility that the next powwow will offer the opportunity to experience it again.

The powwow offers solace to the Waccamaw with the comfort of knowing that they were participating in an event that was widely recognized as "Indian." Pre-powwow community events attracted few outsiders into the area and reinforce the isolation of the Waccamaw. Powwows, however, are pan-Indian or supratribal events and connect the Waccamaw to something larger, something Indians and non-Indians associate with Native Americans. The individuals who participate today in the powwow, especially those who put on the regalia and dance, participate in performances that are both dramatic and ritualized. These performances transforms them briefly into people whose Indian identity is unquestioned.

THE ON-GOING REINTEGRATION PHASE OF THE ORIGINAL POWWOW[4]

The contemporary powwow redresses a set of breach/crisis events that were initiated by desegregation. The breach/crisis events concern Indian norms governing Indian and non-Indian interaction, standards of beauty, economic and occupational traditions, and family-based leadership patterns. Working out acceptable standards through redressive actions of the powwow help the Waccamaw define their Indian identity in a greatly changed social environment.

In the pre-powwow days, Indians married Indians. Indian boys and girls rarely dated non-Indians. In earlier generations, White men and Indian women, unable to marry and live together, were forced by social pressure to reside in separate houses located down the road from each other along the borders of the Indian community. Mixed-blood children, raised almost totally in isolation, "went for Indian" rather than White. Stories of the consequences of interracial dating and marriage related today emphasize the dangerous nature of such relationships. Indian men drove outsiders out of their community and earned a rough reputation. Segregation, discrimination, and prejudice forced the Indians to look inward and they reacted by fiercely defending their social and physical space against unwelcome intruders. Indian schools operated within this enclosed space. Desegregation forced the integration of public schools and public places. The barriers between the races were breached. Indians who opposed interracial mixing saw their community change as their children began to bring home non-Indians, primarily Whites, to live within the community. Mixed blood children, always present in the past, may someday outnumber full bloods as an increasing number of Indian and non-Indian liaisons are made and accepted.

Indian standards of beauty accommodate a wide variety of phenotypical traits reflecting the mixed heritage of many Indians. Dark straight hair, dark eyes, olive skin, and high cheekbones are standards of beauty but curly to kinky hair, light to dark skin are accepted. An Indian is defined not only by looks but by family background. Multicultural and multiracial schools put Indian children in a setting with people whose physical features may overlap with theirs but the standards of beauty are increasingly measured by the dominant culture's emphasis on Northern European physique.

Farming, logging, construction for men and textile mill operator, service positions, part time farmer, and homemaker for women provided a living for the Waccamaw. Breaking into higher paid jobs that require a technical or college education is difficult for children who must first overcome a disadvantaged background in order to succeed. Desegregation of public schools and public places has not ended discrimination against non-Whites who must compete with others for the limited employment opportunities that fall outside their traditional roles.

Family-based leadership patterns have been eroded over the years. The school committeemen were once appointed by the leading family groups. These same family groups provided leaders for the informal tribal council. One of these families provided the men who became the "chief spokesman for the community." The redressive actions of the social drama initiated by the 1964 Civil Rights Act set in motion a process that altered the nature of leadership within the communmity. After 1970, leaders were elected by the community to serve a term as tribal board members. The Chief position became largely ceremonial. Power fell to those who had earned a college degree, entered a profession, or who had been elected to county office following a countywide election. The powwow continues to redress a set of breach/crisis events that are related to the original social drama of 1970 but which developed in the years after the redressive actions were instituted and the reintegration phase began.

I want to end by describing the public version of the 1991 powwow. This is where any visitor to the Waccamaw powwow has to begin—in the present. The 1991 powwow cannot recreate the original communitas experienced at the first powwow. But by taking on some of the characteristics of "ideological" communitas described by Turner (1982a:48), powwows try to recapture the spirit of communitas by providing Indian participants a "being together" experience. Indians, African-Americans, and Anglos may also share a brief moment of communitas resulting from the host and guest relationship.

Friday Evening

The 1991 Waccamaw powwow begins at dusk. As one approaches the powwow grounds (the parking lot of the WSDA and day care), the air reverberates with monosyllabic chants, drum beats, and occasional sharp cries and shouts. These sounds and images of feathers and beads, multicolored and attractive, fill the night air with a tinge of excitement. The powwow grounds are encircled with bright glaring lights strung from the booths of the "Indian traders" whose wares include wooden tomahawks, blue feathers, beaded bands, "silver jewelry," leather belts, arrowheads, and an assortment of "country crafts." There is no mistaking that something very unique is occurring in this small community, miles from the main highway, and on the way to nowhere in particular. Only those coming to the powwow would even pass the area.

The evening events begin with a "welcoming" and opening prayer (primarily Christian in content) by the Chief. Chief Jacobs tells the audience of mostly Indian people that it is good "to be alive again at the 21st annual powwow." She mentions several older Indian people who have died during the year, reminding everyone of how these people will be missed. She ties the major kinship groups directly to the powwow as she mentions those who have passed away. Chief Jacobs then welcomes the Indian people from "tribes throughout the state" to the powwow. She states: "let's not forget our people, especially those in leadership positions that help Indians." Prestigious guests from the North Carolina Commission of Indian Affairs are introduced and asked to say a few words to the assembled crowd. The Commissioner, who is a Lumbee Indian, recalls the past and the former leaders who were so instrumental in organizing the Commission. He says:

> It's good to be back with you today, it's enriching to be with you.
> I remember the early powwows, I remember Chief Freeman, Chief
> Jacob's father, who gave his time, energy, and effort in helping get
> the Commission started. We owe a great debt to Chief Freeman.

This emphasis on the past, on cooperation between Indian people, on the supratribal effort it took to form the Commission, becomes the theme to be repeated during the Saturday afternoon remarks.

Biculturalism, "walking in two worlds," are phrases he uses to describe the code switching at which modern Indians must be skilled in order to exist in the "Indian world" and the "world of shirts and ties." The Commissioner's remarks also introduced the theme of the remaining powwow speakers—"walking in two worlds." Biculturalism, trying to maintain an identity as Indian and make it in the non-Indian world, is repeatedly stressed in speeches throughout the powwow weekend. The powwow is described as the "Indian world here tonight" and the "other world is the world of shirts and ties." The Commissioner enjoins the assembly "to be proud, to have self esteem." He tells them that the powwow does his "heart good," and "recharges his batteries."

The next speaker, the chair of the Commission's Board of Directors, a Lumbee woman, opens her remarks by telling the people that the powwow "refreshes in the Indian way." She demonstrates the progress that Indian people have made in North Carolina by relating an incident that happen to her on her way to the powwow. Driving into the area, she stopped to buy a soft drink at a local store. The clerk, while checking her out, remarked to her: "Oh, you're an Indian [too] and you're on your way to the Waccamaw powwow! I'm going there myself after work." The speaker pointed out that years ago this young lady could not have worked at that store. She alluded to the discrimination directed at non-Whites that was so pervasive at that time. The girl would not have openly admitted in public that she recognized her customer as an Indian or that she herself was an Indian. Progress has been made for Indian people in the state.

Speakers from neighboring tribes continued the theme of Indian unity and progress. Pride in being Indian and participating in an Indian event was stressed. Chief Jacobs spoke again, reflecting on the progress made by Indians who can today "look anyone level in the eye because we are as good or even better than some." Others stressed that pride in being Indian, in participating in the powwow, could keep young people from turning to drugs!

Friday evening fancy and traditional dancers demonstrate their talents. Friends and relatives greet each other while stopping to watch the dancers and enjoy the cool evening breezes. Traders, arriving late, continue to set up their booths and prepare for the Saturday crowd.

The Parade

At ten o'clock Saturday, the parade participants gather two miles down the highway from the powwow grounds at the site of the former Waccamaw Indian High School. This assembly point marks the beginning of the parade route which takes the participants through the "Little Branch" community straight to the powwow grounds. For a moment, the past touches the present where the old high school, opened in 1955 and closed in 1970, marks the beginning of the parade. The high school was the crowning achievement of earlier generations who struggled for years to secure public funding for Indian schools within their communities. Two elementary schools, one opening in 1933 and the other in 1945, and the high school, opening in 1955, became symbols to the Waccamaw of their heritage and their peoplehood. Except for the three Indian Baptist churches, the schools were the most important Indian institutions. So it is particularly fitting that the powwow participants assemble at this point.

Leading the parade, we see the marching band of the regional high school, formerly a White high school, that today includes Indians, Whites, and Blacks.

The band heads the parade of cars loaded with special guests and dignitaries. Bands and parades go together in the minds of the public. But I think that the act of inviting this band to the powwow parade is open to a couple of different interpretations. On the one hand, it may be seen as symbolizing the Indian's efforts to encourage racial harmony. This certainly marks a change from former days when Indians refused to attend schools for African-Americans and were prevented from attending schools designated as White. Racial harmony is a desirable goal in this community, where 13 percent of the spouses are White. African-American intermarriages are also not unknown. On the another hand, the Indian members of the marching band, whose physical appearance may not conform to racial stereotypes of what Indians are supposed to look like, are reinforced in their self-identity as Indian. This is their community, their parade, and their Indian celebration. For the White and Black members of the marching band, participating in this parade acknowledges the Indian community and may symbolize a journey into previously forbidden or dangerous territory. Race relations have not always been as harmonious as those expressed in the parade.

In the car following the high school band, we find the first elected Indian sheriff in the county. This is a considerable accomplishment in a county with only 34 percent minority population (African-American and Indian) and in which a minority candidate has never been elected to either the county commission or the school board. The Indian sheriff's car is followed by a van carrying the Commissioner and board chair of the North Carolina Commission of Indian Affairs. Accompanying the Commissioner is a young woman who is the first Waccamaw lawyer and who is employed by the state attorney general's office. As with the band, achievements are symbolized by the people in the parade. A later car carries the all-White board of education. This symbolizes the complete reversal in relations between the Indian community and the board of education. From 1885 until 1945, this board refused to recognize the community as an Indian community. In 1945, the board funded the second Indian elementary school (first in their county) following years of petitions presented to them by members of the community school committees (Lerch 1988, 1992a).

The Indian pageant winners follow in car after car. Each year, the Waccamaw select a young woman to represent them at local, regional, and state gatherings at which Indian people are present. Miss Waccamaw contestants compete in three age levels: Tiny Tot, Little Miss, and Senior Miss. The families of these girls support their candidacy with financial contributions which pay for their Indian regalia. At each level, the contestants are asked to demonstrate some particular talent (miming song lyrics, singing, reciting poetry or folklore, dancing, etc.) before a panel of judges. The judges are chosen from other Indian tribes and from the non-Indian community. Most of the girls are members of the Indian dance team and perform at public events and fairs during the year. They may also compete for the cash prizes awarded to their age grades at the powwows. In addition to talent, the girls assemble "outfits" of formal wear, street wear, and Indian wear. In the latter case, Indian wear imitates what is presumed to be a Plains Culture style for women. A typical outfit may include a loose fitting shift made of White, tan, or dark brown suede cloth, decorated with colored wooden beads attached to rows of fringe hanging down from the bustline along the front and back of the dress. All the girls wear suede moccasins. Some may carry shawls. Variety is introduced by sewing decorative items such as shells, beads, acorns, dyed corn, or colored feathers onto the shift, or by wearing ankle bells above the moccasins. Little girls and young ladies dressed in Indian wear present a feminine image that blends the Indian princess image with southern images of girlhood.

The parade continues as tractors and tractor-trailer rigs drive by carrying the Indian dancers. The tractor-trailer rigs are used primarily in the logging industry, an industry that has been traditionally important to the local economy. The pine forests that surround the Waccamaw homes were the source of turpentine and tar once so important to a booming naval stores industry that began in the eighteenth century. By the 1910, the South Atlantic States led the country in the value of this type of forest product and North Carolina ranked first in the region. This extractive industry involved small groups of men who during the winter months "boxed" pine trees by removing a portion of the bark and cutting incisions into the tree allowing the resin, crude turpentine, to flow during the spring and summer months. The raw resin was transferred in barrels, made by local coopers or barrel makers, to distilleries. The expansion of the southern railway system also created forest jobs for Waccamaw men, who cut ties for the railroad and floated them out of the Green Swamp, a vast area near the Waccamaw's traditional homes. Such public work supplemented subsistence farming.

Today, the forests are owned by large paper companies but many of the loggers who cut and haul the trees come from the small, privately owned Waccamaw companies. The trucks driven in the powwow parade are also Indian owned and operated, and employ many local Indian men. The semi-truck tractor-trailer rig has replaced the mule- or horse-drawn wagons that were used to haul logs for this industry. Forestry, farming, and construction, as well as other occupations, employ Waccamaw men. Most employed Waccamaw women work in textile mills, social service jobs, or semi-professional positions such as health care worker, farming, and forestry.[5] The trucks driving in the parade send clear messages about employment, economic prosperity, and economic development in the Waccamaw community.

The Powwow Grounds

Following the parade, the powwow grounds once again become the focus of attention. Chief Jacobs welcomes the guests and visitors to the powwow, stressing the themes touched upon the evening before. The Indian princesses from surrounding tribes are introduced. The powwow changes for a few hours into a county fair, or "country chunk down," as the princesses demonstrate their talent by singing or dancing for the crowd. The Waccamaw are Christians, primarily Baptists and Spiritual Baptist. Gospel singers from the local Indian Baptist Church entertain friends and relatives with sentimental religious songs, typical of "country western" music shows.

On Saturday afternoon, before the powwow dancing begins, Chief Jacobs introduces the invited guests. The special guest speaker at the 1991 powwow is the first Waccamaw Indian lawyer. This young woman describes herself to the audience, especially to the Waccamaw children, as being a "typical" Indian because she comes from a large Indian family. She stressed the theme of "walking in two worlds." She pointed out that she wears her legal attire—a business suit—with her Indian moccasins in order to demonstrate the biculturalism faced by Indians in today's society. She tells the crowd that they should "walk in the Indian way, take no more than you need, use what you take." She addresses most of her remarks to the younger generation, telling them to stay in school, stay away from drugs, and work hard to get ahead.

In addition to these messages of success and progress, national identity and patriotism is also a major theme of the powwow. The guest emcee and drum group begin the afternoon dancing with a "Veterans Song," inviting all veterans of foreign wars to join the dance. The crowd is reminded of the many sacrifices that Native Americans have made in defense of their country. The potential tension between being "the first Americans" and "Americans" is mentioned but not dwelled upon.

The traditional and fancy dancing categories, age graded as Tiny Tots, Junior Miss and Junior Boys, and Adults, compete in separate events. The afternoon events culminate with the adult men's traditional and fancy dance competitions. Throughout the late afternoon and evening, the emcee interjects the themes of Indian unity, biculturalism, and pride in Indian identity.

Later in the evening, visitors will leave the powwow grounds. The dancers will take off their regalia. The drum group will get up from the drumming circle. The powwow is over for another year.

THE 1991 POWWOW: PERFORMANCE AND TRANSFORMATION

The social drama played out in the 1991 powwow is summarized in the theme of bicultural or multicultural identity sounded in the speeches of the tribal Chief and invited dignitaries. The "walking in two worlds" theme requires wearing "shirts and ties," symbols of corporate America, and moccasins, a visible symbol of Native American identity. Ecological values, expressed in Native American homilies such as "take no more than you need, use what you take," are coupled with the Protestant ethic of working hard to get ahead. The 1991 powwow reflects the many adjustments Waccamaw make in the redefined social environment following desegregation. The 1970 powwow contrasts with the 1991 powwow on several dimensions.

One dimension is cultural. In 1970 the powwow planners hoped that the powwow would "revive their culture" and educate the next generation about their identity. The closing of the Indian schools created a need for an institution such as the powwow. It would educate and socialize the children as Indians. It would revive the culture and prevent assimilation from eroding the Indian way. By 1991, the powwow planners appear to stress the realities of living in a multicultural environment. Indians must compete, work, learn, and exist in two worlds: the Indian world created by the community and the other world peopled with Whites, Hispanics, Blacks, Asians, and others.

Another dimension involves the sense of family and shared communitas. In the words of Chief Jacobs, the earlier powwows of the 1970s brought Indians together like one family. The Chiefs committed themselves to attending each other's powwows. Most of the people attending the powwows were kin to each other. At least in the early years, few outsiders came. The communitas that they shared was based on their common Indian identity and family connections. The family ties are still mentioned at the 1991 powwow as the Chief reminds those present of old ones who have passed away during the year. But many people are first time visitors to the powwow, and, as guests, know little of the family ties among those they visit. The traders and their booths are primarily owned and operated by Whites. African-American visitors also attend. The visitors represent the non-Indian world and they see a Native American festival as they watch the traditional and fancy dancers decked out in their regalia. The hosts are staging a Native American celebration and the guests are their appreciative audience. The parade defines the Waccamaw as loggers and truckers, as law abiding citizens, as lawyers, as sheriffs, as people who support their children, as a community that coexists harmoniously with members of other races. The dancers perform for a multicultural audience of Whites, African-Americans, and Indians from other communities. African-Americans and Anglos may experience a kind of communitas since they were drawn to the powwow as guests and sought out the experience. Perhaps seeking to "learn about Indian culture" they came to more clearly define themselves. Sharing the powwow experience with Indians may also communicate to African-Americans and Anglos that harmonious race relations are possible. If this possibility is evident, even for a moment, then the potential exists for the powwow to affect and redefine race relations.

The third dimension is performance. Originally, drum groups and dancers contributed their time and talent; today, they are paid or attracted by cash prizes. Indian culture of the past emphasized the family-like contribution of time and talent for the good of the whole. A step closer to Anglo values of compensation for time and talent expended is taken at the 1991 powwow. Certainly, there remain many who have given their time and talent freely to ensure that the powwow runs smoothly. But, as the Chief laments, the powwow is more of a money-making affair today. The Waccamaw spend more time in the non-Indian world today and their powwow reflects this.

A fourth dimension reflects changes in leadership. The democratic system of elections has radically changed leadership patterns, moving from family-based leadership to elected officials. The old Chief served for life, the tribal board members serve a term of two years. The first powwows were initiated and financed by contributions from the Chief and his close kin. Their desire was to "share the culture" with their people and other Indians of the state. Today, powwows are planned by a core of staff people working for the WSDA. Tribal board members and elderly men, who represent the earlier tradition of family leadership, contribute their knowledge and energy, too. Chief Jacobs, a woman, presided as the emcee and she led the opening prayer and dance. The staff set the fees to be charged for the traders' booths, determined the schedule, raised or put up the cash prize for the dancing, paid the drum groups, and invited the emcee to direct the dance competition.

The powwow is a money-making affair. But it also contributes to the self-identity of the participants by publicizing their presence, their history, and their heritage to anyone who cares to look. The pan-Indian and local symbols of identity portrayed in the powwow flow into and out of each other. Public celebrations often symbolize the "essential life" of a group (Turner 1982b:16). This is true of the Waccamaw powwow. The events of their recent history are framed and paraded by for all to see. Following the powwow, the princess becomes Miss Waccamaw for a year. She represents the community at county fairs and public gatherings that include the neighbors of the Waccamaw. The activities and events associated with Indian Day are celebrated in the public schools and recognition is given to the Waccamaw. The struggle for recognition is a daily event in the lives of the Waccamaw people, who place high value on "being known as Indian," within a larger socio-cultural context (Lerch 1991).

The powwow persists today in the Waccamaw community and in other Indian communities in North Carolina because there are continuous challenges to their Indian identity in American culture. The Waccamaw interact daily in social situations in which they are a tiny minority. They seek recognition as Indians at school, at work, and at play. However, they do not always find it. The powwow and parade offer the opportunity to send messages about their collective identity to non-Indians. It links them to other Indians within the state and works to transform sometimes disharmonious relationships into harmonious ones. It also associates them with the larger Native American community and American nation. As hosts of the annual powwow, Indians from around the state and elsewhere in the country attend and participate. The Waccamaw's sense of self is reinforced by this participation. The Waccamaw travel to other powwows where they are recognized and received as guests; perhaps echoing a more traditional sense of a reciprocal recognition that is achieved on the powwow circuit.

NOTES

I want to thank the people of the Waccamaw community who have assisted me over the years in my effort to understand their culture and history. I want to especially thank Chief Pricilla Jacobs for taking the time to discuss the early powwows with me. I am grateful for the help that others have extended but I accept complete responsibility for any errors of interpretation that this chapter might present.

1. *Minute Book IV*, 3 March 1965, Columbus County Board of Education, Whiteville, North Carolina.
2. *Minute Book IV*, 3 March 1965, p. 527.
3. *Minute Book I*, 7 July 1885, p. 5.
4. Reproduced by permission of the American Anthropological Association from *Museum Anthropology* 16(2):27-34. Not for further reproduction.
5. This description is based on a census of occupations that I made in 1985. Out of 258 men surveyed, 42 percent were employed in construction work, 16 percent in forestry, 13 percent in farming, and 24 percent in other occupations. Most women reported being without employment: 55 percent of 239 were housewives, senior citizens, retirees, or unemployed.

BIBLIOGRAPHY

Cornell, Stephen E.
1988 *The Return of the Native: American Indian Political Resurgence.* New York: Oxford University Press.

Howard, James H.
1955 "Pan-Indian Culture of Oklahoma." *The Scientific Monthly* 80:215-220.

Lerch, Patricia B.
1988 "Articulatory Relationships: The Waccamaw Struggle Against Assimilation." In *Sea and Land: Cultural and Biological Adaptations on the Coastal Plain.* James L. Peacock and James C. Sabella (eds.) Southern Anthropological Society Proceedings No. 21. Athens: University of Georgia Press. Pp. 76-91.

1991 "Pan-Indianism and Identity Among the Waccamaw." Paper read at the 89th annual meeting of the American Anthropological Association, Washington, DC.

1992a "State-Recognized Indians of North Carolina, Including a History of the Waccamaw Sioux." In *Indians in the Southeastern United States in the Late 20th Century: An Overview.* J. Anthony Paredes (ed.) Tuscaloosa: University of Alabama Press. Pp. 44-71.

1992b "Pageantry, Parade, and Indian Dancing: the Staging of Identity Among the Waccamaw Sioux." *Museum Anthropology* 16(1):27-34.

Paredes, J. Anthony
1965 "Community Celebrations in Northern Minnesota." Paper read at the 64th annual meeting of the American Anthropological Association. mimeo.graph

Rynkiewich, M.A.

1980 "Chippewa Powwows." In *Anishinabe: Six Studies of Modern Chippewa.* J. Anthony Paredes (ed.) Tallahassee: University Presses of Florida. Pp. 31-100.

Siegel, Sanford J.

1983 *The Emerging Influence of Pan-Indian Elements on the Tribal Identity of the Gros Ventre of North Central Montana.* Ph.D. dissertation. Columbus: Ohio State University.

Thomas, Robert K.

1965 "Pan-Indianism." *Midcontinent American Studies Journal* 6:75-83.

Turner, Victor

1974 *Dramas, Fields, and Metaphors: Symbolic Action in Human Society.* Ithaca, NY: Cornell University Press.

1982a *From Ritual to Theatre: The Human Seriousness of Play.* New York: Performing Arts Journal Publications.

1982b "Introduction." In *Celebration: Studies in Festivity and Ritual.* Victor Turner (ed.) Washington, DC: Smithsonian Institution Press. Pp. 11-30.

Turner, Victor, and Edith Turner

1978 *Image and Pilgrimage in Christian Culture.* New York: Columbia University Press.

7

Anglo-American Mortuary Complex and Cultural Heritage

Pamela R. Frese

Upon death, the multifaceted identity of an Anglo-American is deconstructed, celebrated, and transformed through a complex of culturally prescribed ritual practices and beliefs. This mortuary complex articulates the biological and social processes involved in the transformation of the deceased's identity to rebirth in its eternal forms.[1] The complex includes the rites and ritual symbolism associated with: 1. the death of an individual in an old age home, the hospital, or within the private domestic sphere of the home 2. the embalming of the body and the visitation to the deceased, 3. the ritual burial of the casket, 4. the gatherings of family and friends before and after the burial, and 5. the transformation of the deceased's spirit, material essence, and social identity represented through cultural artifacts. These artifacts include heirlooms and the gravemarkers that perpetuate an individual's identity into the future.[2]

The mortuary complex in contemporary Anglo-American culture reflects an individual's identity on a number of levels that include: gender, age, family status and kinship relationships, and his/her membership in a larger community and/or nation. In addition, the Anglo-American beliefs and practices associated with death are, through extension, commentaries on cultural perceptions of biological and social life. In particular, the mortuary complex is a reflection of the underlying structure of American culture that metaphorizes the cultural categories of Nature and Culture in gendered terms. These categories express, manipulate, and reinvent the gendered spheres that are rooted in Anglo-American history.

While women's roles and female knowledge have always had an important place in all aspects of the mortuary complex, scholars consistently focus on the public dimensions and ignore or even explicitly deny the contributions of women in the domestic sphere. As Annette Weiner found in her exploration of Trobriand mortuary ritual and gendered domains (Weiner 1976) this limited perspective is pervasive in ethnographic studies and also appears as one of the implicit assumptions in the scholarship on American funerals and related mortuary beliefs and practices.

Most scholars concerned with aspects of the American mortuary complex provide fascinating accounts of the historical development of the funeral industry and how the mortuary beliefs and practices mirror economic, political, and technological transformations in American society. These authors assert that at the turn of the century an industrializing society required more mobility of its workers, necessitated smaller houses in urban areas, and urged the adoption of "scientific rationalism" in home and business. As a result of these changes, the funeral and related mourning practices moved from the home into the public sphere to become the province of professionals (Aries 1974, 1976, 1977; Curl 1972; Dempsey 1975; Farrell 1980; Feifel 1959; Habenstein and Lamers 1955; Leming and Dickinson 1985; Metcalf and Huntington 1979; Mitford 1963; Pine 1975; Ragon 1983; Stannard 1976a, 1976b).

Other writers are more explicitly concerned with how the American funeral ritual functions to validate and perpetuate particular social institutions and cultural beliefs. These authors explore how the funeral expresses the social identity of the deceased in terms of: age, sex, kinship relations, class, religious affiliation, and membership in regional and national communities (Crocker 1971; Fenza 1989; Goody 1976; Stannard 1976 [1974]b; Warner 1959; Whitaker III 1980).[3] But, with the possible exception of Warner's pioneering work (Warner 1959), the existing literature on the mortuary complex fails to give any serious consideration to the importance of cultural constructions of gender and the influence of the female domestic sphere in this life-cycle ritual.

NATURE AND CULTURE AS GENDERED DOMAINS

Carroll Smith-Rosenberg has drawn attention to the limited view taken by scholars who ignore the Victorian women's world of friendship and supportive networks as "an excellent example of the type of historical phenomenon that most historians know something about, few have thought much about, and virtually no one has written about. It is one aspect of the female experience which, consciously or unconsciously, we have chosen to ignore" (Smith-Rosenberg 1985:53). These networks and the associated kinds of gender-specific knowledge were especially passed down from mother to daughter at life-cycle rituals. My research on Anglo-American life-cycle rituals (Frese 1982, 1991a, 1991b) supports Smith-Rosenberg's argument that these networks have not disappeared, but still play an important role in perpetuating family identity and integrating community relations within the domestic sphere. These networks still provide "an important sense of continuity in a rapidly changing society" (Smith-Rosenberg 1985:61).

I argue that the public and private spheres exist in complementary opposition and comprise an ongoing dialectic that empowers and recreates the American nation from the Anglo perspective. A gendered paradigm provides a lens through which to obtain a more balanced consideration of the mortuary complex in Anglo-American culture.

Annette Kolodny's (1975) important work on gender metaphors demonstrates that since colonial times the North American continent has been metaphorized as a fertile, sacred paradise on earth and has been assigned female qualities, especially that of virgin/mother. Kolodny convincingly argues that the essential counterpart to female/virgin/sacred nature is reflected in the metaphors that depict the colonist, frontiersman, and pioneer as male/cultivator/polluted civilization. The interaction between "male" civilization and "female" nature in the "frontier" metaphorically reproduces the American nation and the American family. Kolodny concludes that this dialectic underlies and motivates contemporary Anglo-American society as well.

The historic female/nature and male/culture dialectic discussed by Kolodny has influenced American beliefs about other gendered domains for a long time. In addition to its initial role in advertising for the colonization of the New World and as the force behind the expansion of the American frontier, this metaphoric relationship between female and nature was also extended to the cultural perceptions of the family and the home during the 1800s. "Home" was a "paradise on earth," a separate, sacred, natural place viewed as the domain of the ideal woman (virgin/mother) who was referred to as an "angel on earth." Her role was to provide for the physical, moral, and spiritual well-being of the family, all in an area physically and symbolically distinct from the male public sphere of work (see Fowler 1875 [1870]; Welter 1966). Women were metaphorically equated with nature and natural processes, a relationship reflected in fictive kin terms as "Mother Nature" and "Mother Earth."

Anglo-American culture at the turn of the century equated the male sperm with the "hot" life spirit from God/father, while the woman's body was represented the "cooler" sacred natural receptacle (Fowler 1875 [1870]). The woman provided the substance or food for this life spirit to produce the child (Frese 1991b). As mother, the woman nurtured her children in the home, prepared the male child for a life in the public sphere, and helped to develop a girl as an appropriate representative of the domestic world.

Death itself was metaphorized as the natural process overseen by God and imaged as the Grim Reaper or the male harvester of all natural life. The "hot" spirit of the deceased left his/her sacred home on earth to return to the heavenly home above to be reunited with the Father and deceased family and friends. The deceased's material remains were reunited with the "cold" sacred earth or mother nature. Biologically, of course, the decomposing flesh becomes "hot"; it is the life-cycle ritual of the funeral that "cools" it for its return to the "mother."

Intellectuals in the late 1800s warned about the imminent loss of America's pristine female wilderness to encroaching and polluting male civilization. These scholars also adopted gender metaphors to explain the dynamics of social and cultural change (Turner 1961). This fear of losing the essential and dynamic relationship between nature and civilization as a motivating force behind America's progress and her destiny was extended through gendered metaphors into the social realm. As more women left their homes to enter the work force, many scholars argued that their move into the public sphere would be responsible for the breakdown of the traditional family and eventually the nation. The potential disappearance of this "natural" sphere led to an emphasis on the home as the ideal natural refuge for women and the family apart from the male-dominated public sphere.

Feminist anthropologists have been concerned with the cultural categories of nature and culture and their relationship to gender domains for some time. Sherry Ortner (1972) argued that most societies associate male with culture and view female as inherently closer to nature and natural processes. Her controversial article has provoked considerable discussion and debate. Carol MacCormack and Marilyn Strathern (1982 [1980]) took issue with Ortner's assumption of the universality of these oppositions, and argued that Ortner's categories were based in part on her own Western cultural heritage. As MacCormack and Strathern correctly remind us, "nature" is a cultural category and therefore will mirror different concepts of social and cultural phenomena. In a later reflection on this exchange, Sherry Ortner and Harriet Whitehead (1984 [1982]) concluded that the oppositions (female/nature/domestic and male/culture/public) are certainly universal to the extent that the domain primarily associated with males usually encompasses the female domain, and is consistently assigned a higher value (see also Ardener 1972; Barnes 1973; Biersack 1984; Brown and Jordanova 1982; Llewelyn-Davies 1984; Shore 1984 [1980]; Strathern 1984).

Marilyn Strathern (1984 [1980]) argues for a slightly different manifestation of this dichotomy for American culture. Following S.C. Rogers (1978), Strathern argues that male and female have both natural *and* cultural attributes and hints that the power behind this dialectic may be represented in the American image of the frontier.

My research on gender in the Anglo-American life-cycle rituals complements Strathern's thinking in three aspects: 1. the cultural categories of nature and culture apply to both genders, 2. the association of male with the public sphere and female with the private domestic arena, and 3. that which is understood as female is generally perceived to be subordinate to what is associated with male in both domains. The model below presents the Anglo-American gender domains as four areas that stand in complementary opposition to each other: Male/Nature, Female/Nature, Male/Culture, and Female/Culture. I argue elsewhere (Frese 1992) that the symbols associated with the contemporary home and yard reflect this dialectic in American culture and are also those symbols that give meaning to the life-cycle rituals. The paradigm in Figure 1 helps explain aspects of the Anglo-American mortuary complex as well.

The Anglo-American category of nature relates male and female to the gendered relationships found historically in cultural images of the wilderness, Paradise before the Fall, or The Garden of Eden. Here in nature, relationships are pure and innocent of civilization's polluting influence, instinct governs the be-havior of the species, and reproduction is an animal passion for the biological reproduction of the species. In nature, as Kolodny has argued, the female is perceived to be innately seductive and beautiful, and is associated with the virgin, fertile paradise awaiting the dominant male inseminator. "Mother Nature" represents cyclical time where change is represented through the eternal sequencing of the seasons. And even here the seasons of growth (spring, sum-mer, fall) are associated with female powers responsible for reproducing and nur-turing new growth. "Father Time," or the "Grim Reaper," is metaphorized in male terms and reflects the demarcation and end of all cyclical time (seasons of growth, calendrical years, and all natural life) through the actions of the god of agriculture wielding his scythe.

    In this model, culture represents the triumph of civilization over animal in-stinct, of legitimate reproduction over animal passions. In contemporary culture the male domain is still primarily associated with the public sphere of politics, economics, and world relations. Many Anglo-Americans associate woman in

Figure 1
Anglo-American Gender Domains

SACRED NATURE/BIOLOGICAL INSTINCT

MALE	*FEMALE*
Hot, Life Giver	Cold, Life Container
Dominant aggressor	Passive receiver
Inseminator	Seductive, beautiful fertile virgin
Demarcation of Nature, Death	Cyclical Nature, Life
Regeneration of spirit	Regeneration of organic remains
Father Time	Mother Nature, Mother Earth

CULTURE/CIVILIZATION, LEGITIMATE REPRODUCTION

Conquerer, Hunter	Conquered, Civilized, Virgin/Mother
Politics, Economics, World Relations, Law	Home, Kinship and family, traditions and rituals
Exchange Value	Use Value

some way with the domestic hearth and home where kinship and family traditions (and ritual knowledge) are enshrined and perpetuated. Like male in nature, male in culture encompasses the domestic sphere and is awarded a higher social value. For example, woman's work in the domestic domain is ascribed a use value in opposition to the exchange value traditionally attached to a man's labor in the public domain.

This paradigm is reinvented in all aspects of Anglo-American culture. However, while knowledge of these rituals lies in both public and private spheres, it is the public dimension of organized religion and the funeral business that other scholars have examined. The following sections explore elements of the contemporary mortuary complex from a perspective that assumes gender is an important lens for understanding social and cultural phenomena. The aspects of the Anglo-American mortuary complex discussed here include: 1. the funeral ritual as a rite of passage, 2. the flowers, shroud, coffin, and gravestone imagery as expressions of a gendered identity, and 3. the gendered elements or artifacts of the deceased's identity that remain active in society through the passage of heirlooms and the use of gravemarkers in the cemetery.

GENDER AND THE CONTEMPORARY MORTUARY COMPLEX

Funeral Ritual

The funeral ritual functions to break up the deceased into spirit, material body, and cultural artifacts and serves as a vehicle for transforming and reconstructing these elements into their future, eternal condition. The funeral ritual can be divided into several rites: 1. the early preparations of the body after death, 2. visitations of the survivors in the home, 3. the embalming and display of the corpse, 4. placing the deceased in his/her final resting place, and 5. the gatherings of the family and close friends after burial.

A hundred years ago, and in the memory of many older funeral participants, only a close male friend or relative would deal with the business world in arranging for a funeral (Alden, et al. 1907:353; Davis (1880s?):347; *Decorum* 1879:255; *Vogue's Book of Etiquette* 1925:522; Eichler 1921:87). And a recent etiquette book reflects only slight changes in this ritual role in terms of gender:

> A relative or close friend of the deceased (such as a brother-in-law, a business partner, or an adult sister of the deceased) should offer to serve as 'director of funeral events.' As such he or she will be responsible for the overall smooth coordination of the funeral and interment, and also for helping the surviving family in every possible way (Baldrige 1990:333; see also Post 1985:196).

If this person is selected by the family is female, she should be an adult who is able to deal with what Jessica Mitford (1963) reveals as the ruthless business practices of the funerary world.

Traditionally the body was washed and prepared for burial within the home by the women of the family (Habenstein and Lamers 1955, 1977). Today, a majority of Americans die in hospitals or rest homes (Stannard 1976 [1974]a:vii; Sudnow 1967) and hospital attendants and the funeral director have assumed many of these responsibilities. David Sudnow (1967) discovered that hospital rules required that a woman's vagina be plugged, while a man's anus was protected from outside penetration. His studies found that as each body became a passive and potentially sexual object it must have been washed and prepared for the funeral home by a person of the same sex as the deceased. The corpse was then wrapped in a winding sheet and left to "cool off" in the hospital morgue until the funeral director could arrive to claim the body. Today many hospitals no longer plug the orifices of the recently deceased. Each corpse is washed and diapered instead; a practice that, according to one funeral director, recognizes the newborn and genderless status of the body and its initial preparation for transformation into another world.

Much of the contemporary funeral has moved out of the sacred domestic sphere. David Dempsey points out that "90 percent of all burials today are conducted out of funeral homes—[where] the undertaker preempts the supernatural symbols of religion, just as he performs the work of impresario and stage manager once entrusted to the minister" (Dempsey 1975:171; see also Post 1945[1922]; Vanderbilt 1952; Warner 1959). The contemporary funeral director as sacred "ritual specialist" oversees the continued cooling of the corpse through embalming. As Mitford (1963) discovered, embalming is not required by law in most states, but is commonly incorporated into the ritual nonetheless. In addition, funeral directors hire beauticians to apply cosmetics and to style the hair of both male and female corpses. These processes transform the deceased into a "cold," feminized, cosmetically enhanced, passive object. Whitaker argues for one function of the corpse's low temperature in the viewing process; for it is through touching and kissing the cold corpse that family and friends accept that the body is dead (Whitaker III 1980:320). But it is also significant that these functionally "unneccessary" ritual acts prepare the corpse for burial in the "cold" ground on a number of levels.

Historically, the parlor or drawing room was the heart of the woman's domain and served as the appropriate setting for all life-cycle rituals. It was ideally located on the coldest side of the home and, along with the pantry, was perceived as a storage area for the domestic sphere. Sacred family relics and heirlooms, Christian images, and artifacts of nature were displayed and preserved in the parlor. In addition, brass markers engraved with the name of the deceased were removed fom the coffin at the grave site and returned to the fireplace mantel in the parlor to join the other sacred family relics.

The corpse is displayed and visited in the "parlor" of the funeral home, the recreation in the public sphere of the traditional domain of the woman, and surrounded by flowers. This manipulation of the "home," the "parlor," and the frequent addition of a sacred chapel in this symbolic version of the domestic sphere, is yet another area that mirrors how the contemporary funeral parlor has replaced the traditional sacred roles and domains of the woman and the family (Warner 1959:97). The preparation of the body by women in the home occurred in the parlor.

The public version of visitation in the funeral "parlor" includes that "period during which family and friends of the deceased and the bereaved come to 'pay their respects' and to offer condolences. . . . It is the time for the regathering of scattered units, whether these be familial or friendship relationships" (Pine 1975:95). The private dimension of visitation held in the home of the deceased is not mentioned by Pine and is only acknowledged in passing by other scholars (Crocker 1971; Curl 1972; Green 1904; Post 1985; Whitaker III 1980). Private visitation includes the visits to the surviving family members in their home by close friends and family who bear gifts of flowers and food made or purchased by women. A funeral director told me that all kinds of food is brought to the home once people are aware of the death: "generally people bring too much food . . . a lot of it has to be thrown out or given away so it is divided it up and sent with those that have helped." This nurturance by women through ritual food is firmly rooted in the historic past and is represented today in all life-cycle rituals (Frese 1991b; see also Alden, et al. 1907; *Vogue's Book of Etiquette* 1925; Eichler 1921; Kernan 1877). The women of the family, close female friends, and/or the women from the church take over the responsibility for the domestic sphere as long as the funeral ritual continues. In this way, the female social support network affirms the deceased's membership in family and community, nurtures biological and social life, and helps the regeneration of the torn social fabric brought about by death.

The contemporary burial services may be held in the home, in the funeral parlor, or the church. Burial can occur in the family burial ground, the church cemetery, or in the growing number of public "park" or "garden" resting areas. These "garden" cemeteries of today are a part of the rural cemetery movement at the turn of the century that pictured the American burial grounds as "open-air churches where nature's hand alone would dominate" (Jackson 1977:104; see also Blaney 1977; French 1976; Linden-Ward 1989). Scholars have convincingly illustrated that cemeteries are cultural spaces that reflect social organization and cultural beliefs. It is therefore not surprising that contemporary cemeteries and grave markers can be shown to reflect the traditional gender dichotomy presented here.

W. Lloyd Warner's work in Yankee City explored how cemeteries function as collective representations and therefore reflect social organization. He offered an argument for a gendered division of social space that is particularly appropriate here. Warner describes the cemetery as a collective representation in both a city and a garden of the dead. The two symbols fuse and merge in the collective thinking of the people of Yankee City. . . . 'Garden' and 'city' are both feminine images in our culture, the former a dependent symbol of the more ancient Mother Earth. The garden is also a symbol of both life and death. As a *place* it symbolizes life, vitality, growth, and the fertility of the earth. As a symbol of the *processes* occurring there it expresses feelings about man's involvement in the eternal cycle of life and death, its shrubs and flowers come and go and are born again, its life dies, decays, and enriches the soil where new plants and shrubs are reborn and flower again (Warner 1959:282; emphasis in original).

One funeral director explained that "a person's mortal remains turned into black dirt like you would like to have in a garden . . . fertile dirt, back to dust." The deceased is perceived by many survivors to rest in a "garden of Eden" on earth and the contemporary cemetery is described as a natural paradise away from civilization. The women of the family visit regularly, bringing flowers, tending the living plants, and mourning the dead.

There are several options to the embalming and burial of the deceased in a coffin that reflect the paradigm offered here and involve invvovations in processing the deceased's material remains. For example, while cremation has been a recognized alternative to embalming for a hundred years, it is more popular today. However, Sloane finds that "Cremains (the industry term for cremated remains) often are not buried or entombed in cemeteries and memorial parks [and] may be left with the crematory for permanent storage, spread by survivors, or even kept in the family home" (Sloane 1991:228; see also Eichler 1921:99). Cryonics is another option that continues to cool or preserve the body of the deceased: "wrapped in alluminum foil and stored, like frozen food, at a temperature of -70 C" (Dempsey 1975:189) to be defrosted when scientific advancements will let the deceased live again. In addition, it is now accepted to preserve parts of your body within another living person (Post 1985:209).

A contemporary authority on funeral ritual recommends the addition of one more phase to the traditional funeral ritual and encourages a reading of the deceased's will and the redistribution of the material remains while all those concerned are present (Post 1985:219). Like the Iatmul funeral in Gregory Bateson's *Naven* (1958 [1936]), the deceased's identity is in part deconstructed through these objects. My research has found that heirlooms are reassigned along gender lines and serve to perpetuate the memory of the deceased as the artifacts accrue on the new owner. The primary objects that are constantly identified as female heirlooms are those that also define the ideal woman as beautiful bride and prepare her for her role in the domestic sphere: silver, china, crystal, pearls, cameos, and the wedding dress. Female heirlooms also include baby clothes, dolls, and recipes. Heirlooms for men include objects that are also associated in a variety of ways with the groom at marriage and allow the male to participate in the public world: gold, diamonds, cuff links, and pocket watches. Men also inherit train sets, guns, swords, military insignia, and toy soldiers (see Frese 1982).

Heirlooms immortalize certain aspects of the ancestor and in some sense recreate that person in the present. As Marcel Mauss argues: "the thing itself is a person or pertains to a person. Hence it follows that to give something is to give a part of oneself . . . one gives away what is in reality a part of one's nature and substance, while to receive something is to receive a part of someone's spiritual essence" (Mauss 1967:10). Heirlooms can also be discussed as "inalienable wealth" where "the object acts as a vehicle for bringing past time in to the present, so that the histories of ancestors, titles, or mythological events become an intimate part of a person's present identity" (Weiner 1985:210). Only parts of an individual's memory can be perpetuated in any one object and it is through the object and the special value believed to be invested in the heirloom that people "invent" themselves. Heirloom's are part of one's possessions yet never truly possessed; the identities they embody are held in trust for the family.

SIGNIFICANT RITUAL SYMBOLS

The funeral ritual celebrates a process of transformation in which the social rites mirror a biological and cosmic process. The ritual is given meaning in part through the ritual symbols that are used, and they in turn help create the ritual. This section explores the use of ritual flowers, the "shroud," the casket, and the imagery on grave markers with particular attention to these ritual elements as representations of a gendered identity.

Flowers

My research and experience show that women are usually the ones who order the floral offerings for a funeral and female friends are frequently responsible for arranging the flowers for visitations (see also Post 1945 [1922]:274; Crocker 1971:123). Florists add that some flowers reflect the gender identity of the deceased, especially in the colors chosen and in the expected addition of Baby's Breath to a deceased woman's floral piece. In addition, florists and surviving family members interviewed for my research agree that the kinds of flowers in arrangements send a message about the personality of the deceased and the deceased's relationship to surviving family members; especially when ribbons decorated with kinship terms are added to a floral tribute. Certain family members are expected to provide particular kinds of floral arrangements based upon their relation to the deceased. For example, the floral spray is always purchased by the immediate family, displayed at the visitation, placed upon the center of the casket during the funeral service, and placed directly over the casket at the grave site. In addition, some flower arrangements may reflect the occupation of the deceased, and the position of the deceased in the armed forces and/or community.

Flower arrangements may be accompanied by photographs of the deceased as a living person or scrapbooks that capture survivors' memories of the deceased in life. These artifacts of the deceased help the surviving family members reconstruct the deceased individual through selected memories.

Through these objects and floral tributes, the deceased is perceived to still be "present" and this presence of the deceased individual extends beyond the ritual domain as well. Extra flower arrangements are broken apart and taken to dying patients in hospitals and nursing homes, thereby sharing the deceased, through the flowers, with those who are close to death. Gifts of flowers may also be replaced with monetary donations to the deceased's favorite charity or scholarship fund, where the identity of the deceased then rests in his/her ability to participate in ongoing society as money (Post 1985:199), but money that represents his/her social relationships in life.

Shroud

Until the 1920s, the appropriate shroud for men and women was something in which to "sleep" (*Vogue's Book of Etiquette* 1925). The contemporary shroud can be any favorite item of clothing that the deceased wanted to be buried in. However, funeral directors state that women are more frequently buried in a nightgown, a wedding gown, or a dress suitable for church. The shroud favored by men is a dress suit suitable for work or church on Sunday (Crocker 1971:123; Post 1985:201; Vanderbilt 1952:129). When I asked a funeral director why particular kinds of burial clothes were used, he replied: "Well, some people have a different idea of what we are going to be doing in the afterlife." It would appear that men and women must be prepared for different the kinds of work in the afterlife that reflect his/her social role in this world.

Casket

Every funeral director I interviewed explicitly recommended that men and women should use certain styles and colors of caskets over others. These suggestions reflect particular assumptions about gender and gender qualities made by the funeral director that are passed on to those who purchase a casket. These gendered differences are perceived to be based upon the different kinds of material from which a coffin is constructed, the exterior and interior color of the casket, and the decorations placed outside and inside the coffin. The "massive" metallic coffins, usually blue or bronze, or caskets made from the hardest woods are most often purchased for men. The interiors of these coffins should be blue or off-white, and oak leaves and acorns, harvested wheat, or a tree in winter are appropriate decorations. Women are most frequently buried in the more "delicate, fragile" coffins made from softer woods. The interiors of a woman's coffin should be either pink or white and decorated with flowers. Funeral directors agreed that it would be unusual for a woman to be buried in a blue casket or a man in pink. Individual and family identity are included in the burial in one of the corners of the casket that holds a glass vial containing the person's lineage on parchment. This lineage acknowledges the patrilines of both the deceased's mother and father. The public representations on gravestones are different, and traditionally identify, through surnames, only the patriline of the deceased.

A variety of objects may be placed within the casket to accompany the body in burial. These include a man's wedding ring, a watch, a gun, a favorite pipe, and even farm boots. Women are buried with their wedding ring, wedding dress, flowers, a prayer book, pearls, cameos, and in one instance, their favorite childhood doll. Photographs of family members are also placed within the casket. One bereaved woman told me that she had placed a photograph in the casket with her husband because "this picture of me when we got married was always one of his favorites, [with it] I can go with him for a while." Among other meanings that may be assigned to these artifacts, they certainly reflect the underlying gender construct of Anglo-American culture.

In place of, or in addition to the traditional visitation and burial of the deceased, the family may choose to have a memorial service. The deceased may or may not be physically present, but the memorial service reconstructs the deceased's presence for the participants and the ceremony is most often held in a church. The multiple identities of the deceased are represented in music, flowers, a collage of photographs, and a sharing of memories by friends and family members. The participants join for food afterward and comment on how they felt the deceased had "been" there in spirit. Here in the church, the deceased's spirit is honored. The lyrics in the music and the readings emphasize the new dawn and rebirth with the Father in heaven, in a fertile garden of sacred eternity.

Gravemarkers and Gender Identity

The gravestone symbolism and the temporary objects added to the permanent grave site distinguish the identity of the deceased in social life and include: name and lifespan, spouse and marriage date, kinship role in the family, occupation, class, religion, and beliefs about the afterlife. Temporary markers, including American flags on Memorial Day, more frequently celebrate the man's community and national achievements over those of the woman. While the male's patrilineage is still given a higher status than that of the female, some descent through women is acknowledged (photograph 1).

Some gravemarkers are obvious transformations of the paradigm discussed in this paper. On stones from a hundred years ago, the gates of heaven stood ajar,

1. This gravestone illustrates the continued influence of the patriline and the public acknowledgment of the soldier's female descendants. Photograph by Pam Frese.

revealing the heavenly home or sacred city of the Father but the deceased individuals were never represented. Today these gates reveal the sacred eternal home with the representations of husband and wife (photograph 2). These new representations of heaven are accompanied by words engraved on the stone that describe an afterlife: "in the west," "the new frontier," and, "after the sun goes down." One contemporary gravestone particularly reflects the historic Anglo-American paradigm (photograph 3). Other stones feature pictures of the home, a domestic scene, or a church in a variety of possible combinations as the final destination (photograph 4).

CONCLUSION

Previous studies have provided important insights on how aspects of the mortuary complex reflect social change, especially as a result of economic and technological transformations in the public sphere. Social change continues to impact the domestic sphere as professionals in the public domain take charge of many aspects of the funeral ritual. But the opposite is also true. "Home" has been recreated within the public realm.

In most cases however, the male domain still encompasses the female and is assigned a higher value. A story related to me by a funeral director illustrates how participation in the business world can affect the choice of a casket in terms of gender:

> A little old lady came in to buy a casket for herself. She wanted the largest metal one I had. I politely tried to discourage her from this choice. I told her that this was a popular one for men . . . that she 'would be lost in it,' that 'it was overpowering.' She wouldn't have any of it . . . she said that she had worked for it, was successful in her [deceased husband's] business and so deserved it . . . no matter what people thought.

The mortuary complex helps recreate and perpetuate the Anglo-American's tripartate being: spirit, body, and material possessions. The processes metaphorized through the ritual assure that these facets of the deceased's identity are reabsorbed into the domain from which they originated. After the three-day funeral ritual, the soul is safely returned to the Father or to whatever image of spiritual afterlife is shared by the deceased and his/her family and friends. The corpse (male or female) returns to the "mother" through the gradual "feminization" or "cooling" of the corpse, through the bodily fluids flushed into the water systems of the town, and in the material remains committed to the earth to become fertile black dirt from which new life can grow. The deceased's social personae is reflected in gravemarkers and through the artifacts that are passed on to living family members.

2. In Christian funeral services the soul is drawn to the sunrise and spiritual rebirth. The imagery on this stone was explained to me by the couple who purchased it as their future union in the "west" of American paradise. Photograph by Pam Frese.

OGDEN

EDWARD A.
NOV 15 1945
APR 10 1990
TO KNOW HIM
WAS TO LOVE
HIM

LINDA Y.
MAY 4 1947

MARRIED 12.6.69

3. This gravestone represents the rich reinvention of Victorian imagery and the Anglo-American dialectic of nature/culture. Photograph by Pam Frese.

108

4. The deceased buried beneath this stone was a farmer. According to his wife, his "heaven" is represented here where "his lands and his church can be like home for him." Photograph by Pam Frese.

The ritual objects and their symbolism are multivocal; the ritual becomes a powerful multidimensional experience understood by participants in many different ways. The mortuary complex represents ongoing social processes that are learned through participation and experience. The opportunity to participate in this experience is based, in part, upon the inheritance of gendered knowledge and the gender constructs of Anglo-American culture.

In a dialectal process, neither side of the opposition holds permanent power over the other. Both male and female domains are necessary and the interaction is always productive. American culture is not unique in extending gendered biological metaphors into the social and cultural realms (see Bloch and Parry 1982). But Anglo-Americans are exceptional in their continued attempts to control and civilize nature throughout all dimensions of their identity. The multifaceted identity of an Anglo-American is transformed by the mortuary complex into his or her immortal elements. These contemporary eternal forms of an individual ensure that "people pass on, pass away or 'go west'—everything save plain 'die'" (quoted in Bowman 1959:4).

NOTES

1. I use "Anglo" in this paper to refer to White culture in the way non-White Americans do. Anglo also refers to the influences introduced in the powerful heritage of British culture that is reflected in the practices sanctioned in popular etiquette books and popular manuals for the last one hundred years.

2. This paper is based upon ten years of fieldwork on various aspects of the symbolism in the life-cycle rituals, including the mortuary complex. I conducted interviews with surviving family members, florists, funeral directors, embalmers, and cosmeticians. I participated as a member of Anglo culture in six funerals of family and friends. And in August 1992 I participated in the memorial service of a close friend.

3. The journal *Markers* is one of the most extensive considerations of gravemarkers and cemeteries in the United States. However, with few exceptions the studies included in these volumes do not consider contemporary Anglo-American mortuary ritual.

Authors emphasize the gravemarker's identity as a representative of a particular region and/or time period in which they appear (Deetz and Dethlefsen 1966, 1967; Ludwig 1966; Meyer 1989b). Researchers are interested in how gravemarkers represent the social and psychological identity of the deceased (Edgette 1989; Nelson and George 1981; Snyder 1989) or explore the life of the carver or maker of the stone (Clark 1989; Rotundo 1989). Gravemarkers also reflect a particular time period or culture, but a majority of these studies explore past cultures or explicitly "other than Anglo" cultural beliefs and practices (Kelly 1976; Ames 1981; Meyers 1976).

There are a number of different kinds of studies on American cemeteries and most assume that this cultural spaace mirrors society. Popular writers and scholars are concerned with the historical development of cemeteries in particular regions of the country (Francaviglia 1971; Hannon 1989; Jeane 1989; McCowell 1989) and historical descriptions of symbolism in cemetery ornamentation (Gillon Jr. 1972;

McDowell 1989; Murphy 1974). Other studies reflect an interest in how identities of non-Anglo race and ethnicity are expressed in cemeteries (Cunningham 1989; Jordan 1988; Tashjian and Tashjian 1989).

BIBLIOGRAPHY

Alden, Mrs. Cynthia Westover, et al.
1907 *Correct Social Usage: A Course of Instruction in Good Form, Style and Deportment* by eighteen distinguished authors. 8th edition. New York: The New York Society of Self-Culture.

Ames, Kenneth
1981 "Ideologies in Stone: Meanings in Victorian Gravestones." *Journal of Popular Culture* 14(4):641-656.

Ardener, E.
1972 "Belief and the Problem of Women." In *The Interpretation of Ritual.* J.S. La Fontaine (ed.) London: Tavistock.

Aries, Philippe
1974 *Western Attitudes Toward DEATH: From the Middle Ages to the Present.* Patricia M. Ranum (trans.) Baltimore and London: The Johns Hopkins University Press.

1976 "The Reversal of Death: Changes in Attitudes Toward Death in Western Societies." In *Death in America.* David E. Stannard (ed.) Philadelphia: University of Pennsylvania Press. Pp. 134-158.

1977 "Forbidden Death" In *Passing: The Vision of Death in America.* C.O. Jackson (ed.) Westport, CT: Greenwood Press. Pp. 148-152.

Baldrige, Letitia
1990 *Letitia Baldrige's Complete Guide to the New Manners for the '90s.* New York: Rawson Associates.

Barnes, J.A.
1973 "Genetrix:genitor::nature:culture?" In *The Character of Kinship.* J. Goody (ed.) Cambridge: Cambridge University Press. Pp. 61-74.

Bateson, Gregory
1958 [1936] *Naven: A Survey of the Problems Suggested by a Composite Picture of the Culture of a New Guinea Tribe Drawn from Three Points of View.* Stanford: Stanford University Press.

Biersack, Aletta
1984 "Paiela 'Women-men': The Reflexive Foundations of Gender Ideology." *American Ethnologist* 11:118-138.

Blaney, Herbert
1977 "The Modern Park Cemetery." In *Passing: The Vision of Death in America.* C.O. Jackson (ed.) Westport, CT: Greenwood Press. Pp. 219-226.

Bloch, Maurice, and Jonathan Parry (eds.)
1982 *Death and the Regeneration of Life*. Cambridge: Cambridge University Press.

Bowman, Leroy Ph.D.
1959 *The American Funeral: A Study in Guilt, Extravagance, and Sublimity*. Washington, DC: Public Affairs Press.

Brown, Penelope, and Judith Jordanova
1982 "Oppressive Dichotomies: the Nature/Culture Debate." In *Women in Society*. The Cambridge Women's Studies Group (eds.) London: Virago. Pp. 221-241.

Clark, Edward W.
1989 "The Biogham Carvers of the Carolina Piedmont: Stone Images of an Emerging Sense of American Identity." In *Cemeteries and Gravemarkers: Voices of American Culture*. Richard E. Meyer (ed.) Ann Arbor and London: UMI Research Press. Pp. 31-60.

Crocker, Christopher
1971 "The Southern Way of Death." In *The Not So Solid South: Anthropological Studies in a Regional Subculture*. John Kenneth Moreland (ed.) Southern Anthropological Society Proceedings, No. 4. Athens: University of Georgia Press. Pp. 114-129.

Cunningham, Keith
1989 "Navajo, Mormon, Zuni Graves: Navajo, Mormon, Zuni Ways." In *Cemeteries and Gravemarkers: Voices of American Culture*. Richard E. Meyers (ed.) Ann Arbor and London: UMI Research Press. Pp. 197-216.

Curl, James Stevens
1972 *The Victorian Celebration of Death*. Detroit: Partridge Press.

Davis, A. E.
1880s? *American Etiquette and Rules of Politeness*. Chicago: Rand, McNally.

Decorum: A Practical Treatise on Etiquette and Dress of the Best American Society. 1879 New York: J.A. Ruth.

Dempsey, David
1975 *The Way We Die: An Investigation of Death and Dying in America Today*. New York: Macmillan.

Deetz, James, and Edwin S. Dethlefsen
1966 "Death Heads, Cherubs, and Willow Trees: Experimental Archaeology in Colonial Cemeteries." *American Antiquity* 31:502-510.

1967 "Eighteenth-Century Cemeteries: A Demographic View." *Historical Archaeology* 1:40-42.

Edgette, J. Joseph
1989 "The Epitaph and Personality Revelation." In *Cemeteries and Gravemarkers: Voices of American Culture*. Richard E. Meyer (ed.) Ann Arbor and London: UMI Research Press. Pp. 87-106.

Eichler, Lillian
1921 *Book of Etiquette*. Vol. 1. Oyster Bay, NY: Nelson Doubleday.

Farrell, James J.
1980 *Inventing the American Way of Death, 1830-1920*. Philadelphia: Temple University Press.

Feifel, Herman
1959 *The Meaning of Death*. New York: McGraw-Hill.

Fenza, Paula J.
1989 "Communities of the Dead: Tombstones as a Reflection of Social Organization." In *Markers VI*. Theodore Chase (ed.) Lanham, MD: University of America Press. Pp. 137-158.

Fowler, O.S.
1875 [1870] *Creative and Sexual Science or Manhood, Womanhood & Their Mutual Interrelations*. Philadelphia: National Publishing.

Francaviglia, Richard V.
1971 "The Cemetery as an Evolving Cultural Landscape." *Annals* (The Association of American Geographers) 61(3):501-509.

French, Stanley
1976 "The Cemetery as Cultural Institution: The Establishment of Mount Auburn and the 'Rural Cemetery' Movement." In *Death in America*. David E. Stannard (ed.) Philadelphia: University of Pennsylvania Press. Pp. 69-91.

Frese, Pamela R.
1982 *Holy Matrimony: A Symbolic Analysis of the American Wedding Ritual*. Ph.D. dissertation. Charlottesville: University of Virginia.

1991a "The Union of Nature and Culture: Gender Symbolism in the American Wedding Ritual." In *Transcending Boundaries: Multi-Disciplinary Aproaches to the Study of Gender*. Pamela R. Frese and John M. Coeggeshall (eds.) New York: Bergin & Garvey. Pp. 97-112.

1991b "Food and Gender in America: A Review Essay." *Food and Foodways* 5(2):1-7.

1992 "Artifacts of Gendered Space: American Yard Decoration." In *Visual Anthropology*. 5:17-42.

Gillon, Jr., Edmund V.
1972 *Victorian Cemetery Art*. New York: Dover.

Goody, Jack
1976 "Death and the Interpretation of Culture: A Bibliographic Overview." In *Death in America*. David E. Stannard (ed.) Philadelphia: University of Pennsylvania Press. Pp. 1-8.

Green, W.C.
1904 *A Dictionary of Etiquette: A Guide to Polite Usage for All Social Functions*. New York: Brentano's.

Habenstein, Robert W., and William M. Lamers
1955 *The History of American Funeral Directing.* Milwaukee: Bulfin Printers.

1977 "The Pattern of Late Nineteenth-Century Funerals." In *Passing: The Vision of Death in America.* Charles O. Jackson (ed.) Westport, CT: Greenwood Press. Pp. 91-102.

Hannon, Thomas J.
1989 "Western Pennsylvania Cemeteries in Transition: A Model for Subregional Analysis." In *Cemeteries and Gravemarkers: Voices of American Culture.* Richard E. Meyers (ed.) Ann Arbor and London: UMI Research Press. Pp. 237-262.

Jackson, Charles O. (ed.)
1977 *Passing: The Vision of Death in America.* Contributions in Family Studies, No. 2. Westport, CT: Greenwood Press.

Jeane, Gregory
1989 "The Upland South Folk Cemetery Complex: Some Suggestions of Origin." In *Cemeteries and Gravemarkers: Voices of American Culture.* Richard E. Meyer (ed.) Ann Arbor and London: UMI Research Press. Pp. 107-136.

Jordan, Terry G.
1988 *Texas Graveyards: A Cultural Legacy.* Austin: University of Texas Press.

Kelly, Patricia Fernandez
1976 "Death in Mexican Folk Culture." In *Death in America.* David E. Stannard (ed.) Philadelphia: University of Pennsylvania Press. Pp. 92-111.

Kernan, James
1877 *Perfect Etiquette; or, How to Behave in Society. A Complete Manual for Ladies and Gentlemen, Embracing Hints on Introduction, Salutation, Conversation, Friendly Visits, Social Parties, On the Street, In Public Places, In Traveling. . .Courtship, Wedding Etiquette, Christening, Funerals, Etc., with Suggestions How to Dress Tastefully.* New York: Albert Cogswell.

Kolodny, A.
1975 *The Lay of the Land: Metaphor as Experience and History in American Life and Letters.* Chapel Hill: University of North Carolina Press.

Leming, Michael R., and George E. Dickinson
1985 *Understanding Dying, Death and Bereavement.* Chicago: Holt, Rinehart and Winston.

Linden-Ward, Blanche
1989 "Strange but Genteel Pleasure Grounds: Tourist and Leisure Uses of Nineteenth-Century Rural Cemeteries." In *Cemeteries and Gravemarkers: Voices of American Culture.* Richard E. Meyer (ed.) Ann Arbor and London: UMI Research Press. Pp. 293-328.

Llewelyn-Davies, M.
1984 "Women, Warriors, and Patriarchs." In *Sexual Meanings: The Cultural Construction of Gender and Sexuality.* S.B. Ortner and H. Whitehead (eds.) Cambridge: Cambridge University Press. Pp. 330-358.

Ludwig, Allan I.
1966 *Graven Images: New England Stonecarving and Its Symbols, 1650-1815.*
Middletown, CT: Wesleyan University Press.

MacCormack, Carol, and Marilyn Strathern (eds.)
1982 [1980] *Nature, Culture and Gender.* Cambridge: Cambridge University
Press.

Mauss, Marcel
1967 *The Gift: Forms and Functions of Exchange in Archaic Societies.* Ian
Cunnison, trans. New York: Norton.

McDowell, Peggy
1989 "J.N.B. de Pouilly and French Sources of Revival Style Design in New
Orleans Cemetery Architecture." In *Cemeteries and Gravemarkers: Voices of
American Culture.* Richard E. Meyer (ed.) Ann Arbor and London: UMI Research
Press. Pp. 137-162.

Metcalf, Peter and Richard Huntington
1979 *Celebrations of Death: The Anthropology of Mortuary Ritual.* New York:
Cambridge University Press.

Meyer, Richard
1989a "Introduction: 'So Witty as to Speak'." In *Cemeteries and
Gravemarkers: Voices of American Culture.* Richard E. Meyer (ed.) Ann Arbor
and London: UMI Research Press. Pp. 1-6.

1989b "Images of Logging on Contemporary Pacific Northwest Gravemarkers."
In *Cemeteries and Gravemarkers: Voices of American Culture.* Richard E. Meyer
(ed.) Ann Arbor and London: UMI Research Press. Pp. 61-86.

Meyers, Mary Ann
1976 "Gates Ajar: Death in Mormon Thought and Practice." In *Death in
America.* David E. Stannard (ed.) Philadelphia: University of Pennsylvania
Press. Pp. 112-133.

Mitford, Jessica
1963 *The American Way of Death.* New York: Simon & Schuster.

Mourning Etiquette: Hints to Persons in Mourning, Including the Best Social Usage.
1890 New York: Fowler Brothers.

Murphy, Buck P.
1974 "Victorian Cemetery Art." *Design.* 75(2):6-9.

Nelson, Malcolm A., and Diana Hume George
1981 "Grinning Skulls, Smiling Cherubs, Bitter Words." *Journal of Popular
Culture.* 14(4):633-640.

Ortner, Sherry
1972 "Is Female to Male as Nature Is to Culture?" In *Women, Culture and Society.*
M.Z. Rosaldo and L. Lamphere (eds.) Stanford: Stanford University Press. Pp. 67-
88.

Ortner, S., and H. Whitehead (eds.)
    1984 [1982] *Sexual Meanings: The Cultural Construction of Gender and Sexuality.* Cambridge: Cambridge University Press.

Pine, Vanderlyn R.
    1975 *Caretaker of the Dead: The American Funeral Director.* New York: Irvington Publishers.

Post, Emily
    1945 [1922] *Etiquette: "The Blue Book of Social Usage."* New York: Funk & Wagnalls.

    1985 *Emily Post's Etiquette.* 14th edition. New York: Harper & Row.

Ragon, Michel
    1983 *The Space of Death: A Study of Funerary Architecture, Decoration, and Urbanism.* Alan Sheridan (trans.) Charlottesville: University Press of Virginia.

Rogers, S.C.
    1978 "Woman's Place: A Critical Review of Anthropological Theory." *Comparative Studies in Society and History* 20:123-162.

Rotundo, Barbara
    1989 "Monumental Bronze: A Representative American Company." In *Cemeteries and Gravemarkers: Voices of American Culture.* Richard E. Meyer (ed.) Ann Arbor and London: UMI Research Press. Pp. 263-292.

Shore, Bradd
    1984 [1980] "Sexuality and Gender in Samoa: Conceptions and Missed Conceptions." In *Sexual Meanings: The Cultural Construction of Gender and Sexuality.* S.B. Ortner and H. Whitehead (eds.) Cambridge: Cambridge University Press. Pp. 192-215.

Sloane, David Charles
    1991 *The Last Great Necessity: Cemeteries in American History.* Baltimore and London: The Johns Hopkins University Press.

Smith-Rosenberg, Carroll
    1985 *Disorderly Conduct: Visions of Gender in Victorian America.* New York and Oxford: Oxford University Press.

Snyder, Ellen Marie
    1989 "Innocents in a Worldly World: Victorian Children's Gravemarkers." In *Cemeteries and Gravemarkers: Voices of American Culture.* Richard E. Meyer (ed.) Ann Arbor and London: UMI Research Press. Pp. 11-31.

Stannard, David E.
    1976 [1974]a "Introduction." In *Death in America.* D.E. Stannard (ed.) Philadelphia: University of Pennsylvania Press. Pp. vii-xv.

    1976 [1974]b "Death and the Puritan Child." In *Death in America.* D.E. Stannard (ed.) Philadelphia: University of Pennsylvania Press. Pp. 9-29.

Strathern, Marilyn
1984 "No Nature, No Culture: The Hagen Case." In *Nature, Culture and Gender*. C. MacCormack and M. Strathern (eds.) Cambridge: Cambridge University Press. Pp. 174-222.

1984 [1980] "Self-Interest and the Social Good: Some Implications of Hagen Gender Imagery." In *Sexual Meanings: The Cultural Construction of Gender and Sexuality*. S. Ortner and H. Whitehead (eds.) Cambridge: Cambridge University Press. Pp. 166-191.

Sudnow, David
1967 *Passing On*. Englewood Cliffs, NJ: Prentice-Hall.

Tashjian, Ann, and Dickran Tashjian
1989 "The Afro-American Section of Newport, Rhode Island's Common Burying Ground." In *Cemeteries and Gravemarkers: Voices of American Culture*. Richard E. Meyer (ed.) Ann Arbor and London: UMI Research Press. Pp. 163-196.

Turner, Frederick Jackson
1961 *Selected Essays of Frederick Jackson Turner: Frontier and Section*. Englewood Cliffs, NJ: Prentice-Hall.

Vanderbilt, Amy
1952 *Amy Vanderbilt's Complete Book of Etiquette: A Guide to Gracious Living*. New York: Doubleday.

Vogue's Book of Etiquette: Present-Day Customs of Social Intercourse with the Rules for Their Correct Observance.
1925 New York: Conde Nast.

Warner, W. Lloyd
1959 *The Living and the Dead: A Study of the Symbolic Life of Americans*. New Haven: Yale University Press.

Weiner, Annette
1976 *Women of Value, Men of Renown*. Austin: University of Texas Press.

1985 "Inalienable Wealth." *American Ethnologist* 12(2):210-227.

Welter, Barbara
1966 "The Cult of True Womanhood, 1820-1860." *American Quarterly* 18(2):151-174.

Whitaker III, Walter W.
1980 "The Contemporary American Funeral Ritual." In *Rituals and Ceremonies in Popular Culture*. Ray B. Browne (ed.) Bowling Green: Bowling Green University Popular Press. Pp. 316-325.

8

Ritual Cycles of Exchange: The Process of Cultural Creation and Management in the U.S. Borderlands

Carlos G. Vélez-Ibáñez

CULTURAL AND IDEOLOGICAL HOUSEHOLD STRUGGLES

The struggle for the control and autonomy of U.S. Mexican[1] household labor and resources in the Borderlands region is an important feature among others that is responsible for the emergence and development of ritual cycles of exchange among this population and the many cultural expressions and emotive states comprising them. By ritual cycles of exchange I mean a series of calendric and life-cycle events which are partially sacred and partially secular and that seem to operate with some regularity throughout the calendar year among many households. Cultural expressions and states include the actual behaviors such as cooking, repairing, sharing, praying, dancing, singing, observing, joking, story telling, arguing, eating, and sundry other expressed emotive states such as happiness, anger, joy, and sadness.

The ritual cycles themselves are culturally "Mexicanized" in the sense that these events are largely part of a broad system of social exchange in which labor, assistance, information, and support are reciprocated between persons usually part of Mexican household clusters and their constituent social networks.[2]

The results from our study of Mexican/Hispanic households in Tucson, Arizona, show that though the nuclear family is not the primary locality for social life, it is in that setting that *confianza* (mutual trust) is most likely to emerge (Vélez-Ibáñez and Greenberg 1984). Like S.E. Keefe (1979) and S.E. Keefe and A.M. Padilla (1987), we have found that the U.S. Mexican populations operate within a cluster of kin relationships connected to other local households as well as to households across the Arizona-Sonora border. Our data in Tucson, Arizona, show that over 61 percent of our sample have localized kin groups made up of a number of related households involved in extended social and economic exchange relations.

Usually focused on a "core" household of active and largely employed middle-aged to older adults, the peripheral households carry out their life-cycles very much in relation to a centrally located grandparent or parent. The core and peripheral households create social "density" not only from the fact that members of such networks are kin and in their daily lives add layers of relationships based on other contexts. The person to whom one is cousin is also the person with whom one exchanges labor assistance; has a fictive kinship relation of *compadrazgo* (co-godparenthood); shares in recreational activities and visitations; participates in religious and calendric activities; and in many instances lives nearby. That cousin will either recruit or be recruited by a network member to work in the same business or occupation.

Such networks function differently dependent on the situation so that which one of their many functions dominates in a particular instance depends upon the circumstances of the people involved. In the recruitment process mentioned above, our findings indicate that such networks function not only as a reliable defensive arrangement against the indeterminacy and uncertainty of changing circumstances but also to "penetrate" the single strands of employee and employer relations and entangle them within the multiplicity of relationships of the network. In an interesting but not often understood sense, such "entanglement" is a type of social insurance against the vagaries of the employer-employee relationship which is often an asymmetrical one at best and an exploitative one at worst. Especially in the informal sector, which is marked by the lack of protection, security, and wages above the minimum, the network penetration also serves as the only means of minimum insurance against sudden firings.

The Tucson household sample shows these networks in remarkable continuity despite constant disruptive pressures, with a variety of households engaged in frequent exchange relations. Most of these clustered households are continuously involved in child care exchange, house sitting, ritual participation, visitations, and caretaking of persons outside the household's biological unit. Very few of the clustered households relied in any appreciable degree on non-kin network members for child care, recreation, and other emotive functions.

Importantly, as expressions of Mexican identity, the actual activities and exchange processes are in the hands of women and men and play a less important role in both the ritual processes themselves and in maintaining broader relations of exchange between clusters. Men are generally more involved in dyadic exchange between individuals rather than in multiple exchange between clusters as are the women. This condition cannot be only related to a strict division of labor nor to a culturalist explanation. For in fact, among all Hispanic women, Mexican women have the highest percentage of their number in the paid labor force and only slightly below that of all U.S. women. They strongly participate as productive wage earners outside of the household and much of an entire household's survival depends on women's income from informal and formal economies.[3] Decisions regarding major expenditures are usually decided jointly rather than in the stereotypic manner which supports a macho-dominant interpretation.[4] As well, many Mexican households depend on joint income to mobilize resources between household clusters and the expenditures made in the exchange activities are a part of ritual events and behaviors.

Thus the joint labor and limited income of both women and men support individual households as well as broader networks of support within household clusters. Since individual households depend on these broader social networks to cope with the Borderland's complex political and changing economic environment, members are willing to invest considerable energy and resources in maintaining good relations with its members (Vélez-Ibáñez and Greenberg 1992). One way they do this is through family rituals: birthdays, baptisms, confirmations, *quinceaneras* (15-year-old coming-out rituals), showers, weddings, Christmas dinners, outings, and visitations. These events not only bring members of networks together ritually to become involved in exchange relations, but staging them often require members to cooperate by investing their labor or pooling resources. Moreover, such rituals broadcast an important set of signals about the sponsor's economic well-being and the state of social relations with other members—both through lavishness and attendance. The ritual cycle signals the range of acceptable, socially approved relations and mark the changes of those who leave them and/or enter them and so reflect and perpetuate Mexican identity.

However such ritual cycles of exchange cannot be properly contextualized unless we place their performance within broader theoretical frameworks and within the material and economic struggles of U.S. Mexican households within the Borderlands region. Theoretically, I concur with Edmund Leach's long-held axiom that ritual is not only a symbolic representation that occurs in "sacred" situations, but rather rituals express patterns of symbols that reveal the system of socially approved "proper" relations between individuals (Leach 1979:15). However, socially approved proper relations are neither homogeneous, unstratified, nor are they shared in other than in an "equivalent" manner. Socially approved proper relations are distributed according to class, gender, and age, and learned and discarded according to the particular individual needs of participants. Therefore, all rituals, symbols, and emotive expressions are structured as equivalencies rather than as duplications and in the circumstances described here emerge in processes tied to struggles of cultural identity, household maintenance and stability, and economic viability and survival.

HISTORICAL SETTINGS AND CONTEXT

For Mexicans of the United States, these struggles became especially problematic in the late nineteenth century when various types of large-scale, industrially organized technologies and political changes created a border region that now includes a 2,000-mile political border and fifty-two million people in the ten border states.[5] Half of that population lives within a 400-mile-wide belt bisected by that border (Martinez 1988).   The population of the six Mexican border states has increased threefold since 1950, while that of the four U.S. border states has increased from twenty million in 1950 to forty-two million in 1980.

This growth has resulted from uncontrolled industrialization on both sides of the border, created by a series of symbiotic economic and technological relations in manufacturing, processing, industrial agriculture, and labor exchange, and twin plants development.[6] Such relations in the border region strongly shape the conditions of Mexican household formation in both the U.S. and Mexico, as well as its cultural and social responses.[7] A "border subeconomy" is organized by the internationalization of production and the exchange of populations (Moore 1988:16), and from the perspective adopted here, strongly influences U.S. Mexican household development.

U.S. border policy also influences the manner in which Mexican households on both sides of the border cope with changing economic and political fortunes. Whether yesterday's Mexican national becomes today's U.S. citizen is very much dependent upon the economic health of the region. Unlike any other cultural group of the region, Mexicans have been periodically expelled, deported, and "repatriated" during periods of economic stress in the United States at times without regard to citizenship, and always without regard to the population's historical and cultural relation to the region.[8]

Before 1929, the south-to-north movement of persons between border communities was relatively uninterrupted. Cross-border families in fact were common with portions of large extended kin networks residing on both sides. It still is not uncommon for children to attend elementary and secondary schools in the United States while their parents reside in a Mexican Borderland town or city. Such cross-border kinship systems, as Heyman points out, were really "a series of bilaterally related households and networks scattered between similar types of neighborhoods on both sides of the border" (Heyman 1991:7).

As I have shown (in press), after 1929, the cross-border character of Mexican families was somewhat interrupted by the massive repatriation and deportation policies and practices of the 1930s. And as Heyman points out, the new legal context of visa regulation that was instituted during the heyday of the repatriation period "caused the differentiation into distinct branches [and] . . . as state control of immigration and citizenship rights grew, the international boundary increasingly defined two different populations—'Sonora' and 'Arizona'—in the form that had not existed before" (Heyman 1991:120).

After 1929, legal citizenship became the hallmark of cultural identity rather than cultural context, so that for many Mexicans born in the United States, immigration restrictions on Mexican kin created a "they/us" differentiation and interrupted the easy flow of kin between extended cross-border familial systems. As American schools, under the guise of "Americanization" programs, relegated the Spanish language to a secondary position and denigrated the use of the language as well, self-denial processes set in such that some U.S. Mexicans began to change their names, anglicize their surnames, and internalize self-hatred and self-deprecation.

Such differentiation was accentuated historically by systematic deportation, and by voluntary processes in 1954 during "Operation Wetback" and during recent immigration sweeps such as "Operation Jobs" in 1982. In the present, the Simpson-Rodino Immigration Reform and Control Act (IRCA), passed in 1986, was created to reduce undocumented immigration. It has had no striking impact on the labor sectors of which Mexican undocumented workers are a part. In fact, what it has done is to guarantee permanent settlement of Mexican migrants through legalization and has increased the flow of individual workers and families back and forth to the United States with newly acquired legality.

Yet a certain consequence is that the IRCA has created further division between eligible and non-eligible Mexicans. Even within the same extended familial network the legalization of one family member sharply contrasts with the illegality of others within the same network. Together with accompanying immigration sweeps of Mexican workers which seem to coincide with immigration "reform" bills such as the IRCA, further emphasis is made between the "foreignness" of the Mexican population in Mexico and that in the U.S. Such demographic and political splitting between Mexico-born and U.S.-born Mexicans establishes the cultural basis for the creation of an ethnic U.S. Mexican, and the denial of cultural continuity between separate populations.

These dynamic economic, political, and material conditions of the Borderlands region have profound structural, cultural, and ideological impacts on U.S. Mexican households. It is within the household that economic and political forces struggle for control of its labor and energy (Goody 1983; Wolf 1988). As Wolf points out: "by treating kin relations precisely as a battleground in which cultural contexts are fought out, we may gain a more sophisticated understanding of how 'indigenous peoples' may so often survive and cope in political and economic environments hostile to their continued identity" (Wolf 1988:108).

The position adopted here is that the struggle over household labor and production is a constant part of the normal operating procedure of appropriation that all complex systems of extraction seek to establish regardless of their purported ideology.[9] At the household level, the main struggle of its members and especially Mexican women is to defend themselves against the repeated attempts by the state and/or the "market" to exert complete control over its labor and productive capacities. This attempted control is inherent in complex industrial and advanced technological systems; local households respond culturally, socially, and at times politically. The history of Mexicans in the labor movement in the Southwest is replete with organized examples of entire kinship systems and households mobilizing against racial discrimination, low wages, poor housing, and the infamous company stores. The border region is a highly charged and dynamic arena in which new versions of labor and energy-extracting technologies are developed. This struggle is reflected in occupational participation and per capita income gained, and in other household characteristics which are basically aspects of a large working class population.

Most Mexican households are supported by working-class occupations. Only 22.5 percent of the Mexican labor force in the U.S. Southwest is in upper White-collar and upper blue-collar occupations; the largest percentage (75%) is concentrated in the secondary and tertiary labor sectors: low White-collar (21.3%), low blue-collar (32.5%), service (15.5%), and a small portion as farm workers (5.8%).[10]

Such occupational participation is reflected in per capita income. The ratio of Mexican to non-Hispanic White per capita income is .55, and of mean household income it is .78 (Bean and Tienda 1987:199). Therefore, individuals in Mexican households earn slightly more than half as much income as Anglos, and at the mean household level, Mexican households earned three-fourths as much income as did the Anglo households.[11] Thus this is a working-class population and not an "underclass" group.[12]

The poverty rate for U.S. Mexicans in 1980 in the border region was slightly less than 22 percent, a drop of 4.5 percent from 1970 but increased in 1990 to almost 25 percent for U.S. Mexican families (*The Hispanic Population in the United States: March 1989* 1990:16, Table 4). However, poverty was very much concentrated in the southern border counties of the U.S. border region (Stoddard and Hedderson 1987). The probability of higher income is greatest in the western coastal counties and decreases consistently as one moves east toward the Lower Rio Grande Valley of Texas.[13] Poverty among Mexicans is concentrated in female-headed families, persons over 60, and children under 18. The probability of poverty in households headed by a single person is twice as great as in those headed by a married couple (Stoddard and Hedderson 1987:66, 68; Bean and Tienda 1987:355, 371). Of U.S. Mexican households in poverty in 1980, only 17.1 percent were headed by couples and close to 40 percent were headed by single persons (Bean and Tienda 1987:356). Yet despite even worse economic characteristics ten years later for all U.S. Mexican households, home ownership is not only highly prized, but enormous sacrifices are made by Mexican families to purchase their own homes. Among all Spanish-speaking groups, including the "Golden Exile" population of Cubans that has been regarded as the model Hispanic group, U.S. Mexicans have the highest rate of home ownership (47%) and second only to non-Hispanics (66%) (*The Hispanic Population in the United States: March 1989* 1990:5).

U.S. MEXICAN HOUSEHOLD EXCHANGE AND SUPPORT

Additionally, most households are often required to support more kin and friendship relations within and without the household, to maintain ritual and dense multiple social relations, and to mobilize cooperation, reciprocity, and interdependence with others. The core and peripheral households create social "density," and not only from the fact that members of such networks are kin and in their daily lives add layers of relationships based on other contexts. The person to whom one is cousin is also the person with whom one exchanges labor assistance, has a fictive kinship relation of *compadrazgo* (co-godparenthood), shares in recreational activities and visitations, participates in religious and calendric activities, and in many instances may live nearby. That cousin will either recruit or be recruited by a network member to work in the same business or occupation.

Depending on kin or friends, however, is problematic. Besides the uncertainty experienced in the search for work, the frailty of having to depend on others for assistance with child care, household maintenance, and transportation leads people to make very determined efforts to enter primary labor markets. Such formal sector jobs are prized not just for better pay, but because they provide formal benefits that help underwrite the household's reproduction and lessen its dependence on others.

Friends and kin nevertheless often provide a safety net and substantial aid in time of crisis as well as in "normal" times, that is, in the daily activities comprising the life-cycle. Such exchanges occur in such a routine and constant fashion that people are hardly aware of them. These exchanges take a variety of forms: labor services, access to information or resources (including help in finding jobs or housing or dealing with government agencies or other institutions), and various forms of material assistance besides money, such as putting up visitors. Small favors are a constant feature of exchange relations. However, because they are reciprocal, they balance out in the long term, and so are less important economically than is the exchange of information, and special funds of knowledge. Indeed, help in finding jobs, housing, better deals on goods and services, and assistance in dealings with institutions and government agencies is of far greater significance to survival than are the material types of aid these households usually provide each other.

CALENDRIC CYCLES AND THEIR SOCIAL FUNCTIONS

Yet the cultural "glue" that seems to provide a type of consistency to the exchange process are the repetitive yet syncretic series of sacred and secular calendric and life-cycle rituals that operate throughout the year and are largely planned, implemented, and controlled by women of the household clusters. These rituals are the basic templates for all other variations, distributions, and actual operational activities of exchange; who is willing to help stage such family rituals is a measure of whom one counts upon for other things.

In their simplest form these rituals unfold in the manner in which they appear in Figure 1 and are structured along two major calendar rituals: Christmas/New Year and Easter. The former is a terminating and initiating winter ritual, and the latter a summer activity which punctuates the beginning of the second half of the entire cycle but many times is cross-border in function.

Figure 1
Ritual Cycles of Exchange

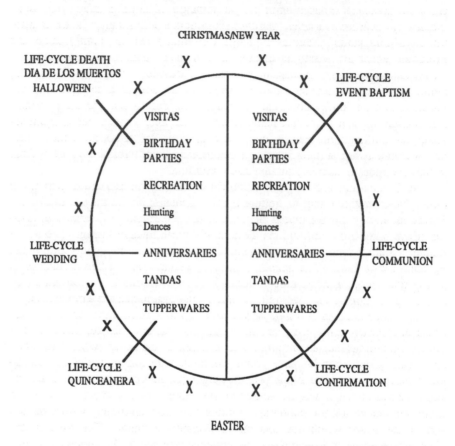

The life-cycle rituals form major secondary templates that are ongoing and always emergent. Marked by Mexican Roman Catholic liturgy most of these will vary in importance and by economic circumstance. The secularized rituals such as visits, Tupperware parties, hunting, and recreational activities are always focused on cooking, preparation of food, commensality, and more importantly some sort of exchange. Nevertheless, like their liturgically-based equivalents, these are held without question, without necessary explanation, nor without much argumentation. However, it would be an error to suggest that these have the same emotive connection but rather have similar social functions as well as significant means of distributing obligations among the clusters of households and their relationships. Even in the hunting domains, which are primarily the provinces of men, women provide crucial support without which the preparation of game collected would be impossible and during which women once more combine to cook, elaborate information, and keep "tabs" on who hunted, helped, and who has what coming to whom.

One important type of variant further removed from the border is that familial clustering of households or extension of families beyond the nucleated household increases with each succeeding generation. I have termed these "cross-border clustered" households because 77.1 percent of our sample have relatives in Mexico and a significant proportion (61 %) organize their extended kin relations in the United States in a clustered household arrangement of dense bilateral kin and maintain kin ties with their Mexican relatives (Vélez-Ibáñez, in press). The life-cycle rituals such as baptisms, confirmations, quinceneras, weddings, and funerals mark a secondary level of minor rituals that fit between the cultural space of the major rituals. Interspersed throughout these are myriad other yet smaller celebrations such as birthdays, anniversaries, housewarmings, Tupperware parties, and ritualized visitations. As Figure 1 shows, the secondary rituals serve as major spatial and temporal punctuation—something like semicolons, while the rest serve as types of commas also serving as punctuation of and for events.

THE CHRISTMAS/NEW YEAR COMPLEX

However, the initial major ritual is a model for most of the social, cultural, and emotive processes essential to the rest. In one manner or another, the Christmas/New Year function sets off most of the characteristics of the other major ritual, secondary life rituals, and minor presentations throughout the cultural and temporal life of many U.S. Mexicans.

The initial Christmas/New Year "arena" from a processual point of view begins and ends the cycle almost simultaneously. Processual analysis emerges basically from political anthropology in which politics are "events involved in the determination of public goals and/or the differential distribution and use of power within the group or groups concerned with the goals being considered" (Swartz 1972:9). The ideas of arena and social field emerge from this tradition as important methodological tools which treat the phenomenon to be understood as always emergent. Human behavior, events, and activities do not have a finality but flow and sometimes jump out of others. Yet for the purposes of analysis all social fields are presumed to have come into existence at some point in time. Their functions, characteristics, evolutions, change, continuance, and decline can be understood as sets of arenas that stack up to form the social field. These arenas are made up of cultural symbols, human behaviors, resources, exchanges, goals and purposes, and economic and material interests. Thus, the research social field is composed of various arenas which must be discovered in order to understand single issues such as "ethics." That discovery technically utilizes an "extended case method" (Van Velsen 1967), which identifies a baseline of human behaviors, activities, events, or goals as an assumed starting point and then traces the boundaries of their arenas in time and space.

For most U.S. Mexicans, the Christmas ritual is focused on children and the "core" household heads. The New Year celebration is mostly for adults and mostly consists of the nucleated households individually either attending or sponsoring parties or dances. On the other hand, the Christmas ritual is for most members of the cluster regardless of age. Most of the expenses incurred are directed towards and support the cluster activities, and great stress is placed on cooperating in the raising of proper funds for a sizable presentation gift to the core heads. Gift exchange between cluster members is "tabbed," mostly by women. That is, an accounting of gift values and their evenness is noted. However, as important is the noting of attention to detail, such as the appropriateness of the gifts according to gender and age of children. This accounting process details whether adult members of the cluster are fulfilling their broader responsibilities of reciprocity. In this manner, this initial ritual also begins the "tabbing" process for the rest of the calendar year.

However, this initial event is also the ritual in which relations are emotively or psychologically reinforced in a distributive manner for the rest of the year. Grandchildren, children, cousins, sisters, brothers, in-laws—the specific parameters of their relationships are all laid out. Since it is impossible for all members of the household clusters to invest in the same specific manner with every person, emotionally, psychologically, or socially, this is also the time in which an individual's favorites are identified, preferences are displayed, and confirmations of the strongest and the weakest of relationships are noted and somewhat cemented. These are then evaluated and further defined and changed as other major, secondary, and minor rituals unfold.

This "distributive" process, however, also allows individuals who by personality preference are identified and given social "breathing space." That is, the non-reciprocal, individualistic, and more egocentric person is somewhat "tabbed." In this manner, such persons are given their social due and, although participants in aspects of both ritual and social exchange processes, they are identified with different sets of expectations.

Making Tamales: Freezing Relations for the Future

Yet among the most important social expectations that are also illustrated during this period are those which children learn contextually. In keeping with other mechanisms that accentuate the expectation for multiplicity and density,[14] children are exposed to participation, gift-giving, negotiating social preferences, and learning the "have to" of exchange during the preparation of tamales (Williams 1984:117-118). Tamales are steamed, corn leaves shucked, and thick Indian corn dough crepes mixed with fillings of red chili and meat, or green chili with cheese, or "dulce" of raisins, sweet cinnamon, and sugar. Part and parcel of the importance of the dish is that recipes are the special province of older women and great pride is taken in the entire preparation. Usually prepared two to three evenings before December 24, tamales are a labor-intensive activity requiring manual labor in the mixing and preparation of the corn paste, the cleaning of corn shucks as the covering for the tamale itself, the cleaning and cooking of fresh chili pods, and the cooking of meats, fillings, and other dishes that accompany the main course. Each tamale is handmade with the corn dough spread on the leaf, the filling applied, and then the entire thing folded neatly into an elongated crepe.

The actual number of tamales made is dependent on the size of the household cluster, the number of friends that eventually will be visited prior to Christmas, and the general finances of the cluster itself. It would not be unusual for fifty to eighty dozens to be made by six to eight women. Yet during the process, it is then that "heads are counted" about who has been reciprocal during the year, the reputation of various household heads, statements of the peccadilloes of men, and the "state" of various exchanges. But importantly for the purposes of this discussion, children are appraised of all of these conversations. It is not unusual for eighteen to twenty-four children from various households to be running about licking spoons, sticking their fingers in the corn dough, and using tortillas to make burritos from available fillings. Children, however, are also exposed to conversations, value judgments, and commentaries which set up for them a context for evaluation of others and reinforces whatever expectations are articulated.

Women basically recapitulate a corporate memory and account for changes, provide new interpretations, and redefine relations. It is during this period in which cross-border relations as well are discussed, relatives who have recently arrived are tallied, and general discussions of the need for gifts for less fortunate relatives in Sonora are held. During this period, relatives from Sonora may also visit and participate. They usually drop off a younger or marriage-eligible member to spend the Christmas holidays. Thus, such events are not unusual during the tamale-making process and reinforce the social exchange processes between those present.

Men, meanwhile, play largely secondary roles. They are usually restricted to the heaviest labor, such as carrying tubs of corn dough, heavy pots of meats and other fillings, and sporadically being present while the actual tamale-wrapping process occurs. Very seldom do men actually ever wrap, cook, or otherwise function in any of the preparatory processes. They may gather to participate in other activities such as helping on some repair job within the household, drinking a beer or two, or watching a football game on television.

Most men perceive the cooking activity as largely women's work and the conversations as "gossip." But men in fact participate in their own "gossip" activities and exchange information about automobile and home repair, leads to employment possibilities, and some discussion of cross-border events and relatives.

The tamales themselves are distributed to each individual household belonging to the cluster. In addition, a number of the tamales are set aside and frozen for the future use of each household, as well as to distribute as part of the general exchange network that unfolds throughout the rest of the year. In an interesting sense, the frozen tamales are the one currency that have no commodity (exchange) value but only social (use) value. In their frozen state they are distributed to those outside of the immediate clusters and broaden relations but as well within the cluster. They remind those present of the labor, effort, and willingness to exchange labor for a share of food itself.

Yet what is of crucial importance is that the entire process is in the hands of women and centrally important to the older women of the household cluster. They are the keeper of the tamale recipes that sometimes have been handed down by generations of other hands, and in fact, each cluster has its own favorite specialty and much is made of the origins and normative character of the recipes. In a way, they are the lineal script by which entire households and their descendants may be recognized. Thus some women will have inherited recipes emphasizing sweet tamales, others pork, others beef; even the kind of chili that is used stands as a cognitive marker for specific families, their location of origin, and their degree of acculturation. Casting individual variation aside, most women will judge the degree of how spicy the chili is in terms of how "Americanized" a recipe is. Thus the older the recipe, the more Mexican and thus will mark how original and legitimate the maker of the tamale is as well. Therefore, older women prize their recipes but even more, pride themselves in handing down "unAmericanized" versions to their children.

The Easter/Semana Santa (Holy Week) Complex

Six months later, a series of transborder Easter activities emerge as the stimulus for the unfolding of the second half of the ritual cycle. This major ritual is especially important in that of all the rituals throughout the year, this is the most likely one to include a large number of relatives residing in the Mexican border states of Sonora, Chihuahua, Baja California, and Coahuilla. Although, many exchanges occur between relatives on each side of the border throughout the first half of the calendar year, including the Christmas/New Year complex, the Easter ritual changes the exchange and focus from gifts to reviving relations across the border and within the household clusters themselves. The Northern Mexican relatives will celebrate "Semana Santa" in the U.S. side by taking advantage of the ten days or so of vacation time to participate in Easter rituals, as well as to vacation with their U.S. relatives. However, this movement north to celebrate Easter has its opposite version with U.S. Mexicans traveling south to celebrate Semana Santa without the usual Easter egg complex, although the closer to the border, the higher the probability for some kind of U.S. Easter artifacts to make their appearance. For the most part, this portion of the U.S. Mexican household population will be first-generation migrants to the United States or persons most recently arrived to the United States. They will also come from the central or Southern Mexican states and not originate in the

Northern Mexican areas. But it is women in households on each side of the border that are responsible for initial communication, preparation of some of the foods, time scheduling, and sleeping arrangements. Like the functions of the Christmas/New Year ritual, this ritual is filled with opportunities for social tallying, rekindling reciprocal relations, the articulation of statuses for women and men, and more importantly, the continued preparation of children for future obligations. While the traditional Mexican observances include adherence to a series of Catholic rituals and restrictive dietary habits throughout the Lenten season, the U.S. versions are strongly influenced by commercialized American cultural practice. This becomes most apparent in the preparation of Easter food and its serving.

Easter Egg Production and Food Preparation

If the tamale-making is functionally important to children and older women, the Easter complex is focused on children once more, but men seem to play a more important role in the actual food preparation. Older women are usually not in charge of the major food preparation activities that require intensive labor, but provide only a single large dish which everyone has enjoyed in the past. Much of the commensal preparation revolves around members of satellite households preparing different foods according to agreements between women while men largely will have their cooking roles confined to the preparation of barbecue and broiled meats. At times, leftover frozen Christmas tamales are brought out as extra dishes.

For the most part, the household clusters will meet either at a satellite household or will gather together at one of the local recreational parks throughout Easter Sunday, usually after having attended Easter services. Yet prior to their gathering, each household will prepare Easter eggs, give Easter baskets to children generally under seven or eight years old, and mobilize the responsibility for specific dishes brought to the gathering. However, meat that will be cooked by men is not made part of the communal pot, but rather, each individual male will purchase meat for their individual household members. While this segmentation may actually break down when the actual cooking and eating begins, nevertheless, the purchase of meat, the preparation for the grill, and the actual cooking is in the hands of individual males rather than a common responsibility of the entire cluster. In an interesting manner, individual food preparation by males is much more in keeping with the values of American individualization and more in keeping with nucleated households than with more reciprocal and communal Mexican values. In a sense, male roles are more like the labor market roles of fulfilling an instrumental function than the affective and instructional behaviors displayed by women. Men seem to reproduce their labor roles in the commodity domain rather than in the social domain of exchange as do women.

There are however instrumental roles that are carried out by women from Mexico. They will generally be integrated into the household routines such as helping with child care, attending to spouses, and preparing food, they do serve a valuable labor function for their U.S. women relatives who are employed outside of the household. In part, they relieve their relatives from double labor tasks—those associated with paid wage production and those with non-paid household production. In a sense, these relatives from northern Mexico, release and provide relief to their U.S. counterparts for a short two-week period of ritual celebration.

As importantly, they also function to maintain the cross-border characteristic of U.S. Mexican households and contribute Mexican cultural funds of knowledge[15] in a highly commercialized "American" process. Spanish is the primary language spoken, largely Spanish-speaking church services are attended, and, more importantly, social exchange and their expectations are directed from these relatives to U.S. Mexican children and adults. They balance out the effects of more American individualistic and commercial acculturation. But obviously this process is a two-way exchange, and Mexico-resident children are introduced by their U.S. Mexican cousins very early to the practice of the U.S. egg preparation and celebration complex and demand an equivalent practice where they permanently reside. Indeed many Mexican stores in the Borderlands make Easter bunny piñatas for Mexican customers.

Thus, among many other cross-border practices which this work cannot discuss, this seemingly unimportant and innocuous "Easter Bunny" practice contributes in a small way to the creation of a regional culture of the Borderlands.

DISCUSSION AND CONCLUSIONS

The Christmas/New Year and Easter events are the major calendric ritual templates on which U.S. Mexican culture is socially displayed. They mark the two halves of the entire calendric cycle and are carefully monitored by the households involved, and give meaning to the social relations articulated through other events. The terminal and initiating complex ends and sets off the energies and behaviors of exchange by processing and tallying who owes what to whom in a general reciprocal sense.

Between this initial birthing and ending of cultural space and time and the next major marker, lie a series of life-cycle rituals as well as more secular practices that are incorporated into the daily lives of persons as "normal" and expected behaviors. They fill out the entire first half but are "distributed" within and among household clusters and individuals according to the indeterminacies and uncertainties of daily life and in the manner in which individuals and clusters are arranged in simultaneously concurrent developmental cycles. Accidents, job losses, immigration raids, addictions, unintended love affairs, the tragedy of the unexpected death of a child—all those vagaries of living may make impossible and sometimes shape the best of intentions and expectations for exchange and for the quality of ritual participation of families and individuals. Coupled to a constantly emerging human developmental cycle, the first half of the calendric process merges into the second with the Easter complex functioning to give new meaning and life to the remaining series of minor secular and life-cycle rituals.

The constant buzz of social activities that comprise the entire calendric cycle are actions by which exchange and reciprocity are carried out in relatively uncertain and indeterminate economic and material conditions. In addition to the exchange activities embossed within the major rituals and the dozens of minor life-cycle versions, are the actual behaviors which articulate the shape and content of what constitute their "socially approved" dimensions.

Thus women's cultural transmission, discussion, and articulation of roles that are part and parcel of both major rituals and their food preparation activities, define them as the interpreters, carriers, and creators of Mexican culture in the United States and the Borderlands. If women's labor and their income are crucial to the maintenance of household stability, their ritual control is central to the maintenance and development of much of the operational and management behaviors that comprise Mexican culture and its exchange activities. Thus Mexican women of the U.S. and Mexico are mostly responsible for the planning, organization, and implementation of not only the activities within household clusters but their cross-border versions as well. If, as Leach has indicated, ritual expresses "socially approved" relations, then it is apparent that women define what constitutes "approval," in their social exchange relations, in the roles that need to be fulfilled including those carried out by men, and in the articulation of these approved versions to children. Yet the perpetuation of such roles and relationships are not merely reflections or cheap reproductions of relations of unpaid labor to a wider capitalist economy. Rather, these are the best methods of thwarting the worst features of economic and political appropriation. These are thinking, active, creative human beings who have negotiated, experimented, and transformed, in the best manner possible, a series of mechanisms, including the rituals described here, to mitigate and "cushion" otherwise destructive and unstabling political and economic pressures.

Since rituals are largely managed by women, this also reflects the central contributions women make to household cultural and social stability. As has been described, the Borderlands is an immensely dynamic region of rapid economic, social development, and dysfunction for Mexicans. Cultural appropriation, economic exploitation, and physical expulsion have been not unusual pressures that Mexicans have had to face. The cultural templates which women operate have been important mitigating factors to these pressures.

Women in this context, from both north and south of the border, transcend nation-state definitions of cultural identity. Rather than to simply accept what constitutes an "American" or "Mexican" according to state myths, women negotiate and manipulate social relations crucial to the formation and articulation of Mexican cultural identity regardless of border.

Women, in fact, negotiate multiple dimensions of cultural meaning through ritual within their household clusters. They define the contexts and operations for gender relations with men and the use of their labor as basically peripheral personnel. They expose children simultaneously to women's versions of social reality including the ability to negotiate, transform, and tally important reciprocal exchanges with relatives and friends. Children learn early on to begin the tally process themselves and what constitute "socially approved" relations.

Lastly, however, women as the central figures within Mexican cultural practices may serve as the key informational sources for larger social and cultural change. What language women use, whether they keep up or fail to keep up exchange relations, whether or not they participate in the expected rituals, and whether or not they manage the operational activities that comprise them, will strongly determine the efficacy of Mexican cultural life in the United States and of the Borderlands region. If this proposition is correct, then not only must future research concentrate on the meanings and defined parameters of ritual but more importantly in whose hands they reside.

NOTES

1. I use the term "Mexican" to describe those born in Mexico as well as those of Mexican parentage born in the United States. Although "Chicano" or "Mexican-American" is also used for those born in the U.S. of Mexican heritage, "Mexican" is the generally preferred term used by the U.S.-born population. See C. Arce (1981), J.A. Garcia (1982), and Carlos G. Vélez-Ibáñez (1983a).

2. Our data show that there is significant residential clustering of one portion of all household clusters which we have termed "primary" household clusters. Primary clusters are those in which exchange relations of kin groups with the interviewed household occur within a residential area of less than a mile. Secondary clusters are those with which exchange relations of kin groups are maintained but are not centered on the household interviewed and are more than a mile away. Half of all household clusters were "primary" and the rest were secondary. There was little significant size difference between the two types: the median was 4.12 households per cluster, and all other socioeconomic characteristics remained constant. For analytic purposes both types may be collapsed for the rest of this discussion except where noted.

Generally, the most frequent exchange within clustered households was baby-sitting for daughters and daughters-in-law. The differences between clustered and unclustered households was statistically significant at the .005 level of probability, with unpaid child care in clustered households being provided by grandparents. There was no statistically significant median age difference between clustered and unclustered households (fifty-two and forty-eight respectively), and the median yearly income for all households was $25,164 with a per capita income of $4,934.

3. See Table 2, pp. 10 and 11 of *The Hispanic Population of the United States*. See also Brett Williams' (1984:114) similar discussion in which she details the manner in which Mexican migrant women who are usually considered as among the most "traditional" are in fact not only productive wage earners, providing half of the household income, but are considered by men as crucial to the function of their own

well-being. Williams points out that the cross-cultural literature shows that "women are the most influential when they share in the production of food and have some control over its distribution" (1984:125). See for example, her references to J.K. Brown (1970); Louise Lamphere and Michelle Rosaldo (1974); and Peggy Sanday (1973). From our studies (Vélez-Ibáñez and Greenberg 1984; Moll, Vélez-Ibáñez, and Greenberg 1990) among Mexican households in Tucson, Arizona, 20 percent of household income is derived from the informal economy of which most was developed by women engaged in swap meet sales, cash remunerated domestic work, ironing, selling tamales and tortillas, embroidery and sewing sales, and taking care of other people's children.

4. See Maxine Baca Zinn (1982), A. Mirande (1982, 1986), and Brett Williams (1984) for a revisionist point of view regarding the participation of women in both decision-making and household income contribution in Mexican households in the United States. As well, recent stratified studies (Vélez-Ibáñez and Greenberg 1984) clearly show that Mexican women play these major roles in the management, operation, and decision-making in Tucson, Arizona.

5. The border region has witnessed the introduction of large-scale irrigation-based farming by the Riverine Hohokom peoples between 300 B.C. and 1450 A.D.; the penetration of mining, farming, and ranching by Spaniards and their entire cultural and political structures; the attempted consolidation by a centralized mestizo population during the Mexican period; and the Anglo introduction of large-scale, industrially organized mining, construction, commerce, and animal production, as well as the present service electronic, military, and modified mining and border-related twin plant production. Most historical periods were also filled with raids, warfare, conquest, and subjection of one population over another. The American period is also marked by large-scale land-clearing, land speculation, control of mineral, water, and natural resources by national corporations, and state ownership of more than half of the available land area.

Throughout the Borderlands areas of Northwest Mexico and Southwestern United States, the Mexican population has been part of major transformations. It has been a population subjected to constant demographic shifts, ecological pressures, and economic uncertainty. The nineteenth and twentieth centuries are replete with periodic large movements of Mexicans moving north and east and west, enlisted or attracted by farming, mining, and railroad recruiting agents and contractors, or pushed out by the Mexican Revolution, depressions, natural calamities, and great economic changes. New capital and technologies that have penetrated these regions have always transformed the regional ecology of the Borderlands. In the modern period, the location in the Borderlands of a labor market necessitating a combination of technical skills and labor manipulability is clear. This has stimulated lineal and cyclical migrations of Mexicans between border states (Vélez-Ibáñez 1980:218). In the period from 1917 to 1921 alone, 72,000 Mexican farm workers were admitted to the United States without the restrictions of the Immigration Act of 1917 (an $8 head tax, literacy test, and prohibition of contract workers). Such restrictions were also waived for non-agricultural workers from Mexico for the railroads, mines, and construction companies. In that period, Mexicans worked in iron and auto works in the Midwest, building trades in Arizona, railroad building in Southern California, and slaughterhouses in Kansas and Chicago (Vélez-Ibáñez 1980). The ten states that comprise the U.S.-Mexico border region are, on the Mexican side: Baja California

Norte, Baja California Sur, Sonora, Chihuahua, Nuevo Leon and Tamaulipas; on the U.S. side they are California, Arizona, New Mexico, and Texas.

6. See the works of J. Diez-Canedo (1981), P. Fernandez-Kelly (1987), J.A. Garcia and M. Griego (1983), B. Gonzalez-Archegia (1987), O. Martinez (1983), A. Salas Porras (n.d.), and S.B. Tiano (1985); all indicate the U.S. orientation of the Mexican border economy. Mexico supplies cheap labor, cheap agricultural products, mostly female-assembled goods, and playgrounds for U.S. sybarites. The U.S. supplies chiefly finished goods and technology. This relationship extends to income in border transactions earned by Mexico. In 1986, $1.2 billion was spent in Mexico by Americans and Mexicans spent $1.5 billion in the U.S. (Gonzalez-Archegia 1987:6).

In 1986, Mexico imported $11.4 billions in goods while exporting $16.0 billion, of which almost 40 percent was oil. The resulting advantage to Mexico is largely erased by the enormous debt burden of $107.4 billion, largely owed to American public and private institutions (U.S.-Mexico Report 1989b:11), and the attending annual interest of $14.5 billion (U.S.-Mexico Report 1989a:18-19).

However, without U.S. investment, the Mexican maquiladora industry (basically American-owned plants used to assemble American manufactured products in Mexico which are then sent back to the United States for sale) could not provide employment for 400,000 persons, mostly along the border. Such employment is in large part responsible for the fact that real income for the six Northern border Mexico states is higher than the per capita income of all of Mexico (Stoddard and Hedderson 1987:59).

7. On the Mexican side of the Borderlands, some of the same structural characteristics apply but with a greater skewing of income distribution and occupational categories. Nationally, 54 percent of the population receive income below the minimum wage while 84 percent live in poverty (U.S. Mexico Report 1989a:16). In 1980, the minimum wage in Mexico was approximately 6,390 pesos monthly, and the exchange rate was 22.50 pesos to $1.00. It should be noted that since 1980 the twin forces of inflation and devaluation have reduced real wages considerably. Thus, for example, in 1980, maquiladora workers in Sonora earned approximately 1,400 M.N. a week, or $62. In 1989, while these same workers averaged 60,000 M.N. a week, the real income was only $24. According to one source (U.S. Mexico Report 1989c), the minimum wage earner's purchasing power has decreased by 70 percent in the past twenty years.

In the six Mexican border states, 72 percent of the population earns the minimum wage of $284 or less monthly. At the upper end of the distribution, only 3 percent of the population earns more than $954, so that approximately 25 percent of the population earns an income between the minimum wage and the upper reported limit. This income distribution is also reflected in the occupational structure of the Mexican Borderlands. Seven percent are in upper White-collar occupations; 18 percent are categorized as self-employed; 69 percent are in blue-collar jobs; and 6 percent in unpaid labor. The category of self-employed captures two different populations. The first is composed of persons who have established their own small businesses and who are largely a part of the lower end of the formal sector. The second is composed of persons who are largely part of the informal sector and who include street vendors, cab drivers, scavengers, street barbers, gardeners, and countless other occupations marked by easy entry, low skills, and the need for few resources (see Eames and Goode 1973, 1980; Lloyd 1982). Finally, 1 percent are officially categorized as unemployed. This figures does not accord with other national estimates of real unemployment which ranges from 30 percent to 45 percent especially if a consideration is given to "disguised underemployment." According to *U.S. Mexico Report* (1989a), fourteen million persons in Mexico are part of an underground economy distributed among industrial and agricultural sectors.

8. A totally new appreciation of the Mexican population of the United States and region may be gained if northwestern Mexico and the southwestern United States are conceived as an area of continuous south-to-north migration, commerce, trade, and settlement from Mesoamerica since at least 1100 A.D. The much later Spanish, Mexican, and American periods themselves accentuated this process. Thus contemporary Mexican populations are another cultural version of this transhumant process.

9. The socialist state's purported ideological intent, to release social labor from the marketplace, is of questionable utility in practice, since the state organizes social labor through conscription and regulation and sets it to work, and wages are set by a privileged centralized management and policy unit. Capitalist systems mobilize social labor by purchasing labor power and sets it to work for wages according to the "market," which is largely asymmetrical, since the buying and selling of labor power is not an even exchange. Under both ideologies the quest for household labor by the state or by market responses is part of a constant struggle against which household members have to balance available labor power, consumption, and exchange in order to meet both culturally constituted "demand" and subsistence needs.

10. See F.D. Bean and M. Tienda (1987:323). I have taken the liberty of recomputing Figure 9.3 and combining men and women in single occupational categories.

11. See F.D. Bean and M. Tienda (1987), p. 199. Our previous work done in Tucson, clearly indicates that mean per capita income in 1980 for 76 percent of the Mexican population was $5,202 and for 24 percent of the Mexican population, $8,398. For the Anglo population the percentages were almost exactly reversed, with only 25.5 percent earning $5,202 and 74.5 percent earning $8,398. In comparing mean household income, 76 percent of the Mexican population earned $14,488 while 24 percent earned $21,994. Only 25.5 percent percent of the Anglo population earned $14,488 while 74.5 percent earned $24,245 (Vélez-Ibáñez, Greenberg and Johnstone 1984).

12. In William Julius Wilson's *The Truly Disadvantaged* (1987:20-62), the creation of a Black underclass results basically from structural economic changes which shift industrial production to services and the relocation of manufacturing out of the central cities. For young Black men this shift meant that they become part of labor force "dropouts" and are deprived the opportunity of suburban industrial employment. This leads to the development of a concentration of poor persons in urban poverty areas who are unemployed, the conditions of which are exacerbated by the flight of middle-class Blacks and their attending religious, economic, and social institutions. Such "flattening" of the social structure results in the creation of sectors of the population who are characteristically unemployed (especially young Black males), poverty stricken, dependent upon institutional subsidies, burdened with out-of-wedlock births, female-headed households, and a shortage of "marriageable" males who are employed. Coupled with non-functional school systems and lack of support of educational achievement as a means of escape by poverty parents, a politically apathetic and passive permanent "underclass" is created largely in poor, urban contexts in which Blacks suffer in disproportionate numbers.

When applied cross-culturally, the concept fails in validity and reveals its limitations especially in discussion of urban populations outside of Chicago and the eastern U.S. "rustbelt." My own work (Vélez-Ibáñez 1983a) in large urban settlements outside of Mexico City that are much poorer, with very high crime rates, in more desperate ecological conditions, with labor markets much more limited, and with unemployment and underemployment rates double and triple those associated in the underclass literature, and with large sets of single parents with children under eighteen—all combine to form characteristics to those associated with "the underclass." Yet these same urban arenas are characterized by hotbeds of political organization and activities, of community resistance to exploitation and political control, of community self-help and communal activities without institutional support, and of familial household clusters of extended and reciprocal relations. In spite of the structural conditions present, the reality of most Mexican urban populations totally contradict the general tone and substance of the "underclass" notion.

13. E.R. Stoddard and J. Hedderson (1987:56, 59). They note a definite trend that selects for higher income in the western coastal counties such as San Diego (California) and decreases very steadily toward the eastern region in the Lower Rio Grande Valley of Texas, such as Starr County, where the percentage of families in poverty is 45 percent!

14. There is one other dynamic aspect that should be considered. Our work shows that Mexican children learn social expectations somewhat differently than Anglo children. Our evidence suggests that these clusters provide U.S. Mexican children with a social platform in which they internalize these thick social relations and learn to have analogously "thick" social expectations. By multiple thick relations is meant that multiple social strands between individuals and groups become expected and activated by reciprocal behaviors. These are learned to be expected early in childhood.

However, because most studies of early childhood socialization have been attitudinal and not observational, the empirical record of process for Mexican children is scant. A recent study by M.T. Vélez (1983) of mother-infant interaction, however, provides some insight into the possible genesis of Mexican expectations and potentialities. Her work provides the probable link between early childhood experience and the formation of these expectations in clustered household settings and establishes the theoretical basis for understanding the phenomenon.

The original postulate in the work asserted there would be significant variations in the mothering styles of Mexican-American mothers and of Anglo mothers that could be attributed to cultural expectations, and that such expectations included the probability that Mexican mothers' providing more proximal stimulation to infants, being more responsive to their infants' signals, and expressing such differences about infant rearing in their beliefs and values (Vélez 1983:11).

In her findings the actual interaction between mothers and infants showed little difference in their frequency or quality. *Of greater significance for the emergence of the Mexican infant's social personality was in the social context of interactions, and the role of others played in the infant's early social experience* (Vélez 1983:80). Vélez found that though she introduced a variety of social and economic controls to match her sample, the Mexican mothers' social density was much greater, contact with infant and mother by other relatives was significantly more frequent, and greater stimulation of the infant by others was also statistically significant. The Mexican infant had a social context packed with tactile and sound stimulation. The child was surrounded by a variety of relatives, and at the behavioral level was seldom really alone. This last finding also was supported by the observation that although Mexican children had their own rooms available, 92 percent of the Mexican children slept in their parents' room, while 80 percent of the Anglo children slept in their own room.

Although this was a working-class sample, we have the impression from our present study that the same phenomenon extends to middle-class Mexican-American households. It would appear that the early "thick" social context that surround Mexican children leads to the emergence of social expectations that are different from those non-Mexican populations that do not have equivalent social characteristics. Such differences we suggest may include the internalization of many other significant object relations with more persons, an expectation of more relations with the same persons, and expectations of being attentive to and investing emotionally in a variety of relations. Such psychodynamic and psychosocial processes entailed in cultural expectations of confianza are those from whence anticipations for exchange relations emerge. Such early experiences give cultural expectation for exchange its substance; expectations that are reinforced by ritual and other forms of exchange throughout the life-cycle.

Such "thick contexts" are the social platforms in which the funds of knowledge of the cluster of households are transmitted. So by examining how such knowledge is transmitted, we gain some insight into the cultural conflicts that may arise when Mexican children confront educational models of the dominant society that seek to reshape Mexican children culturally and socially.

15. The best way to explain what we mean by funds of knowledge is to relate them to Eric Wolf's (1966) discussion of household economy. Wolf distinguishes a number of funds which households must juggle: caloric funds, funds of rent, replacement funds, ceremonial funds, social funds. Entailed in these are wider sets of activities requiring specific strategic bodies of essential information which households need to maintain their well-being (Vélez-Ibáñez and Greenberg 1992).

BIBLIOGRAPHY

Arce, C.
1981 "A Reconsideration of Chicano Culture and Identity." *Daedalus* 110:171-191.

1982 "Dimensions of Familism." Paper delivered at the Pacific Sociological Association, San Diego, California, April 22. Unpublished MS.

Baca Zinn, Maxine
1982 "Chicano Men and Masculinity." *The Journal of Ethnic Studies* 10:29-44.

Bean, F.D., and M. Tienda
1987 *The Hispanic Population of the United States*. New York: Russell Sage Foundation.

Brown, J.K.
1970 "A Note on the Division of Labor by Sex." *American Anthropologist* 72:1073-1078.

Diez-Canedo, J.
1981 *Undocumented Migration to the United States: A New Perspective.* Dolores E. Mills (trans.). Albuquerque: Center for Latin American Studies, University of New Mexico.

Eames, E., and J. Goode
1973 *Urban Poverty in a Cross-Cultural Context.* New York: Free Press.

1980 "The Culture of Poverty: Misapplication of Anthropology to Contemporary Issues." In *Urban Life.* P. Gmelch and W.P. Zenner (eds.) New York: St. Martin's Press, Pp. 42 - 97.

Fernandez-Kelly, P.
1987 "Technology and Employment along the U.S. Mexican-Border." In *The United States and Mexico: Face to Face with New Technology.* Cathryn L. Thorup (ed.) New Brunswick, NJ: Transaction Books.

Garcia, J.A.
1982 "Ethnicity and Chicanos: Measurement of Ethnic Identification, Identity, and Consciousness." *Hispanic Journal of Behavioral Sciences* 43(4):295-314.

Garcia, J.A., and M. Griego
1983 *Mexico and the United States: Migration, History, and the Idea of Sovereignty.* No. 7. El Paso: Center for Interamerican and Border Studies, University of Texas, El Paso.

Gonzalez-Archegia, B.
1987 "California-Mexico Linkages." Paper presented at First Annual California-Mexico Business Conference. Los Angeles: October 28-29.

Goody, Jack
1983 *The Development of the Family and Marriage in Europe.* London: Cambridge University Press.

Heyman, J.
1991 *Life and Labor on the Border.* Tucson: University of Arizona Press.

The Hispanic Population in the United States: March 1989
1990 Current Population Reports, Population Characteristics, No. 444. Washington, DC: U.S. Department of Commerce, Bureau of the Census.

Keefe, S.E.
1979 "Urbanization, Acculturation, and Extended Family Ties: Mexican Americans in Cities." *American Ethnologist* 6(2):349-365.

Keefe, S.E., and A.M. Padilla
1987 *Chicano Ethnicity.* Albuquerque: University of New Mexico Press.

Lamphere, L., and M. Rosaldo (eds.)
1974 *Women, Culture, and Society.* Stanford: Stanford University Press.

Leach, Edmund
1979 *Political Systems of Highland Burma.* 2nd ed. Boston: Beacon Press.

Lloyd, P.
1982 *A Third World Proletariat?* London: George Allen and Unwin.

Lomnitz, L.
(n.d.) *Horizontal and Vertical Relations and the Social Structure of Urban Mexico*. Unpublished MS.

Martinez, O.
1983 *The Foreign Orientation of the Mexican Border Economy*. Border Perspectives, No. 2. El Paso: Center for Interamerican and Border Studies, The University of Texas, El Paso.

1988 *Troublesome Border*. Tucson: University of Arizona Press.

Mirande, A.
1982 "A Reinterpretation of Male Dominance." *Family Coordinator* 28:473-479.

1986 *Chicano Fathers: Response and Adaptation to Emergent Roles*. Working Paper Series No. 13, February. Stanford: Stanford Center for Chicano Research.

Moll, Luis C., Carlos Vélez-Ibáñez, and James B. Greenberg
1990 *Community Knowledge and Classroom Practice: Combining Resources for Literacy Instruction*. Final Report. Office of Bilingual Education and Minority Language Affairs, Contract No. 300-87-0131.

Moore, J.
1988 *An Assessment of Hispanic Poverty: Is There an Hispanic Underclass?* San Antonio: Thomas Rivera Center.

Porras, A. Salas
(nd) *Crisis, Maquiladoras y Estructura Sociopolitica en Chihuahua, Sonora y Baja California*. Unpublished MS.

Sanday, Peggy
1973 "Toward a Theory of the Status of Women." *American Anthropologist*. 75: 1682-1700.

Stoddard, E.R., and J. Hedderson
1987 *Trends and Patterns of Poverty Along the U.S.-Mexico Border*. Las Cruces: Borderlands Research Monograph Series, New Mexico State University.

Swartz, M.J.
1972 *The Processual Approach in the Study of Local Level Politics*. Mimeo. La Jolla: University of California, San Diego.

Tiano, S.B.
1985 *Export Processing, Women's Work, and the Employment Problem in Developing Countries: The Case of the Maquiladora Program in Northern Mexico*. El Paso: Center for Interamerican and Border Studies, The University of Texas, El Paso.

U.S. Department of Justice, Annual Report of the Immigration and Naturalization Service
1954 Washington, DC P. 31.

U.S.-Mexico Report
1989a Las Cruces: Joint Border Research Institute, New Mexico State University, Las Cruces. April. Pp. 16-19.

1989b Las Cruces: Joint Border Research Institute, New Mexico State University, Las Cruces. July. P. 11.

1989c Joint Border Research Institute, New Mexico State University, Las Cruces. February. Pp. 16-17.

Van Velsen, J.
1967 "The Extended Case Method and Situational Analysis." In *The Craft of Social Anthropology*. A.L. Epstein (ed.) London: Tavistock Publications. Pp. 129-149.

Vélez, M.T.
1983 *The Social Context of Mothering: A Comparison of Mexican American and Anglo Mother Infant Interaction Patterns*. Los Angeles: Ph.D. Dissertation, Wright Institute of Psychology.

Vélez-Ibáñez, Carlos G.
1980 "Los Movimientos Chicanos: Problemas y Perspectivas." In *Las Relaciones Mexico/Estados Unidos*. David Barkin (ed.) Mexico D.F.: Editorial Nueva Imagen Pp. 217-234.

1983a *Bonds of Mutual Trust: The Cultural Systems of Rotating Credit Associations among Urban Mexicans and Chicanos*. New Brunswick: Rutgers University Press.

1983b *Rituals of Marginality: Politics, Process, and Culture Change in Central Urban Mexico, 1969-1974*. Berkeley and Los Angeles: University of California Press.

1988 "Networks of Exchange Among Mexicans in the U.S. and Mexico: Local Level Mediating Responses to National and International Transformation." *Urban Anthropology and Studies of Cultural Systems and World Economic Development* 17: 27-51.

(in press) "Plural Strategies of Survival and Cultural Formation in U.S. Mexican Households in a Region of Dynamic Transformation: The U.S.-Mexico Borderlands." In *Diagnosing America*. Shep Foreman (ed.) Ann Arbor: University of Michigan Press.

Vélez-Ibáñez, Carlos G., and James B. Greenberg
1984 *Multidimensional Functions of Non-Market Forms of Exchange among Mexicans/Chicanos in Tucson, Arizona*. Washington, DC: National Science Foundation. Unpublished MS.

1992 "Formation and Transformation of Funds of Knowledge Among U.S. Mexican Households: Contexts for Educational Reformation in the Southwest Region." *Anthropology and Education Quarterly* 23(4):313-335. Dec. Pp. 313 - 335.

Vélez-Ibáñez, Carlos G., James B. Greenberg, and B. Johnstone
1984 "The Ethnic, Economic, and Educational Structure of Tucson, Arizona: The Limits of Possibility for Mexican Americans in 1982." In *Proceedings of the 1984 Meeting of the Rocky Mountain Council on Latin American Studies*. Las Cruces: Center for Latin American Studies, New Mexico State University. Pp. 154-164.

Williams, B.
   1984 "Why Migrant Women Feed Their Husbands Tamales: Foodways as a
   Basis for a Revisionist View of Tejano Family Life." In *Ethnic and Regional
   Foodways in the United States: The Performance of Ethnic Identity*. L.K. Brown
   and K. Mussell (eds.) Knoxville: University of Tennessee. Pp. 113-126.

Wilson, William Julius
   1987 *The Truly Disadvantaged: The Inner City, the Underclass and Public
   Policy*. Chicago: University of Chicago Press.

Wolf, Eric R.
   1966 *Peasants*. Englewood Cliffs, NJ: Prentice Hall.

   1988 "Afterword." *Urban Anthropology and Studies of Cultural Systems and
   World Economic Development* 17(1):105-109.

9

Ethnic Celebrations in Rural California: Punjabi-Mexicans and Others

Karen Leonard

Heralding a "turn to history" in recent research (Kelly and Kaplan 1990:120), many anthropologists are looking closely at rituals in the context of structural change. Sociohistorical research on a biethnic community in rural California formed by men from India's Punjab region and women of Mexican ancestry presents an opportunity to look at what Victor Turner called "the constant cross-looping of social history with . . . ritual" (Turner 1987:77) to see how ethnic celebrations have changed over time. This biethnic community is an unusual one, and one could argue that perhaps it has changed more dramatically than most ethnic groups over the last few decades, propelled by both internal and external forces. The obvious interaction of Punjabi-Mexican identity with larger structural changes in society, however, shows us that conceptualizations of ethnicity and the definition and practice of ritual celebrations always occur within a context, as part of a process of historical change.

THE PUNJABI-MEXICANS

The history of the Punjabi-Mexican community in the Western United States can be given only briefly here (see Leonard 1992). The marriages between Punjabi men and Hispanic women began in the second decade of the twentieth century in California. Since all immigrants from India then were called "Hindus," regardless of the actual religious affiliation, local citizens mistakenly termed the couples and their children "Mexican Hindus." The men were from farming backgrounds in India's Punjab province and most of them came to California between 1900 and 1917. From 1917, federal immigration practices and laws discriminated decisively against Asians and legal entry was all but impossible (Jensen 1988; La Brack 1988). Almost ninety percent of these immigrants were Sikhs, many surnamed Singh; some were Muslims and a very few were Hindus. Most of the Punjabi men were married but had left their wives in India and were prevented by tightening immigration laws from bringing them later on. Those who stayed permanently in California sought to marry local women but were hampered by the state's anti-miscegenation laws which made marriage with women of other "races" difficult. In the Southern Imperial Valley, which lay inland from San Diego along the border with Mexico, however, the Punjabis were able to marry Mexican or Mexican-American women.

The Imperial Valley was a desert until the first decade of the twentieth century, when engineers tamed the Colorado River and the Imperial Irrigation District was organized. The valley was a raw, rough place colonized by farming men from many backgrounds. Native-born Whites were the largest group, but the 1920 census shows large numbers of Mexicans, Japanese, and Blacks, followed by Canadians, Swiss, Germans, English, Greeks, Italians, Irish, and Portuguese. The 1910 census figures showed a county population of 43,453, with 6,414 Mexicans, 1,986 Japanese, 1,648 Blacks; the other named groups ranged from 372 down to 99 (U.S. Department of Commerce: 1920: III, Pp. 109-124). In smaller numbers but otherwise conspicuous were the Chinese and Punjabi immigrant men.

As they settled down to cultivate the land, the farmers tended to seek wives. The Japanese and Swiss men imported wives—"picture brides" and "mail order brides." The Punjabi men turned to Mexican and Mexican-American women, whom they could marry because local officials perceived them to be racially similar. The Punjabi men chose women of Mexican ancestry for other reasons too. Perhaps most important, Mexican immigrants were then entering Southern California, many of them impoverished and pushed by the Mexican Revolution, and many took jobs up picking cotton in the fields farmed by the Punjabi men (Mexicans did not arrive in the northern areas of the state until the 1940s and most of the Punjabi men there stayed bachelors). Mexicans and Punjabis shared a rural way of life with similar types of food, furniture, and other aspects of material culture. And Mexicans and Punjabis shared an initially low class status in California. But individual choice paled before the fact that anti-miscegenation laws prohibited marriages across racial lines in California until 1948. Since most California County clerks saw the Punjabi men as colored, or "brown," the word often sued to describe the men in the blank on the marriage license for race, the women the Punjabis married also had to be perceived as "brown." That generally meant women of Mexican ancestry.

The first recorded Punjabi-Mexican marriages occurred in 1916 and 1917 in the Imperial Valley and eventually there were almost 400 of these biethnic couples clustered in California's agricultural valleys: some 250 couples in the Imperial Valley, 90 in the Sacramento Valley in the North, and 50 in the Central Valley around Fresno (see Appendix I). Another 50 or so couples settled in similar agricultural valleys in Arizona and Texas.

These biethnic families formed a distinct community. Contrary to a popular theory that the Punjabis assimilated to American culture by way of the Mexican-

American subculture (Dadabhay 1954), the Punjabi-Mexican families were not well received by most Mexican Americans. Mexican men opposed these marriages and there were some early instances of violence between Punjabis and Mexicans over them. While some Punjabi men were close to their Mexican relatives by marriage, most were not. Initially separate male and female networks partially combined and both contributed structural elements to family and community life. The friendships of the Punjabi men were one basis of the community, but often farming partners married sets of sisters or women otherwise closely related to each other (Leonard 1992: chapters 4 and 5).

As children were born to these couples in the 1920s and 30s, they were given names such as Maria Jesusita Singh, Jose Akbar Khan and Armando Chand. The children spoke to their mothers in Spanish and to their fathers in English and/or Spanish. Most of them were raised as Catholics, and the fathers, without the time or the training to inculcate Sikhism, Islam, or Hinduism, encouraged this. They saw religion as the women's sphere and many explicitly stated that all religions were ultimately one. The families utilized the Catholic *compadrazgo* system, appointing godparents to sponsor the children at baptism, confirmation, and marriage; most godparents were couples from within the biethnic community, so that Sikh, Muslim, or Hindu men were godfathers to each other's children through the Catholic Church.

The fathers transmitted little of Punjabi culture to their wives and children, save in the culinary and funerary domains, and both of these featured ritual preparations. With respect to food, male and female heritages were combined without difficulty. Growing vegetables favored in the Punjab and cooking "Hindu foods" became household rituals followed to this day by descendants. Chicken curry, bread or *roti*, various vegetable curries, and certain pickles (especially lime pickles in oil) constituted the principal items in the "ethnic" diet. As Arjun Appadurai (1988a) has shown, recipes and menus can be important definers of community, and the wives and children pointed to their food as evidence of "Hindu" ethnicity.

But when it came to funeral practices, competing rituals were sometimes hard to reconcile. It took some time before families were fully included in the Indian men's rituals and before compromises were forged, some of them because of American laws and practices. The disposition of the body upon death was often a matter of dispute. The Sikhs and Hindus practiced cremation and insisted upon it, but cremation was not then an option in America (a 1918 Imperial Valley newspaper reported county officials stopping Sikh farmers who were about to light the funeral pyre of a countryman out in the fields [*El Centro Progress*, August 13]). And cremation then was anathema to Catholics, who believed it to be a sin. Furthermore, back in India, important parts of funeral rituals were conducted by and in the presence of men only, yet funeral homes in the United States featured viewing and services without segregation by sex.

Both conflicts and compromises characterized the death rituals over the years. Some widows buried their husbands' bodies on the Mexican Catholic sections of the local cemeteries, where they themselves would lie, while others were forcibly prevented from doing so by other Punjabis. As the families utilized funeral homes, they posed for photographs which united men and women around the open coffins and which, sent to India, informed relatives there of the death. Often double funeral ceremonies were conducted, one in the American funeral home with a Christian or nondenominational theme and another in a Sikh, Hindu, or Muslim religious setting. The ashes of those cremated could be sent to India or deposited locally, in the Salton Sea or the Pacific Ocean. Punjabi Muslims carried out orthodox burial ceremonies for each other, the men preparing the body and carrying it to the grave. The families of the Muslims attended the funerals, but the early gravestones most typically bore brief inscriptions in the Urdu (Arabic-derived) script indicating the name of the deceased's father's and his village and district in the Punjab. The men were all buried next to each other in a "Hindu plot" which they had purchased jointly, and their wives and children were buried in the Mexican Catholic sections of local cemeteries. In later decades, especially in Phoenix, Arizona, where a "Hindu plot" was not purchased until the late 1930s, some wives and children were buried next to the men, and gravestones added English or were inscribed wholly in it.

The Punjabi-Mexican children struggled socially with their ethnic identity from an early age. Anglos and Mexicans called them "Mexican-Hindus," "dirty Hindus" and "half and halves," and most were sent to "Mexican" or segregated schools. School segregation on the basis of "race" became illegal in California only in 1947 (Cooke 1972 [1948]) and continued in practice beyond that date. Despite the lack of experience with much that constituted Punjabi culture back in the Punjab, most Punjabi-Mexican descendants referred to themselves as Hindu or East Indian,[1] and they were perceived to be "Hindu" and performed as such in the rural California context. Family and community celebrations helped shape this evolving "Hindu" identity (but also American, as we shall see).

RITUAL CELEBRATIONS

Some of the private and public celebrations in which most Punjabi-Mexican families engaged have already been mentioned. The children's generally Catholic upbringing meant the observance of life-cycle ceremonies associated with that church by many families. However, specifically Mexican observances such as the *quinzanyero*, or the fifteenth birthday celebration for girls, were not celebrated. Funeral rituals at first private and confined chiefly to the men, were expanded to include families and others in the wider community. All the Punjabi-Mexican families celebrated major American public holidays enthusiastically: the Fourth of July, Labor Day, Thanksgiving, and Christmas. For the Fourth of July and Labor Day, Punjabi-Mexican families often went together to the mountains or the seaside. They did not celebrate Mexican Independence

Day, but occasions marking India's progress towards independence were central to family and community life. The one statewide Punjabi institution in California in the early decades, the Stockton Sikh temple (founded in northern California in 1913), was the site for meetings associated with the Punjabi anti-British terrorist organization, the Ghadar party, and later the Indian National Congress. The temple served social and political purposes as much or more than religious ones, as scholars looking at that institution over the decades attest (Wood 1966; La Brack 1988). Spouses and children of the Punjabi men, whatever their background, enjoyed meeting each other at the Sikh temple, and annual trips there were a highlight of the year for the better-off families.

The late 1940s brought momentous changes. First came the Luce-Celler bill of 1946, making South Asians eligible for United States citizenship (Jacoby 1958), followed by the birth of two new nations, India and Pakistan, in 1947. The immigrant men and their wives and children celebrated the ending of British colonial rule with great pride. A memorable photo of "the wives of the Hindus" celebrating India's independence in the northern California farm town of Yuba City shows one woman from India, three Anglo women, and sixteen women of Mexican descent. The one photo most likely to be shown to me by families showed Madame Pandit (sister of Jawaharlal Nehru, India's Congress Party leader and first Prime Minister of India) soliciting funds at the Stockton temple, circa 1947, surrounded by Punjabi farmers and Punjabi-Mexican family members. From this time on, the "Hindus" and newly-invented "Spanish-Pakistanis" (the descendants of most Punjabi Muslims renamed themselves because of the religious nature of the partition in India) functioned as representatives of independent Asian nations in their localities.

Even before the independence celebrations of 1947, the Punjabi-Mexican young people had performed as "Hindus" in public celebrations in the farming towns. In the Imperial Valley, the annual Midwinter Fair featured ethnic queens, a "Hindu" queen among them in the 1930s and 40s and, after 1947, a Pakistani queen as well. The other queens were "American," Mexican, Chinese, Japanese, Filipino, and Swiss, the categories emphasizing important immigrant groups in the valley. In Yuba City in the north, a Campfire Girls International fete featured Punjabi-Mexican daughters dressed in *saris* behind a table with a model of the Taj Mahal. And members of the second generation founded a Hindustani Club in the Imperial Valley, just as most of them were coming of age, one of a series of ethnic clubs there sponsored by International Neighbors.

But further legal and social changes have challenged the descendants' claim to be "Hindu." After the 1965 liberalization of U.S. immigration laws, the new immigrant population from South Asia has grown dramatically (see Appendix II). Most of the new immigrants are highly-educated professional people from all over South Asia, and they are settling in urban areas. Some, however, are Punjabi villagers from the very same villages as the pioneers, sponsored by and settling alongside the aged pioneers in rural California. The new immigrants' perceptions of the descendants of the pioneers, and the descendants' perceptions of the recent immigrants, have negatively affected the descendants' claims to Hindu ethnicity and barred them from the new South Asian ethnic celebrations which are now part of the California scene.

The problem is most acute in the North, around Yuba City, where aging bachelor Punjabis have sponsored many new immigrants. Chain migration has brought the Punjabi population from under 400 up to about 10,000 (La Brack 1988). In the Imperial Valley, there are more Punjabi-Mexicans than new immigrants from South Asia. The Punjabi-Mexican descendants in the Yuba City area welcomed the first few newcomers and contributed to the building of the first Sikh *gurdwara* (temple) in Yuba City. Thus one of two benches at the gurdwara entrance reads: "In loving memory of our father Harnam Singh Sidhu, 1891-1974, from children Isabel S. Villasenor, Ray S. Sidhu, Frank S. Sidhu, Pete S. Sidhu, Beatrice S. Myers." But by the mid-70s, the Punjabi-Mexicans were greatly outnumbered and were being dropped from the developing Sikh community there.

The newcomers from South Asia consistently disapproved of and understated the number of Punjabi-Mexican marriages which had occurred. In Yuba City, Bruce La Brack (personal communication) reported that Punjabi wives objected to the other wives cooking in the gurdwara, suspecting that the food was being poisoned! Even if the story is untrue, it is significant that it is being told, and I found descendants arguing that their (Mexican) mothers prepared better chicken curry than recently-arrived Punjabi women. Descendants seldom visit that gurdwara (or other new ones) today. To members of the second generation, the faction-building and heated disputes over leadership at the gurdwaras seems inappropriate to the practice of religion. The so-called "White" or "goora" Sikhs also have trouble with this aspect of Punjabi culture (Dusenbery 1988).

In both the old Stockton Sikh temple and the Muslim (Pakistani) mosque started in Sacramento in 1947, the post-1965 immigrants have reimposed practices changed or abandoned decades ago by the older immigrants: there is now sex-segregated seating, the chairs have been removed and seating is on the floor, and *prasad* (blessed food) is served into bare hands instead of on plates with spoons and napkins (the latter two practices pertain to the Sikh temple). The descendants of the pioneers thought they could be both Catholic and Sikh, or Catholic and Muslim; they now feel excluded. They fight back by accusing the new immigrants of being backward, of spoiling the memory of the pioneers who adapted themselves to their new county in ways ranging from their marriages and beliefs about women to religious practices (Leonard 1989, 1992).

Most members of the second generation still claim a Hindu ethnic identity, but the extent to which outsides know about and support that identity varies depending upon the context. In California's Imperial Valley, farming is still the main occupation, and the small numbers of new South Asian immigrants do not threaten the Hindu identity of descendants. White "Hindu" is still a well-known local ethnic group. It is true that younger people both inside and outside the community testify to a weakening of that perception—to some young people in the Imperial Valley, Singh is now a Mexican name. Some descendants are fighting the Anglo establishment for greater recognition of their heritage. At least one man has tried to get a major local road named "Singh Road"—it would, he points out, cover a great many Punjabi pioneers![2] But "Hindu" has become part of the local language, as an adjective and a verb in the valley. Thus "Hindu" farming means profitable farming but some inattention to outward appearances of the fields and barnyard, and to say he "Hindued it," for example a broken axle, means to make an efficient but makeshift, temporary repair.

In Arizona and northern California, the identities claimed by those who are members of the old biethnic community are no longer acknowledged by non-members of that community; traditions are diverging or contested, and are sometimes converging in a larger, less intimate society. Once similar to the Imperial Valley, Arizona's Phoenix area is now much more cosmopolitan; it boasts a well-established university and frequently hosts national conventions. The second Punjabi-Mexican generation there participates in the expanding urban and suburban culture which has supplanted the agrarian culture of the past. There is still some group feeling among them—they held a reunion in November 1991 which, significantly, was termed a "multi-breed" reunion that avoids the India/Pakistan issue and the old Hindu misnomer altogether. But there are no regularly scheduled rituals or celebrations to proclaim Mexican-Hindu or Spanish-Pakistani identity, and others in the Phoenix area no longer perceive them as a distinctive group. By choosing the anonymous "multi-breed" tag, they collaborate in this process of erasure.

In northern California, the "Hindu" ethnicity is sharply contested. As in the Imperial Valley, Punjabi descendants still rely primarily upon an agrarian economy, but Hindu identity is now both claimed and rejected by the descendants. Food and restaurants are important markers of ethnic and national identity, and descendants are proud of the Yuba City restaurant, El Ranchero, run by a Punjabi Mexican from the Imperial Valley; descendants patronize it regularly and keep Ali Rasul's roti in their freezers for those special family dinners. This is the only Mexican restaurant in California which features chicken curry and roti, since Panchos in Selma in the Central Valley (also run by an Imperial Valley-born Punjabi-Mexican) closed. But the "new Hindus," buying up most of the peach and kiwi orchards, are doing so well that they arouse prejudice. Descendants identify with the "old," not the "new," Hindus, a position hard to maintain with the new immigrants so numerous and so conspicuous.

By the 1980s, there were two major celebrations in Yuba City involving immigrants from India, and they illustrate the dilemma well: a Sikh Parade and a Mexican-Hindu or Oldtimer's Reunion Christmas Dance, both usually held in November. The descendants of the Punjabi-Mexicans might be expected to attend either or both of these events, the Sikh Parade because most of the early Punjabi immigrant men were Sikhs, and the annual Christmas Dance because it began as a reunion for descendants of the Punjabi pioneers. But the Sikh parade is problematic for them. Its clear status as what Falassi calls a "rite of conspicuous display" of the Sikh religion excludes the Punjabi-Mexicans (Falassi 1987:4), and the reaction of other Yuba City residents to the hundreds if not thousands of bearded, turbaned Sikh men marching down their streets brandishing unsheathed sword and signs in Punjabi script (with messages inaccessible to other local people) has been apprehension and resentment.

In contrast, the Christmas Dance falls in the category of "play" rather than ritual or religion (Turner 1987:77) and it has expanded beyond the originally narrow Punjabi-Mexican base and become a self-consciously "American" celebration. It now includes all who went to school with the founders of the dance and their families and has been renamed the Oldtimers Dance. Its organizing committee is predominantly Mexican-American: in 1988, only two of the eight organizers and about one tenth of the attendees were descendants of Punjabis or related to them by marriage. That year, the theme was Hawaiian, with "Aloha" written on a banner above the platform where a mariachi band performed, and the invitation began "Hello/Ohio/Buenos Dias." The emphasis was firmly upon ethnic pluralism in America.

Musing about journalism, scholarly ambitions, and anthropological research in an essay on rodeo, Larry McMurtry asserts that a sophisticated analysis or story can be developed: "provided one makes use of a few techniques taken over from novelists and keeps clearly in mind that it is best to frame the whole against a background of one's personal activities" (McMurtry 1974:9, 20). What follows is almost that slender and the necessary historical research has not yet been done, yet the following brief comparison with other ethnic groups and their celebrations in California's farm towns is suggestive and, I think, useful.[3] Nisei Week in Los Angeles was originally designed to bring the second generation Japanese-Americans back to the Los Angeles center of the produce marketing center for southern California's Japanese farmers, and it has become a public celebration of Japanese culture in the United States. The Chinese "Bomb Day" in Yuba City, characterized by the setting off of firecrackers and originally a celebration of Sun Yat Sen's Republican Double Ten Revolution (October 10, 1911), has become a community-wide celebration in a park set up and maintained by the local Rotary Club. In Imperial County, the Swiss Octoberfest/Schwingfest in Holtville and Mexican Independence Day in Calexico have become events on the County Calendar sponsored by the local chambers of commerce.[4] In Yuba City, the Sikh Parade and the renamed Oldtimers Christmas Dance, produced by successive but essentially discontinuous waves of Indian immigrants, are contending celebrations of immigrant identity, pitting new against old immigrants, religious and regional particularism against American cultural pluralism. There and in Phoenix, the second and third generations are turning to expanded definitions of membership and to "American" ethnicity.

CELEBRATIONS AND ETHNIC PLURALISM

Older notions of bounded cultural units located in time and space and some-times ranked with respect to one another are giving way to a recognition of the difficulties of defining and analyzing such units, particularly in the contempo-rary world. Anthropologists are turning their attention to issues of transforma-tion, to events and historical processes affecting not "cultures" but "connected social fields" (Ferguson and Gupta 1992; Moore 1986:4-5; Wolf 1988). Earlier, the Punjabi peasant immigrants might have been seen as "archetypal natives" (Gupta 1988:5; Appadurai 1988b:36-40), people drawn from their own place by capitalist needs for labor, experiencing social disorganization (Zaretsky 1984:25-31) in their new place (the more so because of the need to marry women of other backgrounds), and forced to accommodate, adapt, or assimilate to the dominant Anglo culture in the United States. Yet the immigrants them-selves and their descendants present a different account. "I'm Hindu, Mexican, and American, and some are not lucky enough to know all three cultures," was a typical statement, one that relates the Punjabi-Mexican experience to its American context positively, and which brings us to the literature on ethnic plu-ralism in the United States.

Ethnicity has been called a weak conception of culture, a conception suitable for organizing divisions within a pluralist state (Clifford 1988:339). John Higham, an historian who writes about American ethnic pluralism, explains the fact that ethnic group behavior varied according to context in the United States by emphasizing the localization of power in this country compared to Europe (Higham 1984:183-184); this certainly fits California's farm valleys. While there has been a deprecation of the celebratory tone of much of the earlier work on ethnic persistence, some charging that ethnic pluralism and democracy are not easily compatible (Higham 1984:198-230; Rabinowitz 1983:28; Steinberg 1981, epilogue), the Punjabi pioneers and their descendants testified to an under-lying consensus that pluralism means equality and diversity rather than repres-sion and delusion.[5]

While the Punjabi-Mexican experience should not be interpreted as a great "ethnic success" or "assimilation" story (see Leonard 1992:chapters 9, 10), it should not be labeled "marginal" and "subcultural" (Dadabhay 1954; Chakravorti 1968) or their current equivalents, "borderland" and "periphery." The Punjabi-Mexican experience (and that of the Japanese, Chinese, Swiss, Mexicans, and possibly others in rural California) certainly exemplify "situa-tional selection of ethnic identity" but not necessarily insecurity or marginality (Nagata 1974:343, 346). The mediating role played by many of the Mexican-American wives of the Punjabis might tempt scholars to follow the lead of the literature developing on women as the inhabitants of borderlands, speaking from the margins, alienated and deterritorialized beings moving in the interstices be-tween groups. In this kind of analysis, because of their "multiple positionality," women and minorities are said to sustain contradictions, invent themselves, and transform their sense of individual oppression into collective resistance (Anzaldua 1987:78-80). These literary, expressive terms do not describe the feelings expressed by the Punjabi-Mexicans about their ethnicity. Rather, the voices of the Punjabi-Mexican-Americans and the history of their private and public celebrations stress the broader American component of their experience and identity.

While this American component defies easy definition, that may be an essential characteristic. It has been suggested that Americans take much for granted among themselves and dramatize and invent ethnicity rather freely. Thus ethnic literary history and discourse best illustrate not each writer's "ethnic perspective" or descent, but the cultural understandings the writers share as they seize upon and exaggerate their differences (Sollors 1986:13-14).

Immigrants are the creative producers of new identities par excellence (Rushdie 1990:3-4), important agents in the shaping of our contemporary world (Appadurai 1988b; Gupta 1988). They are far from being inhabitants of "zero culture transition" zones, as Renato Rosaldo has pointed out (Rosaldo 1988:81). In recent U.S. censuses, an increasing proportion of the American population identifies itself as "American" or "White" instead of specifying an ethnic group. Some scholars view this as "distortion" but nevertheless postulate a new "unhyphenated-White" or "American" ethnic group (Lieberson and Waters 1988). I suspect these phenomena are not restricted to the Euro-American population,[6] and that the selection of Punjabi-Mexicans and others of this "unhyphenated" category at times is not a distortion. In their celebrations, in their self-identity as "biethnic," "triethnic," "multibreed," or "American," the Punjabi-Mexicans dramatize the changing content and form taken by ethnic identity as it crosses oceans, continents, and years. We need to look again at the larger issue of culture, and immigrant celebrations of ethnicity are a promising focus for this exploration.

NOTES

1. The Punjabi-Mexican community was not homogeneous, and members of the second generation responded differently to the choices open to them. The poorer families tended to identify more closely with Mexican-Americans. In some of these families, conflict with the father or his countrymen produced lasting anger, alienating descendants from the Punjabi heritage. Yet even where the Punjabi men were said to have "become Mexican," incoming daughters-in-law found a pride in Hindu ancestry, which denigrated Hispanic ancestry. Only one Punjabi-descended farmer in the Imperial Valley has renounced his "Hindu" name (Singh) and has taken up leadership of the Mexican-Americans there.

2. The words of the organizer of the Imperial Valley Pioneers, the "first settlers" historical association, certainly apply to the Punjabi farmers although they and their descendants formerly were not eligible for membership: [this was] "the greatest of all Valley orders, the Imperial Valley Pioneers, the builders of our empire, competent to grade and irrigate Hell and make another winter garden of it." (Thaddeus Dale McCall,

the organizer, quoted in the *Valley Grower*, summer 1982, 48). The Pioneers has renamed itself Imperial Valley Pioneers Historical Society and broadened its entrance criteria greatly (*Imperial Valley Pioneers Newsletter* 8, March 1984, 5). Some representatives of the Pioneers (including a Punjabi descendant) point to a short street named Singh in El Centro. The street is not long enough to satisfy Bagga S. Sunga, whose November 22, 1978 letter to *The Brawley News* suggested that Dogwood Road (a major road) be renamed Singh Road.

3. For example, the rodeo interpretations made by Frederick Errington (1990) and Elizabeth Atwood Lawrence (1982) might be more finely tuned were they based on detailed sociohistorical study.

4. For Nisei Week, annual schedule, August; for Bomb Day, interviews in Yuba City, 1982, and marker in the park by the Chinese Water Temple, Marysville; *Imperial County Calendar, 1990-1991 Calendar of Events*, Private Industry Council (PIC) of Imperial County in cooperation with Regional Economic Development, Inc. (REDI).

5. Higham refers to the 1960s tendency toward "interpreting pluralism as a repressive condition and a delusive theory" and to the opposing group of American intellectuals "still desirous somehow of upholding both equality and diversity" (Higham 1984:228-229). Higham ends with the assertion that an underlying consensus about basic values is indispensable to a decent multiethnic society and exhorts scholars to help "revitalize a common faith amid multiplying claims for status and power" (1984:232).

6. Regrettably, this work seems again to exclude or marginalize non-Whites. Examining ethnic and racial groups in contemporary America from 1980 census data, Lieberson and Waters found that an increasing proportion of the United States population is of mixed ethnic ancestry and that people were making choices from their various ancestries. Focusing on the Euro-American population, they often use the "unhyphenated-white" or "American" terms interchangeably; more work is needed on non-Whites or people of mixed ancestry (Lieberson and Waters 1988).

BIBLIOGRAPHY

Anzaldua, Gloria
    1987 *Borderlands/La Frontera: The New Mestiza*. San Francisco: Spinsters/Aunt Lute.

Appadurai, Arjun
    1988a "How to Make a National Cuisine: Cookbooks in Contemporary India." *Comparative Studies in Society and History* 30(1):3-24.

    1988b "Putting Hierarchy in Its Place." *Cultural Anthropology* 3(1):37-49.

Chakravorti, Robindra
    1968 *The Sikhs of El Centro: A Study in Social Integration*. Ph.D. dissertation, Minneapolis: University of Minnesota.

Clifford, James
    1988 *The Predicament of Culture: Twentieth-Century Ethnography, Literature, and Art*. Cambridge: Harvard University Press.

Cooke, W. Henry
1972 [1948] "The Segregation of Mexican-American School Children in Southern California." In *Racism in California*. Roger Daniels and Spencer C. Olin, Jr. (eds.) New York: Macmillan. Pp. 220-228. Originally published in *School and Society* 67 (1948). Pp. 417-421.

Dadabhay, Yusuf
1954 "Circuitous Assimilation among Rural Hindustanis in California." *Social Forces* 33:138-141.

Dusenbery, Verne A.
1988 "Punjabi Sikhs and Gora Sikhs: Conflicting Assertions of Sikh Identity in North America." In *Sikh History and Religion in the Twentieth Century*. Joseph T. O'Connell, Milton Israel, and Willard G. Oxtoby, with W.H. McLeod and J.S. Grewal (eds.) Toronto: Centre for South Asian Studies, University of Toronto. Pp. 334-355.

Errington, Frederick
1990 "The Rock Creek Rodeo: Excess and Constraint in Men's Lives." *American Ethnologist* 17(4):628-645.

Falassi, Alessandro
1987 "Festival: Definitions and Morphology." In *Time Out of Time: Essays on the Festival*. Allesandro Falassi (ed.) Albuquerque: University of New Mexico Press.

Ferguson, James, and Akhil Gupta
1992 "Beyond Culture: Space, Identity, and the Politics of Difference." *Cultural Anthropologist* 7(1):6-23.

Gupta, Akhil
1988 "Space and Time in the Politics of Culture." Paper read at American Anthropological Association Annual Meeting, Phoenix.

Higham, John
1984 *Send These to Me: Immigrants in Urban America*. 2nd edition Baltimore: Johns Hopkins Univeristy Press.

Jacoby, Harold
1958 "More Thind Against Than Sinning." *The Pacific Historian* 11(4):1-2, 8.

Jensen, Joan M.
1988 *Passage from India: Asian Indian Immigrants in North America*. New Haven: Yale University Press.

Kelly, John D., and Martha Kaplan
1990 "History, Structure, and Ritual." *Annual Review of Anthropology* 19:119-150.

La Brack, Bruce
1988 *The Sikhs of Northern California, 1904-1975: A Socio-Historical Study*. New York: AMS Press.

Lawrence, Elizabeth Atwood
1982 *Rodeo: An Anthropologist Looks at the Wild and the Tame*. Knoxville: University of Tennessee Press.

Leonard, Karen
1989 "Immigrant Punjabis in Early Twentieth-Century California: A Life History."
In *Social and Gender Boundaries in the United States*. Sucheng Chan (ed.) Lewiston,
NY: Edwin Mellen Press. Pp. 101-122.

1992 *Making Ethnic Choices: California's Punjabi Mexican Americans*.
Philadelphia: Temple University Press.

Lieberson, Stanley, and Mary C. Waters
1988 *From Many Strands: Ethnic and Racial Groups in Contemporary America*.
New York: Russell Sage Foundation.

McMurtry, Larry
1974 *It's Always We Rambled: An Essay on Rodeo*. New York: Frank Hallman.

Moore, Sally Falk
1986 *Social Facts and Fabrications*. New York: Cambridge University Press.

Nagata Judith A.
1974 "What Is a Malay? Situational Selection of Ethnic Identity in a Plural Society."
American Ethnologist 1:331-350.

Rabinowitz, Howard N.
1983 "Race, Ethnicity, and Cultural Pluralism in American History." In *Ordinary
People and Everyday Life: Perspectives on the New Social History*. James M.
Gardner and George Rollie Adams (eds.) Nashville: American Association for State
and Local History. Pp. 23-49.

Rosaldo, Renato
1988 "Ideology, Place, and People without Culture." *Cultural Anthropology* 3(1):
77-87.

Rushdie, Salman
1990 *In Good Faith*. London: Granta.

Social Science Research Council
1989 "The Rise of a New Ethnic Group: The 'Unhyphenated American.'" *Items*
43(1):7-10.

Sollors, Werner
1986 *Beyond Ethnicity: Consent and Descent in American Culture*. New York:
Oxford University Press.

Steinberg, Stephen
1981 *The Ethnic Myth: Race, Ethnicity, and Class in America*. New York:
Atheneum.

"Survey of Race Relations"
1924 Ram Chand interview, June 1, 1924. El Centro; Box 28, No. 232. Stanford:
Hoover Institution Archives.

Turner, Victor
1987 "Carnival, Ritual, and Play in Rio de Janeiro." In *Time Out of Time: Essays on
the Festival*. Alessandro Falassi (ed.) Albuquerque: University of New Mexico
Press. Pp. 74-90.

Wolf, Eric R.
    1988 "Inventing Society." *American Ethnologist* 15(4):752-761.

Wood, Ann
    1966 "East Indians in California: A Study of Their Organizations, 1900-1947."
    Unpublished Master's thesis, University of Wisconsin.

U.S. Department of Commerce, Bureau of the Census
    1920 *Fourteenth Census of the United States: Population, 1920.* Vol. III.
    Washington, DC: Government Printing Office, 1921-23.

Zaretsy, Eli (ed.)
    1984 *The Polish Peasant in Europe and America.* Chicago: University of Illinois
    Press.

Appendix I
Spouses of Asian Indians in California, 1913-1949

Counties	Hispanic		Anglo		Black		Indian		American Indian		Total	
	No.	%	No.	%	No.	%	No.	%	No.	%	No.	%
Yuba Sutter Sacramento San Joaquim	45	50.6	25	28.1	9	0.1	8	9.0	2	2.3	89	23.6
Fresno Tulare Kings	38	76.0	11	22.0	0	0	1	2.0	0	0	50	13.2
Imperial Los Angeles San Diego	221	2.5	12	5.0	6	2.5	0	0	0	0	239	63.2
TOTALS	304	80.0	48	12.7	15	4.0	9	2.4	2	.5	378	100

Sources: Karen Leonard, family reconstitution from county records (vital statistics, civil and criminal records) and interviews.

Appendix II
Asian Indians in California, 1910-1980

Year	Number in U.S.	Number in California	Number in California Cities	% in California	% in California Cities*
1910	2,544	1,948	73	77	3.75
1920	2,544	1,723	75	69	4.35
1930	3,130	1,873	122	59	6.51
1940	2,405	1,476	89	60	6.03
1950	2,398	815	249	34	30.55
1960	8,746	1,586	722	17	45.52
1970	13,149	1,585	546	16	45.45
1980	387,223	57,901	54,447	15	94.00

Sources: Brett Melendy, *Asians in America*, Tables VII, VIII, IX; U.S. Bureau of the Census, *Census of Population 1980*, IB, General Population Statistics, PC80-1-B6 California, 160-170.

*All California city figures include Los Angeles, San Francisco, and Stockton. In 1950, Oakland is included as part of metropolitan San Francisco; in 1960, Oakland and Long Beach are included as part of metropolitan San Francisco and Los Angeles; in 1970, census inadequacies do not permit comparable figures for the metropolitan areas, thus the apparent decline. The 1980 figures includes the standard metropolitan statistical areas (SMSAs) of Anaheim, Garden Grove, Santa Ana; Fresno; Los Angeles, Long Beach; Modesto; Oxnard, Simi Valley, Ventura; Riverside, San Bernardino, Ontario; Sacramento; San Diego; San Francisco, Oakland; San Jose; Stockton; Vallejo, Napa Valley; and Yuba City. In 1980, Asian Indians were not tabulated in SMSAs where their numbers fell below 400.

10

Fishing and Drinking in Kodiak

Rachel Mason

In Kodiak, Alaska, fishermen[1] create and maintain their occupational identity not only through fishing but also through ritual drinking. Although drinking is normatively separated from fishing, the communal ritual of drinking is an essential part of the cycle of fishing life. Both fishermen and non-fishermen in Kodiak say that fishermen have a distinctive drinking style: heavy, loud, and public. The dominant "fishermen's style" of drinking supersedes perceived differences in the drinking of subgroups of fishermen (e.g., skippers and crewmen, or different gear types).

Drinking ritual appears to be a leveler of economic differences because successful fisherman buy rounds for others. At the same time, it is an opportunity for public recognition of a successful fisherman's termporary high place in the hierarchy of fishing success. In the arena of public drinking, fishermen can proclaim solidarity with all other fishermen while working at the same time to create and maintain their individual reputations.

In the last twenty years, accelerated by limited entry to fisheries, increased capitalization, and more regulations and controls, fishing has become more a business and less a lifestyle. Celebratory communal drinking is entering the realm of the mythical past. Now, individual drinking problems are more commonly identified. While many fishermen still see their drinking as a constructive phase of their distinctive lifestyle, drinking as ritual has little positive value for fishermen who are primarily businessmen.

FISHING AND DRINKING

The Kodiak Archipelago is a group of islands in the Gulf of Alaska. The largest community on these islands, the city of Kodiak, had a population of 6,365 in 1990. The population of the entire archipelago, including Kodiak city, a large Coast Guard base, residents of six Alaska Native villages, and people in outlying areas, was 13,309. Thousands of others come to the area seasonally or temporarily to work in the fishing industry.

The economy of the region is dominated by fishing. The main species are salmon, herring, halibut, cod, pollock, sole, sablefish, and tanner crab. Other species which were important in the past but have declined are king crab and shrimp. Salmon and herring are small-boat or inshore seasonal fisheries. Cod, pollock, and other bottomfish are taken offshore almost year-round by larger trawlers and longliners. Halibut is pursued in up to four 24-hour openings a year by boats of all sizes. Tanner crab fishing also includes both large and small vessels.

The inshore versus offshore, small versus large boat distinctions correspond to the ongoing symbolic battle in Kodiak between "lifestyle fishing" and what fishermen see as the inevitable encroachment of big business. Lifestyle fishing is personal, cyclical, and local, while business fishing is impersonal, linear, and extra-local. The ideological opposition between lifestyle and business is subject to manipulation: anyone who fishes for a living in Kodiak is to some extent a business fishermen, but no one wants to admit to being one.

Salmon fishermen are solidly in the lifestyle camp. More than is true of larger boats, they live year-round in Kodiak and skippers own the boats on which they fish. Native Alaskans (about 13 percent of the Kodiak city population), who are the most genuine "locals," fish almost exclusively inshore in small boats.

The most vocal defenders of lifestyle are White men and women now in their thirties and forties who came to Kodiak as hippie adventurers but have stayed to savor participation in the rural Alaskan community. Many now have families and have purchased boats, permits, and land.

The occupational culture of fishing dominates the town of Kodiak, and it includes heavy drinking. There are several cultural sources for the value fishermen place on drinking. It is partly a generic fisherman's model but contains elements of Alaskan frontier ideology. Both fishing identity and Alaskan frontier identity are part of what fishermen call "lifestyle," and public drinking is an appropriate way to show commitment to and membership in the community.

Drinking is also used to establish and perpetuate individual economic positions and fishing reputations; Kodiak fishermen say they need to drink with other fishermen to maintain their place in the fleet. Fishermen must project a rugged, independent, and aggressive occupational self-image. Drinking provides an opportunity for competitive self-expression at the same time that it validates an occupational ethos of egalitarianism.

The fishermen's drinking ritual is distinctive because it does not offer a uniformly ideal representation of culture. For participants who adhere to the fishing lifestyle, it is a proud symbol of rebellion against normal "nine-to-five" society. Drinking done by someone with a "drinking problem" is isolating instead of integrating. It is a private addiction under the guise of public celebration.

Drinking ritual has multiple and sometimes contradictory meanings—culture and anti-culture, solidarity and isolation.

FISHERMEN'S DRINKING STYLE

The bars play an important role in the culmination of a fishing trip. While each of the twenty Kodiak bars has a slightly different ambiance, all of them are meeting places for fishermen. On an evening of drinking, bar patrons do not usually stay in one establishment the whole night. There are migrations from bar to bar, singly or in groups.

The physical layout of most of the bars makes them easy to walk into and look for friends. Interaction with others at the bar takes little effort. A participant can shout across the bar, get up to play pool or put music on the jukebox, and return to his or her seat or stand and talk to somebody else. S/He expects to be acknowledged by and to acknowledge everyone s/he knows who is at the bar. On some occasions small groups go outside to smoke marijuana, or someone with cocaine invites a select few into the restroom or parking lot to share it. Drinkers in groups buy rounds of drinks for their group. It is also common to buy a drink for an acquaintance sitting across the bar.

By law, Kodiak bars can be open from 8 a.m. to 5 a.m., but most of them close by 4 a.m. For those who are still at the bar, closing time coincides with invitations to impromptu parties at people's houses or on boats. Since the party can easily go on all night, it is not surprising that some people are hung over in the morning, or still drunk from the night before, when they drag themselves to work. Some crewmen express pride that, although they drink heavily, they have never missed work because of drinking or been left behind by a boat. However, the quality of their work and their enjoyment of it is appreciably lessened by their condition. The hung-over, tired crewman must struggle miserably through the day of gear work until he can get away for the next night's drinking.

Many people in Kodiak believe that fishermen drink more than normal mainstream Americans, although several pointed out that fishermen do *not* drink more than anyone else; they simply alternate long dry periods at sea with periods of heavy drinking in town. Fishermen's drinking style is defined by the manner, not the amount of drinking. Non-fishermen in Kodiak, especially the wives and families of fishermen, are expected to understand that fishermen need to drink when they get back to town.

Fishermen's drinking style is called "extreme," "without reserve," "binge drinking." There is no moderation: "It requires pounding 'em heavy" (MB).[2] Fishermen drink passionately:

> The fishermen's drinking style is to drink until you get drunk.
> Hooting and hollering, acting crazy. . . . You maintain a high
> energy level when you're drinking. Fishermen fight too—guys

piss each other off, they want to prove themselves, don't want to be called a pussy. We get drunk, so there's more fights. There's camaraderie—we go out partying and a bunch of the crew will go out together (JC).

Fishermen drink publicly, in bars. They usually drink beer, but they also order shots of hard liquor, or mixed drinks. There is a popular idea that drinking beer is not really drinking. When fishermen want to get drunk, they drink hard liquor. They are loud drunks, who use a lot of profanity (VB). Getting drunk has an element of thrill-seeking: "It's more a sport here" (NC). Fishermen want drinking bouts to be memorable experiences.

Fishermen generously buy rounds of drinks for each other and for the whole bar. The goal is to "look like you're doing good [i.e., fishing successfully] even if you're not." Never in my life have I seen a group of people so inclined to buying rounds, even if they're complete strangers that you exchange three words with: "I'm a Fuller Brush man." "Buy him a drink!" (VB) Having money is having power. Making someone else get drunk also confers power.

Drinking is competitive in several ways. There is competition to be the most aggressive spender. Fishermen also strive to emerge from a drinking bout as the most successful, most physically tough, and perhaps the most entertaining fisherman. Fights or loud arguments may arise either from an actual or imaginary trivial incident ("He looked at me wrong"), or from long-time ongoing enmity. The resolution achieved by fighting or competitive drink-buying is temporary at best. Competition while drinking results in fleeting success or humiliation that rarely outlives the next day's hangover.

Would-be fishermen, new in Kodiak, need to learn to act like fishermen in addition to learning the work of fishing. Acting like a fisherman includes drinking like a fisherman. That fishermen have an identifiable and attractive drinking style was illustrated by the comments of a man who had been in Kodiak for about a year. He said that he purposely tried not to drink like a fisherman when he first arrived, but that soon he found himself really getting into it (BE).

Not all fishermen drink heavily. Although the fishermen drinking in public are the ones that are easiest to notice, many others do not drink at all, or drink moderately. A fisherman pointed out that the crowd in bars doesn't necessarily represent *good* fishermen: "They're the ones who aren't professional, aren't very good at it, sit on the barstool and catch a lot of fish. They'd rather sit at the bar than work" (TG). Another man wondered about the accuracy of the local construct of fishermen's drinking: "I'd be interested to know what percent do drink or have alcohol problems. It would be easy to be misled and think a lot more have problems than they do. The image becomes dominant even though it's not a majority of people" (VH). The popular view of fishermen's heavy drinking is a stereotype. Independent of its statistical prevalence, however, it is a cultural construct that motivates and serves as a rationale for individuals' actions (Schneider 1980 [1968]:6).

REASONS TO DRINK

A common feature of Kodiak residents' explanations for fishermen's heavy drinking is that it is seen as intrinsically connected to the work of fishing: fishermen drink because they are fishermen. The different causal links between fishing and drinking can be placed into three categories: drinking as an extension of fishing, drinking as an analogy of fishing, and drinking as an opposition to fishing. "Extension" explanations see drinking as having practical use to fishermen; "analogy" explanations refer to the social functions of drinking; and "opposition" explanations refer to conceptual functions.

Extension

When drinking is viewed as an extension of fishing, it is seen as utilitarian. Drinking provides an opportunity for fishermen to do things that are necessary in order to fish: get a job, hire a crew, or find out useful fishing information. Drinking is also an extension of fishing in that preoccupation with fishing work carries over into non-work life. Fishermen drinking in bars talk about fishing.

Many people said the bars are good places to get fishing jobs. This means finding out about jobs by befriending potential employers while drinking, or simply by hanging around in bars, hoping to be in the right place at the right time. Because the bars are known as hiring halls, a skipper in a hurry to find a crewman might go to a bar specifically to hire somebody. The other standard ways to look for a job are to "pound the docks" (walk up and down the docks asking for a job on boats) or to use one's "connections" (to seek a job through friends or acquaintances). A recovering alcoholic fisherman thought that getting jobs in bars was overrated; he thought it was faster to pound the docks (GC). Another man said that newcomer "greenhorns" wouldn't be hired in a bar except by chance, because they didn't know anybody (QA).

Exchange of fishing information is also an important utilitarian function of drinking in bars. When they are in town, fishermen go to the bars to make an appearance and "touch base" with others. The bars are places for reflection and commentary as well as for forming alliances and plotting new strategies. Drinking is an opportunity to find out how others did on the last trip and to be recognized for one's own success.

Fishermen say they drink to relax or to relieve stress after the hard work and irregular hours of fishing. Some say drinking is to readjust to society after doing dangerous work, recognizing that they could have died in the sea. Back in port, they are temporarily in the safety of home. They drink to "thank the good Lord you made it in" (NG), or, as another man put it, "Drinking is the reward for coming back" (PA).

Drinking also relieves the stress of being with a small crew of people on a boat: "Drinking is a release after restricted social lives on contained vessels"

(AH). Shipboard life is "a dictatorship" (GF) by the skipper, and crew members are frustrated in their dealings with the skipper and with each other.

Fishermen have to do all their drinking in a short period of time (typically four or five days of drinking to twenty-eight days of sobriety, in one fisherman's estimate—TH). There is so little time to drink that they have to drink heavily: "Fishermen have one shot at their Friday night" (GF). Fishermen need a refreshing evening of drunkenness to renew their energy for fishing.

Commonly, it is remarked that fishermen drink because there is nothing else in Kodiak to spend money on, and nowhere to go but the bars. One person said that fishermen typically have no homes, wives, or girlfriends, so they go to the bars. Men might see drinking in bars as an opportunity to pick up women. A non-fisherman wondered if the youthful age of many fishermen were also a factor in their heavy drinking (VH).

"Just being in Kodiak" makes fishermen drink. Several people who live outside of Alaska most of the year said they never drank heavily at home, only in Kodiak when they were away from their families. Some self-identified alcoholics said that coming to Kodiak had caused or exacerbated their problems with alcohol. A fisherman said he rarely attends Alcoholics Anonymous meetings elsewhere, but that in Kodiak he goes frequently, because "Here you're surrounded by it" (i.e., drinking and drugs) (CC). I heard several examples of precariously sober fishermen who were driven off the wagon when they had unusual trouble in fishing, or simply when they got back to Kodiak.

Some said the reason fishermen drink the way they do is that they were already alcoholics before they became fishermen. They thought the occupation attracts people who like the idea of alternating dry periods with drinking binges. The whole state of Alaska is also thought to be a Mecca for alcoholics. An alcohol counselor told me that when he came to Alaska, as a practicing alcoholic, he was delighted to find so many people who drank like him (JF). According to these views, the Alaskan setting and the occupation of fishing provide a welcoming and supportive environment for the heavy drinking that alcoholics would probably do anyway.

Analogy

Explanations for fishermen's drinking which see it as an analogy with fishing focus on the social functions of drinking ritual. Fishermen's public drinking excludes both the non-drinker and the solitary drinker. Just as it is considered unsafe to fish alone, it is undesirable to drink alone. The social setting of fishermen's drinking is analogous to fishing work: drinking, like fishing, is usually done with a few other fishermen (fellow crewmen or fishing buddies), moving from bar to bar the way boats move from one fishing spot to another, within the wider public arena of the whole bar scene, or of the entire sea of fishing boats.

Drinking together delimits ethnic and occupational subgroups (skippers and crewmen, draggers and longliners, Natives and Whites) at the same time that it reinforces a sense of unity of all fishermen. The social unit participating in drinking, the boat crew, is often the same as that working together on the boat. Frequently, though, the skipper does not drink with the crew, or else he goes on to drink with his skipper peers after a drink or two with the crewmen: "Fishermen drink with their own peer group—skippers with skippers, crewmen with other crewmen of the same financial standing" (QA). Fishermen might also drink sentimentally with former fishing partners.

Fishermen mention the special bonding between members of a crew who have been through the dangers of fishing and the rigors of shipboard life together. Fishing is "more than just a job," but carries over into life in town. Getting drunk together, and compulsively buying drinks for one another, reinforces the bond. Fishermen who quit drinking miss this camaraderie.

Drinking can be either to celebrate a good trip or to "piss and moan" after a bad one. After a twenty-four-hour halibut opening, for example, when everyone has done well, there is an atmosphere of congratulation in the bars. If the opening was poor for almost everyone, there is a spirit of commiseration. In presenting their fishing outcome to others, fishermen feel obliged to pretend they did well if they did poorly, and to be modest about their success if they did well. Public drinking is the accepted setting for these face-saving exercises.

Fishermen's communications while drinking are also analogous to communications during fishing work. While boats are on the fishing grounds, information is offered and received by visual scrutiny (others can see where a boat is fishing or guess where it is headed) and over the radio, which everyone can hear but can be covertly controlled by coding messages or switching channels. On shore, communication in bars is partly based on public display, but also includes private conversations and alliances (which others might overhear or try to barge in on). In both milieux, fishing grounds and on shore, the desirable information can be summarized as "Who is getting all the fish, where are they getting them, and how can I position myself so *I* get them?"

The reckless manner of drinking is analogous to the dangerous, intense work of fishing: "The finest high in my life is being scared to fucking death" (TH); "The kind of guy with fishing in his blood, there's no half measures" (GF). One man said that fishermen like to gamble and have risky hobbies, in addition to fighting while drinking: "They're into risk-taking." According to another man, fishermen's drinking style is "very extremist, in the same manner as fishing— the competition, the one-upmanship" (QA).

Drinking ritual marks a contrast between fishermen and people who belong to "normal" society. Fishermen grow single-minded about fishing, perhaps due to their isolation from "land" society, and they have a hard time relating to non-fishermen (LB). Drinking brings fishermen into contact with one another, but further separates them from other people.

Many respondents thought that fishermen are obliged to drink in order to properly represent their occupational image: "They have to do everything more than mainstream Americans" (CC); "They want to be different" (MB); "They have to be male, loud, and obnoxious" (NC). Fishing self-image is one of independence and proud separation from normal life. CH, a state trooper, said that when he was working in Anchorage he occasionally stopped fishermen for traffic violations, and they would say indignantly, "But I'm an Alaska fisherman!" as though this excused them from observing traffic rules.

While fishing is fiercely competitive, there is a strong ethic of helping other fishermen if a boat is in trouble. Breaches of the law are tolerated within standards of fairness to other fishermen. The fishermen's aggressive self-image and admiration of risk-taking (within limits of responsibility to other fishermen) applies to drinking behavior as well as fishing work. If one member of a drinking party gets in a fight or some other kind of trouble, his drinking companions are expected to help him out. Despite their independence, "Fishermen has got to stick together" (LC) while drinking and fishing.

Opposition

The category of opposition as an explanation for drinking is one that deals with conceptual separations. Drinking should be separated from fishing work. Some people were offended to hear that I was conducting research on fishing and drinking, because, they insisted, the two activities are mutually exclusive. They pointed to cases of men who are drunk whenever they are in town, but who never drink when out fishing. Many boats forbid drinking on the boat, but in practice some alcohol creeps in:

> A lot of people smoke pot baiting up, but they don't drink. A lot of skippers let you have a beer. . . . I'll have a beer with a meal, maybe, or before I go to bed. Running the hydraulics, stacking crab gear, or operating a skiff—can you imagine doing that drunk? (JC)

Some boats keep a few beers to drink on the way in. One skipper ritually drank a beer every time he went around Cape Chiniak on the way back to Kodiak, and threw the can at the cape (PF).

Even in town, the boat is not a place for drinking or being drunk. Typically, crew members of boats docked temporarily in town are supposed to show up in the daytime and do gear work. Although skippers tell crewmen that "It doesn't matter what you do in your own time" (GF), crewmen find it difficult to find their own time, even in town. The obligation to spend many hours drinking with other fishermen might prove as burdensome as working with them.

Drinking is so much a part of the cycle of fishermen's working life that some fishermen do not even consider it a leisure activity (Mars 1987:93).

Drinking is a ritual that marks the transition between the limited social and mental fishing life and "land life." Even fishermen who do have families or spouses in town make an obligatory stop in the bar on the way home. Drinking offers ritual license, "time-out" from social norms (MacAndrew and Edgerton 1969). The license includes behavior that wouldn't be tolerated in working life, such as fighting or being put in jail. On the other hand, drinking is safe and relaxing compared to the life-threatening dangers of fishing. While fishing is isolating and competitive, drinking is a communal activity that creates solidarity.

Sometimes fishermen long to get out of the town phase of their fishing and drinking cycle. They are glad to go fishing in order to dry out, and dread coming back to town from fishing. The fishing-drinking cycle works best when there are only a few days of drinking to several weeks of fishing. Problems arise when boat trouble, strikes or closures, injury, or unemployment cause the fisherman's drinking days in town to stretch into weeks or months.

Attitudes toward drinking and fishing in Kodiak have changed. The extremes of total sobriety and total drunkenness are thought to have softened since the heyday of Kodiak's wild drinking days. With this change, there is perhaps more acceptance of *moderate* drinking while fishing, for example having drinks at cocktail hour on setnet sites or keeping a six-pack of beer on a boat to drink on the way in to town.

SPENDING MONEY

Money is an attraction to fishing and is the primary criterion of successful fishing. It is a frequent and favorite topic in fishermen's conversation: how much they have made and how much they hope to make. Spending money is an integral part of the drinking ritual. Communal drinking, and reciprocal buying of drinks, are effective means of leveling fishermen as equals. The heavy spending in drinking is a kind of "capital destruction" (Mars 1987:100), or aggressive consumption which gives prestige to the spender.

"Highliner," the name given to a boat that brings in the most fish and makes the most money, is a temporary distinction. A fisherman either has a good season or a bad one. Drunkenly squandering the money made on the last trip (or *appearing* to squander it) returns fishermen to an equally low economic position. Each new fishing trip can be anticipated with hope of being the top boat in the ephemeral hierarchy of fishing success.

Blowing money is part of the fishermen's self-image. A fisheries observer said he had heard people brag about blowing $3,000 in a single night (II). Blowing money is often associated with drinking binges of several days or more. The claim to fame of a fisherman I worked with was to have spent $25,000 in a single weekend.

Skippers and crewmen are paid in shares of the catch rather than hourly wages or a salary. Payments to fishermen come in large checks or large amounts of cash instead of as a regular salary, a type of payment common to many jobs in Alaska. Fishermen get their pay in large settlement checks at the end of fishing. Before the season is over, crewmen can receive "draws," several hundred dollars at a time, from skippers. Draws require special verbal application and often involve a trip to the skipper's house so that his wife can write a check. Draws are used to stay temporary needs, and are typically used for drinking money while a boat has a short stop in town.

Although the insecurity of the fishing industry does not normally allow fishermen to turn a better profit every year, fishermen are often optimistic in their estimates of how much they will make in the coming year or season. Long-term purchases must made based on what fishermen think their income is going to be. The fisherman with business foresight puts his income into better fishing opportunities: a boat, a permit, or better gear and more up-to-date technology. There is pressure to fish successfully, in order to keep up with payments.

Since fishing settlements come in irregular chunks of money, there is a tendency to see them as windfalls rather than as one's regular income to be used for regular expenses. Some people eking out a living in Kodiak spend money on drinking or drugs, but have difficulties meeting long-term expenses. Purchase of high-priced and quickly-consumed cocaine is a particularly efficient way to squander money and have nothing to show for it. The most conspicuous consumption, however, is drinking.

Some Kodiak drinking traditions are associated with blowing money. One is "ringing the bell," or buying a round of drinks for the whole bar, which is what someone flush with money is expected to do. The bells still ring occasionally in Kodiak bars, and it is common for bar customers to buy drinks for several others. It is rare, in fact, for someone to buy only a drink for himself. In the past, another way to accelerate spending was to buy someone six drinks at a time.

Fishermen exchange cash for services and substances while they are drinking, but they have a real or feigned carelessness about the cash transactions. Although fishermen while they are working constantly calculate how much they will make, drinkers do not keep a tally of the amount of cash they are spending or the amount that is being spent on them. It would be in very bad form to respond to the offer of a drink with a request for the cash instead.

Although blowing money is conceived as an individual act, it is important to note that there are usually many volunteers to help an individual spend his money. People run in the door of a bar when they hear the bell ring. Blowing money, a means of displaying individual power while achieving community solidarity, is necessarily a social act.

Crewmen, not skippers, are generally expected to blow money. It is significant that crewmen are more transient and more likely to be single than skippers; becoming a skipper marks a movement toward adulthood and is often associated with increased family responsibilities. While fishermen who are single can blow their money with impunity, it is considered bad for married men to waste money. Fishing wives rightly see expenditures on alcohol or drugs as siphoning off money that could have been spent on necessities or family leisure. However, blowing money on alcohol or drugs is not really a personal expense, either, since others are implicated in the social consumption.

Blowing money on drinking with other fishermen is a social investment. If you spend all your money in Kodiak you are committed to the community, perhaps literally because you do not have the means to leave, and must keep fishing. There is hostility toward people who take their entire paychecks away from Kodiak with them. Drinking is a productive expenditure insofar as it establishes a commitment to fishing lifestyle. If a fisherman puts his money back into his own business of fishing, it is a private investment; the community is not included in his spending. In business fishing, personal success is separate from communal occupational identity.

DRINKING PROBLEMS

Even when it is a valued part of fishing lifestyle, fishermen's drinking does not always produce solidarity. Individual drinkers have to tread a fine line between drinking that enhances their self-image in the occupational community, and drinking that hurts their reputation as fishermen. Heavy drinking is a drinking problem if it interferes with fishing work.

Many Kodiak respondents think that there is a more "generous" or "tolerant" definition of alcoholism among Kodiak fishermen than there would be in other groups. Drinking behavior that would be considered abusive elsewhere fits into the normal range in Kodiak. Residents perceive a general pattern of alcohol abuse without necessarily labelling participants as alcoholics. Conversely, there is also recognition that heavy public drinking can serve positive social functions even if some of the participants are alcoholics. Use of the term "alcoholic," implying individual dysfunction, itself represents an ideological move away from a communal lifestyle into a business world where individuals need to be uniformly functional.

Some of the traits Kodiak residents associate with alcoholism are in keeping with the clinical criteria used by treatment personnel. Addiction to alcohol, for example, is considered a defining characteristic. Except among people schooled in alcoholism (i.e., counselors and recovering alcoholics) there is little identification of *sporadic* heavy drinking with alcoholism; more often, alcoholism is associated with constant intoxication whenever alcohol is available.

In contrast to the disease model espoused in treatment and in Alcoholics Anonymous, Kodiak residents do not have a consistent perception of the progressive nature of alcoholism. While some say that drinking problems inevitably get worse and worse, others think that an alcoholic's drinking behavior stays fixed at one point. There is a view that heavy drinking is typically cyclical, and fishermen and others speak of people whose drinking "got really bad" for a while, for example during a divorce or other circumstances of personal disaster.

For most fishermen, apart from a few adherents to religions that ban alcohol, there is little moral stigma attached to drinking itself. Drinking is bad only if it detracts from work or sociability. Solitary drinking is frowned upon in Kodiak, because it indicates that the drink itself is more important than its ritual setting. The alcoholic is not interested in bar sociability, but only in satisfying his craving for drink.

Diminished ability to work is the most important indicator of alcoholism. If a fisherman's drinking is more important than fishing work, it will eventually hinder his fishing reputation. There are different criteria for reputation damage for skippers and crewmen; because skippers have more responsibility, they are permitted less drunkenness.

Skippers frequently fire crew members for not showing up for work, or for showing up drunk. Because of drinking, deckhands can also be late, fall asleep, or get lazy on the job (AH). Even when the boat is in town, crewmen's drinking can be a problem. However, "Fights and stuff are OK," a woman said (LB), as long as work is not affected. The trouble with alcohol-impaired deckhands is that they are unpredictable. It might be harder for a deckhand to get a job if word gets around to potential skippers that his abilities have deteriorated.

Knowing that a would-be deckhand has a reputation for drinking, a skipper can choose to hire him anyway. Some people are known to get drunk whenever they have the opportunity, but they have valued skills which cause employers to seek them out:

> PB is known as one of the best web men around, but it's also
> known that he'll take one trip and fuck up, disappear, quit. But
> when they suddenly need someone for the net, they go looking for
> PB. And he manages to hold out for good jobs too. He'll be out
> of work for a long time and then get something really good (JC).

The alcohol-related things a skipper could do to damage his fishing reputation include: "if he got drunk and wrecked a boat, missed a whole season or got somebody hurt" (GF). Many thought it would take longer for a skipper's reputation to be affected than that of a crewman who was in trouble with alcohol. Not many fishermen think poorly of a skipper as long as he catches fish. It would not damage a skipper's reputation if he had a string of bad luck; anyone could have a bad season: "There has to be something wrong consistently" (KE).

Skippers with good reputations, however, are not thought to spend a lot of their time drinking. Some well-known "party boats," run by drunken skippers, are not considered reliable or safe. A skipper's irresponsible drinking is sometimes the reason crewmen quit their jobs.

Surprisingly, fishermen's motivations for sobriety are typically *not* that they or someone else discovered their fishing work was impaired. Sober fishermen's stories of their impetus to sobriety vary from person to person. In some instances, fishermen decided to quit drinking, at least temporarily, because they were embarrassed by their drunken behavior on a particular occasion. One man was frightened into sobriety by his alcohol withdrawal symptoms as he left to go fishing after a prolonged drinking binge. Others said they were tired of waking up and wondering where all their money went. Some said they quit drinking or cut down simply because they "grew up"; drinking wasn't as fun anymore (TG). Heavy drinking was commonly seen as a phenomenon of youth that naturally disappeared in middle age.

Many pointed to a number of respected skippers in Kodiak who used to be known as heavy drinkers, but are now sober. While an increasing number of fishermen in Kodiak have achieved sobriety through participation in Alcoholics Anonymous, others have simply "turned their lives around" in what is perceived by others as part of a normal process. There are also some skippers and crewmen who achieve sobriety for months or even years, then go back to drinking.

DRINKING, LIFESTYLE, AND BUSINESS FISHING

As Kodiak fishing becomes more and more like the business world everywhere, individuals' abusive drinking is noticed more than it used to be. Kodiak has become less tolerant of heavy drinking. What used to be an exciting, communal bar scene has now become seedy and depressing: "I remember it being three deep in the bar, pandemonium, bell ringing, you had to wrestle your way up to the bar. Now it's sparsely populated in the bar, more like Skid Row. . . . I find the bars more depressing than I used to. I have increased intolerance for the drinking environment and social contacts with drunk people" (VH).

The decline of some of Kodiak's fisheries since the 1970s has coincided with an expansion in state and federally-supported alcohol agencies, and with the identification of more drinking problems in the community. When fishermen are unsuccessful, the lifestyle model of drinking becomes unsuccessful as well. If there is no money to squander, and no hope of catching *all* the fish, there is no reason to celebrate fishermen's self-image by drinking. If there is no fishing, there is a danger that drinking might expand to fill all the available time. The unemployed fisherman who drinks despite the fact that he has no money is more likely to be defined as an alcoholic, by his fishing peers and by others in Kodiak, than the temporarily rich fisherman who goes on a drinking binge following a fishing trip. The unemployed fisherman is also more available for treatment and AA than the fisherman who is busy fishing.

According to the director of Kodiak's alcoholism treatment center, the clients seen in treatment tend to be "marginal, lower-class people" (IE). Social class is becoming more important in Kodiak, despite the egalitarian frontier ideology that continues to prevail. Unlike the past, when communal drinking served as a leveler of hierarchical relationships between highliner and lowliner, skipper and crew, today's class hierarchy cannot be resolved by communal drinking. Although some fishermen still drink as intensely as they used to, the community no longer smiles upon them. Fishermen continue to enjoy the myth of Kodiak's lifestyle past. However, people currently living this myth by drinking heavily and sporadically are increasingly identified as alcoholics.

Heavy public drinking is more appropriate to lifestyle fishing than to business fishing. Fishermen's drinking has symbolic meaning only to someone who sees fishing as a way of life, rather than as an isolated category of work. Ritualized drinking can only be an extension of lifestyle fishing. In business fishing, jobs are filled by people who best fit the position, not by friends the skipper runs into at a bar. Bar socializing and exchange of information while drinking are more appropriate to the lifestyle community than to impersonal business fishing.

In lifestyle fishing, drinking is an appropriate analogy to fishing. Business interests, however, do not encourage a self-image that is counter to "normal" society. The cult of independence and risk-taking that characterizes lifestyle fishing and fishermen's drinking has no place in the rational world of business.

Lifestyle fishing is cyclical. The goals of business fishing are linear: to efficiently invest profits into more profits. Drinking ceases to be a conceptual opposition to fishing as business concerns become more important. In business fishing, work is separate from leisure, but there is no call for ritual separation as part of a fishing and drinking cycle. Business fishing allows the possibility of "moderate" drinking, instead of an alternation of complete sobriety and drunkenness.

Stories about the good old days of drinking in Kodiak are similar in tone to reminiscences about the old days of fishing. Just as it is important to celebrate the myth of lifestyle fishing, it is important to keep alive a vivid oral tradition of fishermen's drinking. Fishermen fondly remember the bygone times when the bars in Kodiak were packed, and highliner fishermen rang the bells all night, buying rounds of drinks for everyone.

Drinking ritual resolves some contradictions of occupational identity, but perpetuates others. As a forum for expression of both group and individual self-image, it allows fishermen to express their egalitarian ethos together while they jostle for temporary prestige, and to celebrate a common occupational identity while preserving their normative individual autonomy. However, as economic changes have occurred and fishing profits are concentrated in the hands of an elite, the value of a common lifestyle identity has decreased. The temporary leveling that occurs through competitive treating and money-blowing in communal drinking cannot result from half-hearted gestures of limited generosity. As a result, drinking ritual loses its relationship to fishing work it becomes an assemblage of individual drinkers.

NOTES

1. Both men and women participate in Kodiak's commercial fisheries, although fishing is still aggressively male-dominated. Most women who fish prefer being called "fishermen" to "fishers," "fisherwomen," or "fisherpeople" (Miller and Johnson 1981:138).

2. The names of Kodiak people quoted in this paper have been replaced by pseudo-initials: AB, AC, and so forth.

BIBLIOGRAPHY

MacAndrew, Craig, and Robert B. Edgerton
   1969 *Drunken Comportment: A Social Explanation.* Chicago: Aldine.

Mars, Gerald
   1987 "Longshore Drinking, Economic Security and Union Politics in Newfoundland." In *Constructive Drinking: Perspectives on Drink from Anthropology.* Mary Douglas (ed.) Cambridge: Cambridge University Press. Pp. 91-101.

Miller, Marc L., and Jeffrey C. Johnson
   1981 "Hard Work and Competition in the Bristol Bay Salmon Fishery." *Human Organization* 40(2):131-139.

Schneider, David M
   1980 [1968] *American Kinship: A Cultural Account.* 2nd Edition. Chicago: University of Chicago Press.

11

Coronation in San Antonio: Class, Family and the Individual

Michaele Thurgood Haynes

INTRODUCTION

The young woman in an elaborately trimmed velvet gown and a twelve-foot-long train embellished with hundreds of glass stones and beads is helped onto the runway by two older men in full evening dress. She starts down the runway with slow, measured steps. The "duchess" meets her duke, dressed in full evening dress, at center stage. With some trepidation she executes the extremely low "formal court bow" in which her head almost touches the floor. The duchess rises without assistance from her duke and acknowledges the applause with a smile. She climbs the steeply raked steps to a small pedestal while her escort and two younger girls help with the train, for she cannot pull the weight herself. They arrange the train so that its full splendor may be seen, while she and the other twenty-three duchesses, each in similar raiment, wait for the appearance of the princesses and the queen.

The young woman is not part of an Elizabethan tableaux staged in honor of the Queen's birthday but is one version of a San Antonio, Texas debutante. She is taking part in "Coronation," an annual event sponsored by the Order of the Alamo, a men's social organization. Each year the new duchesses/debutantes are presented and two from the previous year are crowned "Princess" and "Queen." Each Coronation has a theme, and the set, royal robes, and narration are carefully researched and designed to conform to it. It has been performed by young elite Anglo women since 1909 and is one of the oldest events in "Fiesta San Antonio," the city's spring festival.[1] The wearing of the specially designed robes in the pageant legitimizes their claim to the crown—the crown of socio-economic domination.

This essay explores the specific ways in which the pageantry of Coronation, as exemplified in the royal robes and played out within the context of Fiesta, acts as a prime mechanism to define and affirm identity as members of an elite social class and of specific family lineages.[2] Coronation serves to identify and unite the economic pinnacle of a hierarchical society. But the Coronation class is also an aristocracy bounded by rules of relationship and not just income level, for relationships can be traced consanguinally or affinally for most members. The Coronation is based upon American perceptions of English royalty and European aristocracy, and provides a secular annual ritual around which shared values and interrelationships can be enacted.

Ritualized social events are important sources of information about the construction of social identity since rituals are not just passive reflections of interrelationships but are themselves agents of individual and communal identity. Clifford Geertz (1973) and Catherine Bell (1992) provide the frameworks within which to understand the importance of Coronation. Geertz characterizes ritual as being not just a model "of" but a model "for" reality (Geertz 1973:93). Presentation in the faux royal court identifies the elite social class but also creates a means by which the participants and their families are identified as the elite. Catherine Bell, through a practice based framework of ritualization, analyzes the efficacy of ritual activity. She focuses on the creation of reality through "redemptive hegemony," the way ritualized activity makes the participant cognizant of the social order and her/his potential personal empowerment (Bell 1992:84). The ritual of Coronation reifies the social hierarchy and the participants' assumed rightful places in it. Pierre Bourdieu's (1984) argument's help inform the specific ways in which the elements of the pageantry of Coronation—setting, royal robes, and text—act as a model of the hierarchical order.

THE ELITE AS ETHNOGRAPHIC SUBJECT

The literature of the social sciences, particularly anthropology, is rich in ritual studies, but it is relatively limited regarding studies on the American elite. Since the development of an elite perspective to explain agency in the late nineteenth and early twentieth centuries (Pareto 1935; Mosca 1939), sociologists have been virtually the only social scientists to research the upper class or the elite as a powerful social organization (see Domhoff 1967, 1971, 1974; Mills 1956). Although there is a body of anthropological work on stratification in complex societies, it is largely confined to work in colonial societies (see Barth 1959; Cohen 1981). In 1964 Laura Nader called for anthropologists to "study up" in order to understand the processes of exercising power and responsibility in the United States, but relatively few have followed her directive.

Two recent researchers of American culture related to this paper are John Dorst (1989) and George Marcus (1983, 1987, 1992). Dorst explores the numerous texts of Chadds Ford, Pennsylvania, through which its citizens create and maintain the idea of itself as a community as both a historic site and the home of American's most well-known family of artists, the Wyeths. Marcus' work with one of the oldest and wealthiest families in Galveston, Texas, examines the relations among kin and affines and the private memoirs and papers which attempt to create a legacy, but which are superseded by external legal and financial agencies (Marcus 1987:6).

Dorst reads documents both private and public domains and the site itself for his interpretation of the creation of an identity, while Marcus depends heavily upon the reading of documents for his understanding of family dynasties. Neither looks closely at the social events which permeate the lives of Chadds Ford and Galveston. However this is not unusual, for social events, such as charity balls or debutante parties, are in general only covered journalistically (Amory 1960; Birmingham 1958, 1987). Investigative access to elite organizations and occasions is often limited, but perhaps more importantly, social events which focus upon young women in costly dresses are often marginalized by academics. They are not recognized as serious contexts in which issues of identity, power, and influence are negotiated. In contrast, this paper explores the ritualized event of Coronation as it reflects, creates, and maintains status for members of San Antonio's elite.

THE HISTORY OF FIESTA AND CORONATION

Coronation is one of the oldest components in San Antonio's version of a spring festival, Fiesta San Antonio. For ten days in April, over a hundred events, including parades, a band concert, a carnival, military reviews, a pilgrimage to the Alamo, and the Coronation, take place at sites all over San Antonio. Fiesta was begun in 1891 by a group of socially elite Anglo women. They staged the "Battle of Flowers" parade to honor the veterans of San Jacinto, the final battle in Texas' 1836 war for independence from Mexico. Although the contemporary parade is a celebration in memory of the successful battle, the overall tenor of Fiesta is always affected by the fact that the Alamo, the site of Texas' most important defeat, is located in San Antonio. Several events and organizations commemorate the deaths of the "defenders of the Alamo" and all parades pass in front of the Alamo. Although many events have been added over the years, the "Battle of Flowers" parade is still the high point of the festival for most San Antonians, and the original emphasis on patriotism and history prevents the development of a carnival atmosphere.

The patriotic and historical orientation of Fiesta San Antonio places it in the realm of pageantry or "a major way to construct a popular view of history" (Glassberg 1990:1). Many Fiesta events, from the original parade in honor of the Battle of San Jacinto to the Pioneer Ball, emphasize the history of Anglos in San Antonio. The historical pageantry of Fiesta is an attempt to justify the gradual political and cultural annexation of Mexican Texas, while the pageantry found in Coronation is a mythologized ethnic and class history which justifies the hierarchical positioning of its Anglo participants; albeit, the intentionality may be subconscious in both cases.

ORDER OF THE ALAMO AND ITS CORONATION

The sponsors and organizers of the Coronation pageantry are the men and women associated with the Order of the Alamo. In 1909 John Carrington gathered a small group of his friends to form the nucleus of the Order of the Alamo, a private men's social club whose sole purpose was to elect a queen crowned in an elaborate coronation and to sponsor accompanying social events.[3] A romantic and would-be writer, Carrington was apparently influenced by his family's English ancestry and landed-gentry Virginia background in creating the Order of the Alamo, and the Coronation are modeled on the English court and its aristocracy. The name of the organization and titles of the participants, such as Mistress of the Robes and Lord High Chamberlain, are all taken directly from British royalty and ceremony.

San Antonio was settled in the eighteenth century by Spaniards from the Canary Islands, but they were eclipsed both numerically and economically in the following century by Anglo settlers from the southeastern United States and by German immigrants.[4] Order membership (and the right of daughters to be in the Coronation) denotes those who are descendants of the nineteenth-century banking and entrepreneurial families who came to dominate San Antonio business. Although a number of families who did not arrive until the twentieth century do participate in the Coronation, the majority of the duchesses and a preponderance of the queens and princesses still come from the dozen or so nineteenth-century families. Royal status in Coronation does mark one's economic status due to the costs of the gowns and the accompanying parties. More importantly, it marks the royalty as the "right people," those with ties through kinship or friendship to old monied families who share certain conservative values and "appreciate the tradition" of Coronation. Fortunes may rise and fall, but the wearing of royal robes affirms the family's aristocratic heritage.

No more than twenty-four new members are accepted yearly, and preference is always given to "legacies"—sons, grandsons, and nephews, so there are relatively few spots available for "new blood." Sons-in-law may be taken in as married members, a smaller category since unmarried members are needed to act as escorts for the court royalty. The sole guarantee of an invitation for membership is to marry a former queen or princess or to be the father of one (however, it is quite rare that a father is not already a member). Without kinship or affinal connections, the only way to become a member is to grow up and attend school with the sons of older members. Almost all members live in one of the three suburbs developed in the 1920s for San Antonio's elite. They attend the same schools up through college, often pledging the same fraternity. Although many members of the Order claim to be open to the acceptance of "outsiders," even those with Hispanic surnames, in reality the necessary connections simply are not made due to residential, educational, and social de facto segregation. There is only one member with a Spanish surname on the current membership list of 832.

The members of the Board of Directors of the Order of the Alamo head the committee responsible for producing the Coronation. The twelve-member board is hierarchically arranged and usually the directors automatically succeed one another. The Coronation chairman makes all final decisions regarding the Coronation and automatically becomes president the following year. The set and lighting are handled by professionals while members of the Order act as director and other positions normally associated with a theatrical performance.

The Coronation chairman issues the invitations to be a member of the court after consultation with other members of the board. The ideal court is made up of twenty-four duchesses, equally divided between the in- and out-of-town courts. However, numbers may be changed according to existing circumstances since the guiding principal of court selection is aristocratic: the young women with the oldest family connections to the Order always have priority.

The aristocratic character of Coronation can be seen throughout the make-up of the court. Many of the old families intermarried, and cousins are often members of the same court. It is said that at any one time at least ten of the people on stage are interrelated. The small children who make up the queen's and princess' entourages are usually nieces and nephews, and pages are often related to someone on stage or on the board of directors. Many informants have strong memories of being a runway page at seven or eight and dreaming for weeks of their future roles as duchesses.

A royal family background is even more important in the selection of princess and queen. The 1987 queen had twenty-six family members, both male and female, who had taken part in previous Coronations. A former princess said that she could count and name all of the former queens and princesses in her lineage, but she would not even try to enumerate the duchesses because there were simply too many.

Queens and princesses are selected from the previous year's list of in-town duchesses and are voted on by the entire membership. The ballot must be delivered personally at the August meeting, always held in the Alamo, San Antonio's most sacred spot. The ballot simply consists of three blank lines which are filled in order of preference. Although there are no official candidate lists, behind-the-scenes politicking does take place. The family must be able to afford the approximately $50,000 it takes to place a crown on a daughter's head due to the costs of the royal robes and attendant social activities. However, the Queen of the Order of the Alamo is an ascribed position. The queen is the young woman with the oldest family line, the most female royal relatives, and lastly, the father who has been active in the Order. The runner-up becomes princess. There have been a few princesses and queens who were not from the old lineages, but they were elected in years in which there were no available or willing candidates from the "proper" families.

The Coronation chairman hires a professional designer for the set, but the gowns and trains are designed by the Mistress of the Robes. She is the wife of an Order member, known to be interested in fashion, art history, or a related area, and is chosen by the chairman long before the duchesses are selected. She and the chairman decide upon the theme: she then spends approximately two years in research. Themes in the early decades were often based on nature, "The Court of Spring," or literature, "The Court of Aladdin." Recently, themes are more often historically based: "Court of Embellished Dreams" (the history of needlework), "The Imperial Court of Faberge," "The Court of Spanish Empire," and "The Court of Imperial Patronage" (history of porcelain). The research is so extensive that Mistresses can usually relate the exact origin of every motif used on a gown or train to a historical source, whether it be from a classic painting or a little-known piece of statuary.

The trains and headpieces that have always been a part of Coronation are based on the British requirements issued by the Lord Chamberlain's office regarding the dress of ladies at Court (Arch and Marschner 1987:57). However, the San Antonio trains are far longer, reaching a maximum length of fifteen and a half feet, for they provide the surface upon which the theme of the court can be most easily represented.

The Mistress writes the script in collaboration with the chairman, or sometimes with a professional who volunteers his/her expertise in a field related to the theme. The Mistress of the Robes is also involved in the choice of musical selections. A court artist is hired to make the scale drawings, and in many cases, actually does most of the real design work. However, she, too, is often a former duchess or wife of an Order member.

After receiving the designs from the Mistress of the Robes, the court members and families select one of the seven approved dressmakers. The Mistress must approve any changes in design or color, but the dressmaker and the family make the decisions as to specific fabrics and how much beading and rhinestone highlighting will be done. Most dresses and trains are designed so that there is a good deal of leeway in the level of possible elaboration and detailing.

DESCRIPTION OF CORONATION AND ASSOCIATED EVENTS

A description of a particular Coronation and the associated reception, parade, and Queen's Ball reveals the specific ways in which class and family identity are established through the social ritual. The 1991 "Court of Imperial Spain" is typical of most Coronations.[5]

Any given Coronation actually begins years earlier as the future Coronation chairman begins to consider a possible Mistress of the Robes and themes. After those choices are made, he thinks about an appropriate Lord High Chamberlain or narrator, who may or may not be a member of the Order. The young women of the court feel that their participation in the April Coronation really begins in the previous September when they receive their sketches for the gown and train from the Mistress of the Robes and begin the six-month process of consultations and fittings.

The ritualized event always takes place on Wednesday night of Fiesta Week in the historic Municipal Auditorium. The backstage area is filled with Order of the Alamo members in full evening dress and purple baldrics, symbols of membership. The women's dressing area is filled with court members and their assistants, both paid and voluntary. While dressmakers, hairdressers, and make-up artists work on the duchesses, princess and queen, the mothers of the pages and entourage members help their children get ready.

The young women arrive at the auditorium wearing casual outfits. They are first zipped or hooked into merry widows (the modern equivalent of a corset) which change not only the outline of the upper body, but also posture. They are then zipped into closely fitted floor length dresses which may weight as much as twenty-five pounds due to the heavy fabrics and the attached stones. The sheer weight of the gown and the length of the train radically affect physical movement. The princess and queen also wear large standing "Elizabethan" collars built upon a metal frame and worn over the merry widow. When the thirty-five pound train is attached and the headpiece or crown in place, the wearer is transformed into a regal young woman.

The parents of the royal women are easily recognized backstage or in the dressing rooms because they wear six-inch-long "tags." These are miniature simplified versions of the trains made for each parent (and step-parents if attending) and worn throughout Fiesta week. Fathers simply pin theirs onto their tuxedos but mothers select their gowns carefully to compliment the "tags."

Although the tickets are moderately priced and are readily available, few people attend who do not know someone who is involved in the Order or the Coronation. The vast majority of observers are friends and relatives of the court members, but the difficulty of the deep bow makes the young women apprehensive about performing for the 4,000-member audience.

After the San Antonio Symphony plays the overture from *Carmen*, the curtains open, revealing an elaborate stage set depicting a plaza in Segovia. Heraldic banners are suspended from the balconies of the buildings, and the backdrop shows the countryside complete with a Roman aqueduct. The stage is filled with thirty-six young girls, ranging in age from seven to sixteen, who act as court pages. They are posed in a tableaux from a Goya painting and dressed in burgundy velvet dresses trimmed in black and gold lace, based upon a Velasquez court painting. The narrator, the Lord High Chamberlain, is dressed as a seventeenth-century Spanish nobleman. His opening proclamation sets the tone of the evening:

Here is Segovia's Plaza de los Festivales, a place flooded with light
and vitality, from which will emerge a vision of Spain's brilliant
evolution from mysterious, half-mythical country to illustrious
European power. We shall circle the earth with Spanish Explorers
and watch Spain assume her sovereign role in the community of
nations.

The younger pages take their places along the ramp to disengage trains in
case they catch on the footlights, and the older ones stay on the stage where they
assist the duchesses in arranging trains to the best advantage. The Lord High
Chamberlain beckons the ladies of the "Royal Household" who represent historical periods of Spain. The in-town duchesses proceed down a runway erected
above the center aisle, and cross over the orchestra pit before stepping on the
stage. Royal titles include "Duchess of Tartessian Opulence," "Duchess of
Visigothic Adornment," "Duchess of the Spirit of Pilgrimage," and "Duchess of
the Age of Reason." They enter individually while the narration elucidates the
titles, and music is played to compliment each dress. While many of the musical
selections are from Bizet, others are more obscure.

The "Duchess of Visigothic Adornment" wears an amethyst velvet dress with
gold lamé trim on its dropped shoulder neckline and a formal A-line skirt whose
shape "recalls the dress depicted in the Visigothic manuscript of the Codex
Remilianenis." The gold lamé train is covered with designs "inspired by the arm
of a great processional cross of repousse gold encrusted with cabochon rubies."
The narrative explains:

Spanish delight in ornament began with the Visigoths, lavish decoration penetrates the very essence of every work of art.
Establishing Toledo as their capital, Visigothic aristocrats, with
their long hair and massive jewelry, created the Spanish monarchy,
and at the same time an independent culture with its own personality.

Each duchess makes her extremely low bow turning her head to the audience
(although facing her duke) and proceeds to her place on stage.

After the in-town court is in place, the "Princess of the New World
Treasures" enters from the runway, preceded by her entourage, three children
dressed in simplified miniatures of her dress. The narrator quotes Columbus:
"May the Lord in His mercy guide me and make me find this gold . . . for gold is
excellent, and he who has wealth may do what he will in this world and even
send souls to Paradise." The princess wears a silver embroidered purple velvet
dress adapted from a Spanish portrait of Isabel de Bourbon. The purple velvet
train has silver and gold appliqués in the form of a giant jewelled urn: "embossed with foliage and double headed eagles, inspired by a nineteenth century
South American wall appliqué."

A flamenco dance is performed after the princess is seated. The Lord High Chamberlain returns, now wearing the costume of a conquistador in jeweled armor. The out-of-town visitors are then introduced, representing treasures of the New World, both physical and ephemeral. They enter from the wings directly onto the stage. Titles include "Duchess of Rio de la Plata," in bright red glitter crepe dress and silver lamé train, and "Duchess of Ornate and Exhilarant Artistry," whose train is covered with the tracery of vines in the "exhilarant Manueline style of embellishment." "The Duchess of Empires Reclaimed" representing treasure-laden shipwrecks has a train covered with large "ornate golden chains that evoke memories of the treasures discovered at the bottom of the sea."

The President of the Order of the Alamo arrives to crown the queen. He wears full evening dress and a floor length black velvet cape with the Order of the Alamo crest made of silver and topaz rhinestones on the back. His five-year-old son and nine-year-old daughter wear black velvet knee breeches and jacket with a gold lamé dress respectively. They carry the Queen's crown and scepter. The U.S. Third Infantry Old Guard Fife and Drum Corps of Washington act as the queen's honor guard. The Lord High Chamberlain proclaims:

> Like the great navigators of old, we have circled the globe, following the rainbow of Spain's destiny . . . let us celebrate the Soul of Spain; brilliant synthesis of all that is bold and glorious. . . . Empire upon whose boundaries the Sun never set. In honor of Spain's rich heritage and enduring legacy in Europe and in the New World, Her Gracious Majesty, Queen of the Court of Spanish Empire.

The queen arrives followed by her royal attendants, three very small children and her younger brother, all dressed in deep red velvet, gold lamé and lace to compliment the queen's dress, itself "inspired by a gown worn by Queen Isabella II." The train is completely covered with jeweled heraldic emblems accented in Spanish gold and bordered with the "Chains of Navarra." In addition, "The Bourbon fleau dais, the Stripes of Cordova and Aragon, the castle of Castile and the crown of the Queen of Spain were also beautifully depicted in her ensemble." Her Prime Minister, in full evening dress with jeweled baldric, escorts her to His Excellency, the President of the Order. She kneels before him and accepts the vow to reign over her kingdom according to the laws of happiness and joy. She promises to "bring mirth, melody and sweet music to this, your Kingdom" just as five of her relatives have done before her.

After the entertainment the court is ordered to retire. The duchesses withdraw in pairs escorted by their dukes with the out-of-town duchesses making formal bows to the queen as they depart. The louder applause given to several of the duchesses as they return up the runway hints at the identity of the next queen.

An official reception immediately follows and is the most private of the Coronation-related events. The President of the Order, the queen and princess and their escorts form a receiving line on a small raised platform while the duchesses form parallel lines in front of them. The young women rest on tall stools with the trains spread out in front. Guests come by to speak, and most importantly, to closely examine the trains. After an hour or so, the duchesses remove their trains, leaving them in place, while they go into the other rooms to eat and socialize. One informant refers to the reception as "viewing the bodies." People continue to view the trains even when the wearer is absent, for the train is a metonym for the duchess and her family.

The only really public appearance of the royal robes is in the Battle of Flowers parade on Friday. The queen and princess each have a float and the other twenty-four duchesses are divided among eight floats which are decorated with large paper flowers and plastic "petal paper." The bright colors seem to compete with the dresses rather than compliment them. The whole effect under the bright sunlight is one of flashiness and glitz. No subtlety of design or detailed work can be seen by the parade watchers due to the distance. Even though each girl is carefully identified by name and title, the average observer pays little or no attention, only judging the court members and their clothing according to her/his own standards of beauty.

The last time the royal robes are put on is for the "little coronation" which takes place at the Queen's Ball on Saturday night. It is held early in the evening in the patio at the hotel. The young women wear their gowns and trains (although they change afterwards) and are presented once again by the Lord High Chamberlain. They walk around the open area providing one more view of the gowns and then repeat the low court bow. The significant difference is that they are escorted by their fathers rather than their dukes. Each couple then goes up on a large balcony to observe the rest of the presentations. The fathers unhook the trains and hang them over the balcony rail creating the effect of medieval baronial banners.

On Monday morning, the royal women have to decide how to fill their days now that their social year is over. A decision must also be made regarding the gown and train. If they are not donated to the local museum (there is a required $5,000 contribution), where they will be "properly cared for and displayed," they are usually stored in a box under a bed. The owners cannot find a use for them but "cannot bear to get rid of them." Some spare bedrooms have three generations of royal robes in their closets.

ANALYSIS OF THE CORONATION

Class Identity

The themes, narration, and robes are all essential to the successful creation of an elite ritual which is used to legitimate particular interpretations of social reality. The selection of Spain and European royalty as a theme provided a particularly rich array of events and motifs in a pageantry context with which to create and affirm identity. The San Antonio elite could identify with a glorified Spanish history, culminating with Spain as conqueror and extractor of the wealth in the New World. The Royal Household members were named for periods of Spanish history, from the ancient Tartessos to the eighteenth century "Age of Reason." As in the pageantry tradition, at no time was reference made to any war, ethnic strife, or political conflict—elements of the history of most countries. Rather, the narration was filled with references to "zenith of power," "time of prosperity," and "new zest for creativity." Even the Visigoths were characterized as monarchs with artistic tastes, not as the barbarians and invaders that they truly were.

The out-of-town court, the Noble Visitors, depicted "Spain's global dominions," the result of Columbus' arrival: "the greatest revolution ever effected in the history of mankind." Columbus' discovery is read as the beginning of attainment for Anglo culture, not as the beginning of loss for indigenous peoples. In all cases, the correlation between the elite class and economic conquerors and inherited position was central to the sense of identity validated through the Coronation.

In addition to the general theme, details in the setting, text, and royal robes created a specific class identity for they relied upon a certain degree of knowledge about Spain for greater appreciation of the "authenticity" of the presentation. Coronation is an excellent marker of class distinction for it is built upon the attainments which make up Pierre Bordieu's (1984) cultural capital: education, knowledge of the arts, and social skills. The setting could be read easily as a representation of a plaza or public place in Spain, while the heraldic banners suggested a historic period. However, the inclusion of the Roman aqueduct presupposed knowledge of Spain's history. The titles of the duchesses, with references to Visigoths and Rio de la Plata, assume some historical and geographical knowledge of the viewers. The queen's train with its "Chains of Navarra, Stripes of Cordova and Aragon, and Bourbon feau dais" is a visual Spanish history. The costumes and arrangements of the pages with their origins in Goya and Velasquez paintings reflect the art history background of the Mistress of the Robes and the viewers of her work.

The ability to point out that a design "recalls the dress depicted in the Codex Remilianenis" or the "exhilarant Manueline style of embellishment" clearly demonstrates the superiority of those who design and create the Coronation. The emphasis on classical music played by the San Antonio Symphony also

188 Celebrations of Identity

strongly marks possession of cultural capital, for "nothing more clearly affirms one's 'class,' nothing more infallibly classifies, than tastes in music" (Bourdieu 1984:18).

Although the theme is carried out in the setting and text, the focus in Coronation and the following reception are on the elaborate robes. The gowns and trains automatically mark membership among the elite, but additionally, they offer one of the relatively few times that members of the aristocracy may be ostentatious. Generally, old wealth maintains an extremely comfortable lifestyle, but one that is essentially restrained and in "good taste," representing the "brilliant synthesis of all that is bold and glorious." In contrast, the rhinestones, sequins and lamés of the royal robes are "flashy." They are clearly used as a means of displaying wealth. Thorstein Veblen (1934) provides the classic terms, "Conspicuous Consumption" and "Conspicuous Waste," to refer to displays of upper class ranking through clothing, particularly that of women. According to Veblen, it is the duty of a wife to become "the ceremonial consumer of goods which he produces" (Veblen 1934:83), but daughters are also capable of displaying a father's ability to clothe his loved ones in finery.[6] The sheer size and elaborateness make the royal robes conspicuous. The yardage demanded by the design and train length, in addition to the limited wearing before being consigned to a storage box, clearly demonstrates waste.

The insistence upon all embellishments being done by hand is an additional way in which the royal robes reinforce class distinctions. The hand labor itself denotes honorific value for it is a more wasteful method of production (Veblen 1934:159). Members of the family and close friends see the robes in the home environment, and other members of the Order of the Alamo are able to appreciate the detailed handwork at the private reception following Coronation. The fine details can only be appreciated by those most intimately associated with the wearer, they are not for the benefit of the casual viewer. Therefore, the display of cultural capital is primarily a means of demonstrating inclusiveness and creating a feeling of a shared aristocratic culture.

The gowns and trains are marks of wealth but connote differences primarily to those who wear them. Bourdieu specifically states that "art and cultural consumption are predisposed, consciously and deliberately or not, to fulfill a social function of legitimating social differences" (Bourdieu 1984:7). However, as has been pointed out, Coronation is attended primarily by members of the Order of the Alamo, their families, and friends. Like the court spectacles of the Renaissance, coronation is an event for its peers, rather than a means of aweing outsiders. Even the public display of Coronation gowns in the "Battle of Flower" parade fails to unduly impress the average spectator.

Family Identity

While socio-economic group identity is the overall result of Coronation, the ritualized spectacle is based upon the participation of families rather than individuals, for as Marcus argues "family background is still a major factor in attributions of elite status" (Marcus 1983:44). Bourdieu notes that family names are properties which are overtly designated to be signs of distinction "especially the names and title expressing class membership" (Bourdieu 1984:482). The young women of the court do benefit in many ways, but the woman is selected as a representative of the family, not as an individual. Her family name is the prerequisite, not her physical or mental achievements. Old family names are still emblazoned on buildings, businesses, and streets all over San Antonio. Court members are quite aware of their relative unimportance as individuals and are willing to play their part in carrying on the family tradition.

The Coronation and its long-established rules of participation provide a model for aristocracy and its emphasis upon genealogies (however, unlike the British monarchy, the aristocrats themselves become royalty). Coronation families, as in many old-line families, do strongly mark lineage through use of the mother's maiden name as a middle name for both sons and daughters and by the repeated use of family first names over many generations. When a duchess is announced, she is referred to as "Martha McCloud (mother's maiden name) of the House of Thomas" so that both the middle and last names are emphasized.

As in England, San Antonio aristocratic families often have family crests. These are occasionally used on the trains, particularly for the princess and queen. Sometimes initials or motifs will be added to the design which have special meaning to the family. One young woman had the animal symbol of her father's oil company added to the back of the gown (hidden by the train to the casual observer) since it was the source of the money for the dress. Even when family references are not deliberate, families may find something within the design of the gown which has special significance to them. The train of the "Duchess of Spirit of Pilgrimage" had symbols referring to St. James on it, and the family read it as personally identifying, for they felt strong ties to the saint.

Coronation provides an annual reemphasis on the family; it is a time for recounting family participation. A young woman who is recalcitrant about becoming a duchess may be reminded of how many of her female relatives have been royal and how important it is to carry on the family tradition. Young girls are chosen to be pages or entourage members for an aunt, godmother, cousin, or sibling. Adults recall being in "my cousin's court when she was queen" rather than being in the "Court of Faberge." The most obvious reference to family is the "tag" worn by parents (and an occasional grandmother if she paid for the dress). All parents, as representatives of the family, can be recognized even when not with their daughters, and be credited with the financial and genealogical ability to be part of Coronation.

CONCLUSION

The entire ritualized event, within the specific periodic context of San Antonio's Spring Fiesta, is the necessary underlying structure within which the identities of the socio-economically elite and family lineage are negotiated and validated. Coronation is a manifestation of Bell's definition of ritualization: the utilization of a structured space with limited access, codes of communication to heighten the formality, distinct and specialized personnel, objects, texts, and dress (Bell 1992:204-205). The choice of theme and its subsequent interpretation in the setting, clothing, and narration is central to the achievement of Bell's redemptive hegemony. Coronation is successful in Bell's terms because it presents a social order that overall represents dominance, but also has an internal hierarchy which allows the participant to be cognizant of the ordering of social relations and his/her ability to achieve personal empowerment through "activity in the perceived system" (Bell 1992:84).

Sons of Order of the Alamo members grow up expecting to become members, if they so choose. They also know that if they want to work their way through the hierarchical board of directors to become president, there will be no problem in acquiring a board position. For many daughters of the old families, it is never a question of "if I am a duchess" but "when I am a duchess." The process by which a girl can move up from ramp page, to stage page, to duchess and even higher is a natural progression.

Young royalty have the privilege of growing up knowing that they will become part of the elite and carrying on family lineage. As Bourdieu points out, there are both the economic and social advantages of old money because it functions as cultural capital by providing an advance (both a head start and a credit) and enables the new generation to acquire both wealth and the basic elements of culture "in the most unconscious and impalpable way" (Bourdieu 1984:71). A male informant claims that "Our girls are just born knowing how to walk into a drawing room." Coronation not only provides a model of stratification but a model for the social and economic achievements of the upper strata which is the birthright of Coronation royalty and their parents.

Geertz argues that ritual is not just a model "of" but a model "for" reality. Rituals give meaning to social and psychological realities "both by shaping themselves and by shaping it to themselves" (Geertz 1973:93). The pageantry and the construction of the Order of the Alamo and the Coronation all are part of this ongoing dialectic.

The text and the artistic interpretations of the themes of Coronation are always highly Anglicized reassemblages which make beauty, power, and attainment of material and intellectual riches seem to be the natural order of things. There is never any reference in the themes to the realities of ethnic or class divisions which are inherent in stratification. As David Glassberg argues, pageants present an idealized view of history by ignoring class and ethnic divisions and tensions in a community, yet pageants suggest "categories for our understanding the scale of our social relations and the relative position of groups in our society" (Glassberg 1990:1). Even if a specific element of the theme does refer to an aspect of the non-elite, it becomes co-opted. In the 1968 Court of Mexico, the in-town dresses represented the folk arts of Mexico. A train was covered with motifs painstakingly derived from a piece of Tzintzuntzan pottery which was made in a potter's dirt-floored home. However, there was no hint of the connection with real clay and the potter by the time the design was transferred to satin-backed velvet and outlined with Austrian rhinestones.

The themes of Coronation both present a model of Anglicized domination and history and reflect the real world of the Anglo elite in San Antonio. The Coronation and all of its cultural capital is presented for the Order of the Alamo, family, and close friends. It is inwardly directed, not outwardly; it is a model for and of a closed community. The three contiguous neighborhoods in which the Coronation class lives are highly homogenous and distinctly separate from the rest of San Antonio. The neighborhoods are legally incorporated as independent entities with separate political structures, including fire and police departments. The three share an independent school district and all needed goods and services are available within their boundaries. It is possible to stay under the protective shade of the towering oak and pecan trees of the area and rarely have to confront the class and ethnic divisions which are found throughout San Antonio.

Like the Visigothic aristocrats in the narration who "created an independent culture with its own personality," the ancestors of the Coronation families came to San Antonio in the nineteenth century and gradually established themselves as the elite socio-economic class. Their descendants perpetuate the entitlement to those privileges through the annual ritual of Coronation which both models and reflects their identity as members of an elite culture. The ritual emphasizes aristocratic lineage, but the cost of the elaborate royal robes makes a certain level of wealth also necessary.

The Order of the Alamo is sensitive to criticism about the costs of Coronation. However, the general attitude is that it is a private organization and receives no public monies; therefore, it should be able to continue its traditional practices, no matter how expensive they have become. The quotation from Columbus in the 1991 Coronation in which he appeals to God for success in his search for wealth is fitting here: "for gold is excellent, and he who has wealth may do what he will in this world and even send souls to Paradise."

NOTES

This article is based upon fieldwork carried out in San Antonio, Texas from January 1991 until the present. I thank Mike Coggeshall for introducing me to Pam Frese and thank my invaluable and tireless readers: Carol Canty, Dan Gello, David Haynes, and Shirley Mock.

1. The term "Anglo" is used to designate members of the core culture (Feagin 1978:58). "Elite" is used to denote a specifiable group characterized by agency and exclusivity (Marcus 1983:7-13).

2. This essay is drawn from a dissertation in progress. The longer work covers the myriad gender issues, including the classification of a debut as a rite of initiation, the place of women as gatekeepers, and the public/private domain dichotomy.

3. In 1926 Carrington began another men's club to sponsor the election and crowning of King Antonio; thus Anglos controlled and filled both the king's and queen's thrones. However, monarchs have slowly been added to Fiesta activities including Miss Fiesta, Miss Soul, and the Charro Queen. Increasingly since the early 1980s the position of Rey Feo, representative of the Mexican-American community, has been considered of almost equal importance to that of King Antonio. His inclusion has undoubtedly been responsible for the relatively little criticism directed at the Anglo King Antonio.

4. Like all frontier settlers, immigrants to Texas came from a variety of backgrounds and for a variety of reasons, although most were at least lower middle-class. The Germans were largely middle-class and the southeasterners were primarily planters (Fehrenbach 1985:296-304). Both groups were highly successful, intermarried and continue to dominate San Antonio socially and economically although they have lost their political dominance. For the best analysis of the reasons for their successes see David Montejano (1987).

5. The Mistress of the Robes was personally interested in Spain but using it as a theme the year preceding the quincentenary was viewed as serendipity since the connection was not realized until well after the decision had been made. This Coronation description is based upon one I observed in 1991 while those of the private reception and ball come from informants. The quotations in this description are taken from the script and from the text in the printed program. Every member of the audience receives a detailed program, but several months later members of the Order receive a "yearbook," with full color photographs. The text includes a recounting of the event and the full script. Every fifteen or twenty years, the yearbooks are reissued in a hardbound collection. Such multiple records of Coronation reflect the importance of being able to revalidate one's own participation or that of family members.

6. Other relatives, particularly grandmothers who had been in Coronation themselves, sometimes pay for the royal robes, but it is assumed that the father signs the checks.

BIBLIOGRAPHY

Amory, Cleveland
    1960 *Who Killed Society?* New York: Harper.

Arch, Nigel, and Joanna Marschner
    1987 *Splendour at Court.* London: Unwin Hyman.

Barth, Fredrik
    1959 *Political Leadership Among Swat Pathans.* London: Althone Press.

Bell, Catherine
    1992 *Ritual Theory, Ritual Practice.* New York: Oxford University Press.

Birminghan, Stephen
   1958 *The Right People*. Boston: Little, Brown.

   1987 *America's Secret Aristocracy*. New York: Berkley Books.

Bourdieu, Pierre
   1984 *Distinction*. Cambridge: Harvard University Press.

Cohen, Abner
   1981 *The Politics of Elite Culture: Explorations in the Dramaturgy of Power in a Modern African Society*. Berkeley: University of California Press.

Domhoff, G. William
   1967 *Who Rules America?* Washington, DC: American Council on Education.

   1971 *Higher Circles: The Governing Class in America*. New York: Random House.

   1974 *The Bohemian Grove and Other Retreats*. New York: Harper and Row.

Dorst, John
   1989 *The Written Suburb*. Philadelphia: University of Pennsylvania Press.

Feagin, Joe R.
   1978 *Racial and Ethnic Relations*. Englewood Cliffs, NJ: Prentice-Hall.

Fehrenbach, T. R.
   1985 *Lone Star*. New York: Macmillan.

Geertz, Glifford
   1973 *The Interpretation of Cultures*. New York: Basic Books.

Glassberg, David
   1990 *American Historical Pageantry*. Chapel Hill: University of North Carolina Press.

Marcus, George
   1983 "A Review of Ethnographic Research on Elites in Complex Societies." In *Elites*. George Marcus (ed.) Albuquerque: University of New Mexico Press. Pp. 7-61.

   1987 "Constructive Uses of Deconstruction in the Ethnographic Study of Notable American Families." *Anthropological Quarterly* 60:3-16.

   1992 *Lives in Trust*. Boulder, CO: Westview Press.

Mills, C. Wright
   1956 *The Power Elite*. New York: Oxford University Press.

Montejano, David
   1987 *Anglos and Mexicans in the Making of Texas, 1936-1986*. Austin: University of Texas Press.

Mosca, Gaetano
   1939 *The Ruling Class*. New York: McGraw-Hill.

Nader, Laura
   1964 "Perspectives Gained from Field Work." In *Horizons of Anthropology*. Sol Tax (ed.) Chicago: Aldine. Pp. 148-59.

Pareto, Vilfredo
   1935 *The Mind and Society*. New York: Harcourt, Brace and World.

Veblen, Thorstein
   1934 *The Theory of the Leisure Class.* New York: Modern Library.

12

The Ritual Cycle of the American Monarch

J. R. McLeod

The study of political ritual has long been a mainstay of political anthropology.[1] The traditional view of the relationship between political complexity and societal emphasis on ritual has held that the two phenomena are inversely related (McLeod 1991b:107-109). That is, the more complex and diverse the population of a single polity becomes, the less important rituals are in political integration. In this view, political complexity lessens the importance of ritual in the political process. This point has been made by G. Almond and G.B. Powell (1966), M. Gluckman (1965), A. Southall (1965), and a host of others. The concept that is typically used to analyze the diminution of ritual is secularization. As Almond and Powell contend: "Secularization is the process whereby men (sic) become increasingly rational, analytical, and empirical in terms of their political action" (Almond and Powell 1966:24).

This theory holds that there is little reliance on mystical authority for the reinforcement of the political system in developed state societies—and that the concomitant of state evolution is *secularization*. In such societies, political power is held centrally, and the use of force by one segment against another is effectively precluded by the monopoly on the use of force which the central government possesses. As Southall argued: "The organic structure of society renders people ineluctably interdependent and ritual is less necessary to hold them together in solidarity. Specialized authority roles enable order and security to be achieved by larger groups over wider areas. The ritualization of social relationships is not only less necessary but less possible" (Southall 1965:125). Such state-level societies have been defined by M. Fried as stratified, or "a system by which the adult members of a society enjoy differential rights of access to basic resources" (Fried 1967:52). However, Gluckman contended: "If this analysis were correct, I decided that I would not find ritualization of social relations in any high differentiated society, particularly where the existing structure of society is not accepted as hallowed. This 'prediction' was fulfilled when I checked the political rituals of the more developed states" (Gluckman 1965:286). As this author has demonstrated elsewhere (McLeod 1991a; 1991b) the selection of the American president is highly ritualized and these rituals serve similar functions to political rituals in traditional societies.

THE INAUGURATION AND THE RITUAL CYCLE

The Presidential Inauguration is the keystone in a cycle of ritual events leading to the installation of the American king (Kertzer 1987; Novak 1974). While the Inauguration is a critical element in this cycle, it cannot be understood in a vacuum. Its full cultural and political significance can only be seen in the context of wider political phenomena, and its true meaning to the American people lies in its power to create their identity, certify their king, and end civil conflict through ritual. L. Durbin explains:

> 'Before he enters on the Execution of his Office,' reads the last sentence in Article II, Section 1, of the Constitution, 'he shall take the following Oath or Affirmation:—"I do solemnly swear (or affirm) that I will faithfully execute the Office of the President of the United States, and will to the best of my Ability, preserve, protect, and defend the Constitution of the United States."'
> It was a simple formula for the Inauguration of a President when it was written in 1787, and it remains so today. Time honored traditions now surround the oath taking, but the unpretentious ceremony is, in essence at the very heart of the democratic process, the grand experiment initiated by the Founding Fathers. A private citizen repeats the 35 word oath and in that dramatic moment becomes the President of the United States, endowed with the awesome duties and powers of that office, elevated by his fellow citizens—both those who have elected him and those who have willingly acquiesced to the verdict of the election by the people (Durbin 1977:ix).

The point has often been made that the American Presidency is probably the most powerful elected office on earth. But a crucial aspect of the power of the Presidency lies in the ritual of selection of the candidates, the rhetorical and symbolic wars which the candidates fight, and the confirmation of the victor through the Inauguration itself. The election of the President is a four-year ordeal, both for the candidates and for the American people. In that quadrennium, the American people are cajoled, persuaded, analyzed, and bombarded with information and rhetoric concerning the qualifications of the candidates. The candidates themselves (and would-be candidates) are subjected to the most rigorous public scrutiny possible by a horde of media specialists; every aspect of their lives is investigated, every possible scandal is reviewed. The closer they get to the prize, the more detailed and difficult the scrutiny becomes. The candidates are comparable in some ways to those undergoing initiation in tribal societies (La Fontaine 1985; Richards 1982; Turner 1967). Subjected to difficulties and trials in order to judge their virtues for admission to one of the most exclusive band of initiates in the world, the candidates compete to become one of those who have been initiated as Presidents of the United States. At the time of this writing, this included only forty-one members of a very exclusive society. All have been men, all White, and all have been chosen by the various elective procedures laid down by the changing Constitution over the past 200 years. The direct popular vote and universal suffrage are relatively new in this process, as is the participation of Blacks and other minorities; but the cycle of ritual selection has been in place since the first inaugural in New York City on April 30, 1789. There has never been a failure of this succession process, whether it be through war, depression, assassination, or "hung" elections.

However, this essay is not a history of the Inauguration process; even less is it an attempt to review Presidential candidates. As an essay in the social anthropology of ritual, what we attempt here is a comparative overview of the problems of ritual accession to office as they have existed in cross-cultural and cross-temporal perspective. For the race for the Presidency in the United States is not simply a process of rational political choices; it is also a complex symbolic and highly ritualized event. Even in the first completion of the cycle of Presidential ritual, symbolism was highly important, as the government document "George Washington: Journey to the Presidency" makes note:

> April 30. (1789). Day breaks to the sound of artillery and church bells. In honor of American industry, Washington dresses in a suit of brown broadcloth spun at Hartford with buttons displaying a wing-spread eagle. At 12:30 p.m. a military escort joined by a procession of dignitaries and citizens accompany Washington's coach to Federal Hall. Upon arrival, Washington proceeds to the Senate chamber where the two Houses of Congress wait to greet him, then onto the outer balcony in front of the Senate Chamber. Chancellor Robert Livingston administers the oath to Washington, who holds his right hand on the Bible and responds: 'I swear, so help me God.' Livingston then turns to the cheering crowd and proclaims 'Long live George Washington, President of the United States.'

There is no direct mystical appeal to unseen forces beyond sensory observation in the oath of office itself—but virtually every President has appealed to God for faith and help in either their affirmation of the oath or in the Inaugural Speech. As such, the Inaugural ceremony fulfills Max Gluckman's criterion as a ritual rather than as a ceremony. According to Gluckman (1965:295), "ritual" is here distinguished from "ceremonial," highly conventionalized performances in which this mystical element is not present. Both the accession to the Presidency and the appeals which are made throughout the campaigns embody highly emotional symbolism and appeals to legendary heroes, such as the Founding Fathers, the spirits of departed presidents, and a host of non-rational elements. In his Inaugural Address, George Bush made the first act of his Presidency a ritual of invocation for the future of the United States:

> *The Inaugural Address—January 20, 1989*
> I've just repeated word for word the oath taken by George Washington 200 years ago; and the Bible on which I placed my hand is the Bible on which he placed his . . . and my first act as President is a prayer, I ask you to bow your heads.
> Heavenly Father, we bow our heads and thank you for your love. Accept our thanks for the peace that yields this day and the shared faith that makes its continuance likely. . . . God Bless America.

ANTI-THESIS: PRESIDENTIAL RITUAL AS FALSE CONSCIOUSNESS

The ritualization of the American Presidential cycle can alternatively be seen as an exercise in "false consciousness." This conception identifies the Presidential race as a mystified class struggle. From this point of view, the Presidential campaigns and the final element in the Presidential cycle, the Presidential Inauguration, constitute a kind of mystified cultural discourse. The political economy of Presidential selection and installation is certainly germane to our comprehension of the power of the Presidential cycle as a social force. In terms of this conception, the Presidential election cycle constitutes an ideological discourse, expressed through the medium of rhetoric and symbol, and aimed at the maintenance of a particular class and power structure. Marx made a similar point when he wrote:

> The ideas of the ruling class are, in every age, the ruling ideas; i.e., the class which is the dominant material force in society is at the same time its dominant intellectual force. The class which has the means of material production at its disposal, has control at the same time over the means of mental production, so that in consequence the ideas of those who lack the means of mental production are, in general, subject to it. The dominant ideas are nothing more than the ideal expression of the dominant material relationships, the dominant material relationships grasped as ideas, and thus of the relationships which make one class the ruling one; they are consequently the ideas of dominance (Marx 1964:78).

The question of the class-domination effects of political ritual relative to the cultural-integration effects of these ritual events has been argued before in other cultural contexts. E. Shils and M. Young (1953) argued that the coronation of the British monarch had significant effects in creating a sense of integration and social solidarity among the British people. This was later criticized by N. Birnbaum (1955), who argued that the coronation was a class-based phenomenon, and a distraction from the realities of the class and power struggle. In essence, Birnbaum argued that the power of the monarchical symbol system was the result of false consciousness.

Sir Raymond Firth attempted to make sense of this argument by analyzing both sides from the point of view of the function of the monarchy as a "master symbol." Firth pointed out that Shils and Young held that the coronation did much to integrate British society, while Birnbaum held the ceremony only to result in the kind of "cult of adulation built up around certain film stars." However, Firth endeavored to synthesize the two views by pointing out that symbolic coronation of the Queen attracted massive public attention whatever the underlying mechanics of ritualization might have been. Firth wrote:

> In essence this was a difference of opinion about the acceptance of a
> 'master symbol' at face value. Both parties agreed that the symbol
> was accepted in the sense of attracting public attention in general.
> To Shils and Young the coronation was interpreted by the public as
> a justifying symbol, positively representing the values aspect of
> the power structure as 'an act of national communion.' But to
> Birnbaum, it was interpreted as a diversionary symbol, a distraction
> from the realities of the power struggle. I do not think there is
> enough evidence to come to a firm conclusion on this issue (Firth
> 1973:89).

The symbolic power of the British Monarchy or the American Presidency can only be understood within the historical and ethnographic context of the cultures which spawned them. To relegate all ceremonial and ritual action to the realm of false consciousness is to isolate the rites and ceremonials from their cultural context. While the installation of the monarchy and the Inauguration of the American President have significant similarities, they are not the same process. They do not mean the same things to the members of their respective societies, nor are the processes of selection to these offices similar. Simply to say that these ritual processes are illusory, and then to dismiss them as aspects or mystifications of productive forces, ignores the specific cultural meaning of these events.

The interpretation of the function of key symbols (Ortner 1973) as a means of implementing false consciousness closely approximates R. Barthes' (1972) and M. Bloch's (1977) distinction between revolutionary consciousness and mystified consciousness, as B. Lincoln (1989:5-10) has noted. In this view, ritual action is illusory, as it mystifies social consciousness (La Fontaine 1985:35-36). Such analyses contribute to our understanding of socio-cultural phenomena, but they are not completely explanatory. Lincoln expresses the following reservations:

> Thus, like Barthes, Bloch located a non-mystified and potentially
> revolutionary mode of thought and discourse within the experience
> of productive labor, and here, of course, they both follow Marx.
> This they dialectically oppose to another mode of thought and dis-
> course that serves only to mystify and thereby perpetuate the socio-
> political status quo. This latter category they locate in myth (R.
> Barthes), ritual (M. Bloch), and ideology (B. Marx). There are
> problems with their common line of analysis (Lincoln 1989:6).

The ritualization of the American presidency includes appeals to many types of symbolic forms and not all of these are directly reducible to class relations. In the 1992 acceptance speech by Bill Clinton for the Democratic Party's Presidential nomination, Mr. Clinton used the Pledge of Allegiance as a ritual device to demonstrate his party's loyalty to the ultimate goals and value attitudes of the United States. Mr. Clinton also invoked emotionally compelling appeals to the "American Dream" and the "Horatio Alger" myth through his "Man from Hope" infomercial and his acceptance speech (McLeod 1993). These powerful political symbols involved political persuasion and political rhetoric based on a system of fundamental beliefs about what it means to be an American. This system of political symbol and ritual is therefore related to economic forces but also distinct from them (McLeod 1991b).

This is not to say that productive forces are not at the root of most sociological phenomena, nor that rituals are divorced from their economic context in some kind of "superorganic." It is, however, to argue that the study of why and how such rituals are effective within their cultural context is at least as important an area of study as the question of their relationship to productive forces. Both aspects of the ritual process need to be understood if we are to have a viable social anthropology of ritual. As A. Cohen has concisely noted:

> Power relations are objectified, developed, maintained, expressed or
> camouflaged by means of symbolic forms and patterns of symbolic
> action, both of which are referred to here as 'symbolism.' In most
> of the systems that anthropologists have studied, kinship and ritual
> have been the main form of symbolism; they are deployed alterna-
> tively or combined together as articulating principles that are di-
> alectically related to power relations (Cohen 1979:89).

From this point of view, the study of symbols is never complete until it is related to the problems of production (economic forces). The problem for the symbolic anthropologist is that many kinds of symbols are irreducible directly to the accompanying modes of production, distribution, and exchange. While most anthropologists would agree that symbolic persuasion is ultimately based on economic factors, the use of economic or coercive force by political elites can have consequences which can undermine political legitimacy and cultural predictability. This is why the realm of the symbolic is so critical to the political anthropologist. In sum, productive forces alone cannot explain social relationships, nor can they be used as the pre-existing basis for all sociological explanation. Those economic forces themselves are conditioned by other factors which are culture specific and value derived. To put it differently, rituals work to both create and to mystify social action. Understanding how this system of mystification works as a social process is equally important to understanding the genesis of the process of mystification itself.

LIMINALITY AND PRESIDENTIAL POLITICS

Following the work of V. Turner (1967, 1974), H. Herzog (1987) demonstrates clearly that American Presidential campaigns are liminal events and that the unrecognized assumptions of the electorate are part of the ritualization process. These unrecognized assumptions act as guideposts or symbolic identifiers which allow politicians to seek office and gain access to power through the manipulation of symbols.

The Presidential selection cycle as a ritual can be examined by two interrelated perspectives: 1. the perspectives of the participants directly involved in the election cycle itself, and 2. the perspectives of the wider society. For those participating in the electoral campaigns, no explanation of the importance or existence of the Presidential cycle is necessary. For those who do not vote or participate, a large number of the American population, the cycle still holds importance in terms of the calendrical measurement of cultural time and the role of the Presidency in American symbolic space (Warner 1959). From this point of view, the election of a President to office clearly defines a transformation of national character and social status. The American presidency may not be a monarchy in terms of the process of selection, but the symbolic space occupied by the President has significant aspects of kingly authority. Even democracies demand emotionally charged symbols, and the Presidency serves this function in the United States.

The degree to which the Inauguration processes act as ritual events that unite the country is probably minimal in and of themselves. But when considered as an aspect of the entire Presidential election and installation process, the overall integration effects are significant indeed. However, the election/Inauguration process also acts as a means for the introduction of new values and symbolic elements into the civil religion. Values are rearranged, re-examined, re-developed, and re-integrated into a new synthesis. The candidates become the vessels through which these values are tested, examined, and claimed by the electorate. When the process is over, however, as ordained and sanctified by the Inauguration ceremonies, the system is still that which was outlined in the sacred literature (Kluckhohn 1968:153) and maintained through experience, history, and traditional system of belief (McLeod 1991b). As H. Herzog states:

> As a liminal period, campaign time is a social setting in which many symbols are experienced. The voters and the politicians interact around and within a symbolic environment. Manipulating and altering meanings and creating symbols are the main activities during such a period. All of this is carried out in a competitive environment. The context may reflect symbols of the existing social structure and at the same time may be a seedbed for negotiation over the meaning and legitimacy of symbols (Herzog 1987:571).

The overt purpose of Presidential campaigning is the acquisition of power through the election process. The covert purpose is the reintegration of society through a kind of integrative catharsis (Gluckman 1963:110-136). Election campaigns and the Inauguration rituals serve to allow the expression of sectional and hierarchical disharmonies within a culturally approved matrix of mudslinging, negative campaigning, personal investigations, and dramatic presentations. As such, they are the means by which American society comes together through quasi-violent symbolic attacks which ultimately reinforces cultural stasis. Lincoln has pointed out: "he [Gluckman] attempted to demonstrate that when sociopolitical tensions and conflicts of a potentially violent and disintegrative nature are set within ritual discourse, they are thereby rendered harmless and result only in continuation of the status quo" (Lincoln 1989:53).

The process of Presidential electioneering serves a similar function for the political and economic framework of American culture. In 1992, H. Ross Perot promised to spend $100 million to get elected President if necessary. The costs of Presidential electioneering are staggering—and the stakes are nothing less than the crowning of the American king (Novak 1974). From a wider cultural perspective, election campaigns are much more than this. The national discourse manipulates views of the normally disarticulated minorities for the ritual moment and integrates them into a system of rhetoric and symbol. Bill Clinton's comments on Sister Souljah's anti-White rap lyrics in 1992, for example, are a classic case of elevating the interests of the oppressed into the arena of Presidential ritual and rhetoric. From this point of view, the election ritual allows the expression of what James Scott has termed "the hidden transcript": "discourse that takes place 'off stage,' beyond direct observation by powerholders. The hidden transcript is thus derivative in the sense that it consists of those offstage speeches, gestures, and practices that confirm, contradict, or inflect what appears in the public transcript" (Scott 1990:xii).

This perspective allows us to understand why "rap" music became an issue in the Presidential campaign of 1992; and conversely why "Willie Horton" became an issue in the campaign of 1988. During the campaign stages of the ritual of installation, no holds are barred in the contest for power—so that a Democratic candidate can attack a rap singer in order to appeal to the dominant white American worldview (McLeod and Goh 1991) or a Presidential candidate can use a quasi-racist appeal to gain office (McLeod 1990a, 1991a). At the close of the contest, however, the rules of succession must be firmly applied, and the rival candidates subdued. This is the purpose and the promise of the Presidential Inauguration, and the importance of the ritual installation of the President to the culture. As S.F. Moore and B. Myerhoff observed:

> Every ceremony is par excellence a dramatic statement against indeterminacy in some field of human affairs. Through order, formality, and repetition it seeks to state that the cosmos and the social world, or some particular small apart of them are orderly and explicable and for the moment fixed. . . . In other words, a dialectical relationship exists between the formed and the indeterminate. Ritual is a declaration of form against in determinancy, therefore, in determinancy is always present in the background of any analysis of ritual (Myerhoff 1977:17).

In this sense, the act of supporting a particular candidate creates an emotional bond between the voter and the "prince." This support also identifies the individual supporter with the symbols of the campaign as expressed through Presidential rhetoric (McLeod 1990b, 1991b). In the case of the United States, the rival princes for the throne (Presidency) are the major Presidential candidates who strive to ritually kill one another off through the process of campaigning.

During this period, the ordinary rules of political exchange are voided in favor of effective political killing strategies (McLeod 1990b). From this point of view, political campaigns in the United States are "rituals of rebellion" (Gluckman 1963) in which the voices of the constituent units of the society are vented publicly through the liminal process of campaign-engineering and rhetoric. The Inauguration is simply the end point of the process of ritually choosing the right prince for the throne during the subsequent electoral process. It is impossible, therefore, to understand the ritual significance of the Presidential Inauguration without considering the campaign processes which lead up to it as a ritual event. The United States is disarticulated during the election campaign through the use of very powerful symbols of unity, disunity, order, anarchy, chaos, and institutions; and then it is rearticulated through the processes of the Inauguration and Presidential installation. From this point of view, the ritual installation of the President is similar in function to that observed for the Swazi Incwala ritual, the classic ritual of rebellion analyzed by M. Gluckman (1963, 1965), H. Kuper (1947), and finally reanalyzed by Lincoln (1989). In his analysis of the Incwala ritual of kingship as a ritual of resistance to colonialism, Lincoln observed the following:

> The Ncwala of the colonial period served as such an instrument whereby the Swazi nation was rallied, its political institutions reaffirmed, and those who threatened it—either with fission (i.e., the Dlamini princes) or an unwanted fusion—were triumphantly expelled from the ritual ground. At that moment society itself was disarticulated and rearticulated, literally, taken apart and put back together, as two different groups—that some sought to merge— were dramatically separated in space and in sentiment: those who were considered and in that very moment defined themselves as loyal Swazi and those whose sentiments of loyalty to the Swazi king being suspect were accordingly labeled alien (foreigners) (Lincoln 1989:75).

Without carrying the analogy between the Swazi ritual of installation and the Presidential Inauguration too far, it is worth pointing out the similarity in terms of function. The constituent units of society in both cases have divergent interests, both economically and politically. Both systems recognize a central head figure in whom the ultimate decision-making power rests. In both cases, that central figure cannot make decisions without taking into account councillors, advisers, and the will of the people over whom the leader has suzerainty. In both cases, the rituals of installation are subsidized by the people at large, not voluntarily but through taxation and tribute. Finally, in both cases, the rhetoric and symbolism of the occasions invokes the interests of the members of the society in symbolic terms and through common condensing symbols (Kertzer 1987). As Gluckman pointed out for African societies: "These common values refer to fertility, health, prosperity, peace, and justice, everything which gives life and happiness to a people. They are the safeguards of both the material needs of existence and the basic relations of social structure" (Gluckman 1965:279).

THE RITUAL CYCLE IN PERSPECTIVE

The rituals of contestation and installation of the American President provide a cultural template which is predictable and symbolically meaningful for the members of the American polity. As M. Fortes and E.E. Evans-Pritchard noted for African societies:

> Members of an African society feel their unity and perceive their common interest in symbols, and it is their attachment to these symbols which more than anything else gives their society cohesion and persistence. In the forms of myths, fictions, dogmas, rit-

ual, sacred places and persons, these symbols represent the units
and exclusiveness of the groups which respect them (Fortes and
Evans-Pritchard 1970:17).

While there is no doubt about the political economy of Presidential electioneering, it is critical to realize that it is the symbolic world of American voter
which is activated during the liminal process of Presidential contests. During
these contests, economic, sectional, racial, and ethnic issues are stressed. The
unity and exclusiveness of each grouping or region of the country is expressed
through symbolic discourses about the "American way." Candidates have an
acute knowledge of the legends, histories, symbolic icons, and worldviews of the
American people, past and present. In this sense, the quadrennial cycle of
Presidential rituals performs an important cultural function as a symbolic anchor
in times of social upheaval and distress. The Presidential cycle is both rule-gov-
erned and predictable. That predictability is in itself an asset in a world as uncertain as that in which Americans find themselves. The Presidential contest has a
definite past and a secure future and it will be extant as long as American culture
lasts.

Rule governance is central to the functioning of the Presidential ritual cycle
as a symbolic anchor for Americans. Politicians may be corrupt, Presidents may
lie to Congress, the American family may be in decline, but the ritual of
Presidential selection and Inauguration provides a set-point in the continuing cycle of American symbolic time (Warner 1959). M. Novak argues that: "Every
four years, Americans select a king—but not only a king also a high priest and
prophet. It does not matter that we are a practical and sophisticated people, no
longer (we think) influenced by symbols, myths, or rituals. To what our president represents, we react with passion" (Novak 1974:3).

American Presidential politics is generally known as a "dirty business," and
the securing of the Presidential prize has led to some very nasty business indeed.
The conduct of Presidential warfare has included Donald Segretti's dirty tricks on
Edmund Muskie, the Watergate scandal, buying votes from the Mafia an the
Dailey Machine in Chicago, selling infidelity stories to tabloids for enormous
sums of money, and using political commercials which obscured the truth
(McLeod 1990b). The rhetoric used in campaigns has also been extremely un-
pleasant, ranging from implications concerning the patriotism of a candidate's
wife to quasi-racist appeals and the manipulation of facts for political advantage
(McLeod 1991a). However, when these phenomena are put in perspective, they
emerge in quite a different view. The cycle of Presidential campaigning and ritual installation should be seen for what it is; an alternative to civil war for the
accession of the American king.

A. Oberg described the accession practices of the Ankole kingdom:

The brothers (the rival princes) spied upon one another in order to
creep up during the night and get the other unawares. They put

> poison in each other's food or stabbed one in his sleep. Magic and the help of foreign allies was resorted to. . . . During the accession war which might last for several months, the country was in a state of chaos. Every man resorted to his kinsmen for protection. . . . One by one, the princes were either killed or driven into exile until only one remained (Oberg 1970:158).

In the place of these cycles of ritual warfare, the American people have the quadrennial cycle of Presidential campaigning. The Presidential contest thus constitutes a kind of dramatic ritual discourse which is expressed to the public through an emotionally compelling series of organized and institutionalized dramas of social order and disorder (McLeod 1991a; Kertzer 1987). As H. Duncan has observed:

> But whatever it is called, and however it is done, successful appeals to the people are now recognized as the basis for all power in modern society. . . . How to appeal to the general public, not *whether* we should appeal, is the modern problem in communication. Elites who reach decisions of their own, and then tell the people how to carry them out, are now obsolete. In their place we now have elites who are masters in the art of communicating to general publics through mounting frequent and intense dramas of social order (Duncan 1968: 95; emphasis in original).

Although framed as a secular ritual discourse, the Presidential cycle also possesses significant extra-mundane appeals. Praying for God's blessing during the campaign, publicly attending church, and associating with religious figures before, during, and after the campaign process, are all aspects of the mystification of American political culture. Sacred songs, such as the National Anthem and "God Bless America," are part of the cult of the divine America (McLeod 1991b) and critical to the ritual cycle. As a result, Presidential campaigns and Inaugurations must be considered as something more than a simply secular occasions. One can argue that in comparison to other ritual events in which sacrifice, direct and obligatory appeal to the ancestors, or direct appeals to mystical beings beyond sensory observation constitute the bulk of the ritual event, American political rituals are relatively secular institutions. However, American political culture is not secularized, especially when it is compared to the political culture of other industrialized nations. American political culture is highly ritualized and these ritual events are important markers in the cycle of American culture. Even though American voter participation is very low, the Presidential cycle acts as a reassurance that the culture of the United States will persist through time. The process guarantees order, stability, and permanence for the members of the culture, uniting present with past, and allowing the culturally approved expression of disunity and dissent.

The Presidential election campaign is in fact a kind of controlled ritual warfare in which the candidates act in similar fashion to rival princes in traditional African kingdoms. The weapons are rhetoric, symbol, and televised debates; but the goal is the same, that is, to defeat your opponent and be installed as king. The means of selection are also divergent; voting versus outright warfare—but the number of Presidential candidates who have described the system of electoral selection as a kind of warfare is legendary. The uncertainty of the outcome in both the African cases and the American Presidential elections underpin the political liminality which makes the installation of the monarch that much more satisfying when it is accomplished. No matter how securely the rules of succession are defined, there always exists a contributory element of insecurity, as Yamaguchi explains:

> It can be noted that there is in practice an uncertainty about the rule
> of succession even in societies where the rule of succession is, in
> principle, clearly defined. It is this practice which is commonly
> observed among traditional African states, notably in Buganda,
> Ankole, and Bunyoro. . . . In these societies, the death of kings is
> followed by ritual combat, or ritual civil war controlled by the
> prime minister of the deceased king. Princes fought among them-
> selves with the support of their respective maternal family
> (Yamaguchi 1972:56-57).

American Presidential contests are the expression of the civil religion, quadrennially played out in the rivalries between national princes. This satisfies a deeply felt cultural dimension, which can be interpreted as the attempt of a democratic society to fulfill its symbolic function in terms of cosmic imagery:

> Over the disparate elements of American society, uniting all, is as
> it were a single arc of sky, a canopy, a limited symbolic horizon.
> The nation has sacred obligations—not to be merely selfish, not to
> be decadent, not to be wasteful, not to be vicious—sacred obli-
> gations to try to be a *good* nation. The nation has its holy calen-
> dar, it's sacred cities, and monuments and pilgrimages, its conse-
> crated mounds, and fields. It has as its president a priest, a prophet,
> and a king.
>   What, then, is the civil religion? It is a public perception of
> our national experience, in the light of universal and transcendent
> claims upon human beings, but especially upon Americans, a set
> of values, symbols, and rituals institutionalized as the cohesive
> force and center of meaning uniting our many peoples (Novak
> 1974:127; emphasis in original).

However, it must be considered that the process of electing the President, with all the primaries, speeches, campaigning, and myth-making, is the essence of the ritual cycle. The "holy calendar," of which Novak writes, cycles year round and reaches a liminal peak every four years with the Presidential election campaigns. One would be naive indeed to argue that the Inauguration in and of itself worked to bind Americans into a seamless web of political culture and organic American beliefs. But to ignore the existence of such a dominant American political culture is to invite political catastrophe, as both Walter Mondale and Jimmy Carter found out to their distress. More recently, appeals to that dominant and organic American value system propelled George Bush into office when he established Michael Dukakis as a value-neutral technocrat and himself as the incarnation of American values (McLeod 1990a:3-15). This was accomplished through a complex system of rhetoric and symbol, including political commercials, speech-making, Presidential posturing, and image building (McLeod 1991a). The goal is the Inauguration of the American monarch, as the Carter Inauguration committee noted: "The oath-taking, of course, punctuates a moment that is like the passing of monarchs: the king is dead, long live the king. Indeed the Inauguration ceremonies, as they have evolved over the years, have been called by an English historian American's quadrennial coronation" (Inaugural Committee 1977:72). Furthermore, the recognition by political candidates of the importance of this "symbolic agenda" was reiterated during the 1992 campaign in the controversies over "Murphy Brown" as a parental role model and the attempts by both Bill Clinton and George Bush to portray themselves as pro-family in their acceptance speeches to their parties, albeit on different grounds.

An important example of the role of values and worldviews in the cycle of American political ritual can be seen in the singing of the National Anthem by Roseanne Barr in July 1990. Although not a Presidential election year, the furor she created by attempting to make comedy out of the American sacred song was substantial (McLeod 1991b:102-106). Her attempt at a humorous rendering of the National Anthem to a crowd of over 30,000 at a baseball game between the Cincinnati Reds and the San Diego Padres was a significant violation of sacred symbolic space. If there were no dominant organic American political culture, the entire incident would have passed without any comment or notoriety. As it was, her attempt at a humorous rendition of the most important sacred song in the cult of the Divine America was considered by many Americans as the vocal equivalent of flag burning. As Robert Merrill, opera star and fellow singer of the National Anthem at nine World Series games noted "I almost upchuked my dinner . . . it was to me, like burning the flag" (*USA Today*, front page article, July 27, 1990). The flag and the President are both symbolic icons of the republic, and it is noteworthy that such symbols become issues in virtually every Presidential election. The importance of the flag to Americans and importance of symbols in Presidential campaigns was underscored in 1988 in the debates over the Pledge of Allegiance, the Flag Amendment, and other patriotic themes

(McLeod 1991b:110-115). D. Kertzer has advanced the following summary of the ritualization of the American Presidential cycle:

> The greatest political sociodrama and the most elaborate competi-
> tive use of ritual in American politics come each four years with
> the campaign for the Presidency. The metaphor of a journey guides
> the entire enterprise; campaign as pilgrimage. The population is
> supposed to get to 'know' the candidate through his highly ritual-
> ized appearances, while the candidate uses the rites to present a cer-
> tain image of himself and to use symbols to both define and to ig-
> nite the emotions (Kertzer 1987:108).

The importance of ritualizing accession to office in state-level societies lies in the pubic recognition of leadership. Even in those societies which are puta-tively rational, the significance of these ceremonies underlies cultural pre-dictably. Not all societies possess state-level institutions, nor do all societies have monarchs, elected or hereditary (Mair 1970; Middleton 1966). But for those which do possess such institutions, rituals of installation are critical. Yamaguchi argues that:

> Kingship, therefore, is nothing more than the dramatic space which
> is capable of being stabilized in the imagination of peoples as a
> symbolic universe symbolizing the inner life of the individual. . . .
> This explains why kingship furnishes the most widely used model
> of ritual political and mythical transcendence, even in those soci-
> eties where this was already overtaken by other phenomena as a po-
> litical institution (Yamaguchi 1972:68).

Rituals of installation to office vary widely from culture to culture but their function remains relatively constant. Rituals of installation in state level soci-eties legitimize the role of the political leader vis-á-vis followers within the po-litical community (Bailey 1969). As La Fontaine notes: "usually power and au-thority are associated, for power is legitimized by an appeal to moral principles, and authority given access to economic and political power. Ritual is concerned with legitimacy, reaffirming the divisions and hierarchies that are indispensable to authority" (La Fontaine 1985:17).

In this way, rituals of installation provide symbolic affirmations for political community which the leader serves or directs. The impact of these rituals is en-hanced by their appeals to worldviews, symbols, icons, and other discourses which are culture-specific and emotionally compelling. The ritual event provides an expressive metaphor of power to unify complex political systems. The degree to which political rituals impose themselves upon the political culture of the governed is a critical aspect of the study of political ritual in complex society.

In a previous paper (McLeod 1991a) I identified a threefold continuum of political ritual in Presidential campaigns in the United States: secular, phatic, and sacred ritual events. In the ritual cycle of Presidential selection and Inauguration, all three types are present. The Inauguration itself is simply the end point of the ritual cycle of the American Presidency. The selection of the President and the ritual installation of the winner constitutes a Presidential ritual cycle which is one of the most important identifiers of American political culture. The Inauguration, therefore, cannot be understood without seeing this ritual as the resolution of a complex system of political conflict. In *The Inaugural Story, 1789-1969*, this point was clearly recognized by the Inaugural Committee: "The Inauguration of a President is the high point in the four year cycle of American government. It is a solemn occasion; it is a gala occasion; it is a time of pomp and circumstance, and of pageantry and gaiety of parades, balls and receptions" (1969:7).

KINGS AND PRESIDENTS: THE AMERICAN MONARCHY IN PERSPECTIVE

The problem of succession to high office is a critical one for all forms of complex political systems to one degree or another. This problem is particularly acute in systems which possess a single high political office in which authority is vested to a large degree. In some of these systems, the role of succession has a unifying force in the society is underpinned and by the belief that the highest official in the culture is semidivine or derived directly from a legendary or mythical figure (Ohnuki-Tierney 1991; Hughes 1969, 1982). In other systems, the highest political office is seen as directly related to the ancestors, and the relationship between the power-holder and the ancestral line is stressed. This is true for the Bunyoro (Beattie 1964), the Zulu (Gluckman 1970), the Swazi (Kuper 1947), and a host of others (Mair 1970:214-270). For example, Gluckman describes the dynamics of Zulu kingship:

> What tradition and history was common to all Zulu had to be told in the names of the Zulu kings, and it was largely their common sentiment about the king which united all Zulu as members of the nation. At the great first fruits ceremonies and war-rites, the king was strengthened and cleansed in the names of the ancestors, and the welfare of the country was held to depend on them. This ceremonial position of the king was backed by his ancestral spirits (Gluckman 1970:30) .

L. Mair (1970:240-270) notes important differences between those societies which recognize the paramount chief or king as a mystical figure and those in which it is the relationship between clanship and power which is at issue. In either case, mythology, worldview, and ritual are all interconnected parts of that complex whole which constitutes the political aspect of culture in these societies. But succession is often a trying process for these societies, and rival princes can and do contravene the process of the installation of the king. Often, this difficulty is overcome by adopting a rule of succession which invokes either primogeniture or ultimogeniture. Though sound in theory, these rules often fail in practice.

The Western tradition is also replete with stories concerning the difficulties of succession to high office. As the succession of King David demonstrates, the difficulties of determining an appropriate heir are inherent in the monarchy. The woes of Absalom (2 Samuel 16) and the claims of Adonijah (1 Kings 11) are proof of this, as are the prayers of Solomon (2 Chronicles 6-7) concerning the problems of rulership. The problems of succession to the Imperial office of Rome (Gibbon 1952; Graves 1970) also exemplify the intrinsic quandries that succession poses: "In elective monarchies the vacancy of the throne is a moment big with danger and mischief" (Gibbon 1952: 101).

These problems have also attended the English monarchy, as the persistence of the Robin Hood legend clearly attests. While there is little doubt that Richard should be the king according to the cultural rule system, John, his half-brother and rival prince, is clearly not satisfied with this situation and tries to rewrite both history and culture for his own benefit. Kertzer cites another telling example from British history:

> A man becomes a king because he comes to be treated as a king. Ritual is used to constitute power, not just reflect power that already exists. This becomes most evident where authority is under attack. In 1485, the Tudors were struggling in England against their rivals armies and it was not clear just who would win. The ritual coronation of Henry VII at Westminister in that year, and his subsequent marriage to Elizabeth, symbolically uniting the rival houses of York and Lancaster, were important parts of his victorious political campaign (Kertzer 1987:25).

M. Southwold's (1968:128-147) analysis of the problems of succession among the Ganda princes and commoners analyzes a similar dilemma in the political culture of an East African kingdom. The rise and fall of Chinese dynasties throughout the long imperial history of China clearly indicates the problematic nature of the succession to power (Fairbank, Reichshauer, and Craig 1978:1-278), as does the maintenance of the Pharaonic tradition over 2,500 years in Egypt, albeit through a multitude of dynasties or ruling families (Wenke 1990).

The Japanese developed an expressly binary answer to this problem of succession to a divine office. After the reign of the Fujiwaras (858-1160), the system of ritual and political power in Japan became bifurcated between the Regents and later the Shoguns who held the military and political power, and the

Emperor, who came to be the source of ritual authority and the symbol of the state.[2] With few exceptions, from that time on, the political/military role of ruler was carried out by the family who held the Regency or the Shogunate, while the symbolic power rested in the hands of the Imperial line. The two lines were often intermarried, it is true; but the distinction between ritual and political power instituted by the Fujiwaras is a key to the continuity of the Imperial line to the present day. It should be noted that this constitutes the longest continuous monarchical line on the planet. As J. Fairbank, E. Reichsauer, and A. Craig point out: "Despite their great power, however, the Fujiwara never made the slightest move toward usurping the throne. The concept of hereditary authority and the special religious aura of the Imperial line were too strong. It gradually became accepted, however, that the emperors reigned but did not rule" (Fairbank, Reichsauer, and Craig 1978:351). This formula was ultimately accepted in Britain as well, although at a much later date: "She (the Queen) does not steer the ship, but she must make sure that there is a man (sic) at the wheel" (Jennings 1972:43).

This desire for permanence and predictability is demonstrated by the ritual of the Presidential cycle. The need for a central symbol which can unite the nation in times of stress is only one side of the equation, however. The other obligation of the President's national symbol is to maintain the symbolic integrity of the Presidential office. When the rules of that integrity are violated, the power of the symbol system may not be enough to prevent the downfall of an incumbent president, icon or not:

> For if a leader must judge the loyalty, courage, and devotion of his
> followers, his followers, in turn, must judge that leader's majesty
> and power. When the followers have been taught to believe deeply
> in transcendent principles which uphold social order, they watch
> carefully to see that their leaders play roles in keeping with such
> principles (Duncan 1968:203).

Lyndon Johnson's decision to not seek re-election is a clear example of the fact, as is the exit from office of Richard Nixon over the Watergate scandal.

Unlike monarchs in other cultures, the electoral system in the United States guarantees that symbol and performance are related through the power of public opinion and the ballot box. This does not mean, however, that the process of choosing our "king" is entirely rational; it simply means that the process of selection of a President differs from that of choosing a monarch. The symbolic space both occupy after they have been chosen is relatively similar. The Inauguration is essentially a reintegration rite:

> The Inauguration is something of a catharsis for the American peo-
> ple—an act of healing after the divisiveness of a political cam-
> paign. Through all the pageantry and whoop-di-do comes the mes-

sage that one side has lost, the leader on the other side is going to do everything possible to unite the nation behind him.   The Inauguration is the most visible affirmation we have of our faith in institutions, and when it is over, one more symbolic act is taken. The new President's home that night is the nation's home—the most historic building in Washington, D.C.—and he sleeps where every President since John Adams has rested. Because he is there, that house is a symbol of power and sovereignty, but it is also the home of a man and his family—the one man who represents us all (Inaugural Committee 1977:72).

THE CLINTON INAUGURATION OF 1993

An important watershed was reached with the Clinton Inauguration of 1993 in terms of reaching out to the multicultural realities of the new America of the post-industrial age. Wendell Ford, Senator from Kentucky and Chair of the Inaugural festivities, presided over the most integrative Inauguration in the history of the event. In 1905, Geronimo and Quanah Parker had both participated in the Inaugural Parade, but this was more a reminder of the closing of the frontier than a real attempt at the recognition of the multicultural realities of American culture. In the Inauguration festivities of 1993, more than 125 ethnic groups participated in the parades, and for the first time, gay and lesbian groups were officiallly included in the process. Groups represented Polish-Americans, Italian-Americans, Hispanic-Americans, and a host of other "hyphenated Americans," heralding the ritual inclusion of the multicultural groups which characterize America of the 1990s. The Inauguration of 1993 was a ritual of inclusion.

There were standard elements in the Inauguration ritual as well that reflected the historic roots of contemporary American culture. The Reverend Billy Graham led the ritual prayer, and Bill Clinton repeated Washington's "So help me God" prayer as Mrs. Clinton held the Inauguration Bible. This Bible was steeped in family tradition, having been presented to Clinton by his grandmother while he was still a very young child. The Ballard High School choir sang favorites of the old South, including "My Old Kentucky Home," while the Marine Corps Band played the music of John Pillip Sousa both before and after the formal ceremonies. Celebrities of all kinds were present, from Bishop Desmond Tutu of South Africa to Jack Nicholson of Hollywood; from Newt Gingrich on the Republican right to Ron Dellums of the Democratic left. An atmosphere of celebration and hope pervaded the ceremonies and the continuity of the traditional Inaugural oath insured the transfer of power to the forty-second President of the United States.

But there were other, less traditional elements as well. Just before Clinton was sworn in to the office of President, the strains of the music of "Monty

Python" were played—harking back to President Clinton's generational loyalties as the first President of the so-called "baby-boom" or post-Vietnam generation. The all-Black Philander Smith College Choir performed the song "City on the Hill" written especially for the Inauguration by Black artist and scholar Marvin V. Curtis. The concentration on non-Whites was also evident throughout the television coverage of all four networks: ABC, NBC, CBS, and CNN. Many faces from the non-Anglo population were shown in the television coverage of the Clinton Inaugural. This emphasis on minorities was highlighted by the ritual selection of Maya Angelou, Black poet and scholar from Wake Forest University, to be the keynote speaker following the Inauguration speech.

Clinton's Inaugural speech was a profound reiteration of his consistent campaign appeal for *change* (McLeod 1993:1-11). In the speech, he saluted the America of George Bush, but ritually identified his new status by saying that ". . . a generation raised in the shadow of the Cold War assumes new responsibilities." He also appealed to what he called "the mystery of American Renewal" by stating: "This ceremony is held in the depths of winter, but by the words we speak and the faces we show the world we force the spring. A spring reborn in the world's democracy." This call to revitalization was summarized in his rhetoric that the people of the United States must "Reinvent America." His call for change was reinforced through the rhetoric of inclusion of all people in the American Dream. Clinton stated that "We must do what America does best—offer more opportunity *to* all and demand more responsibility *from* all."

Clinton's Inauguration rituals reinforced the theme of multiculturalism and inclusion, and ceremonially infused new symbols into the national civil religion. Whether or not these symbols will have lasting force for the future has yet to be seen; but clearly, the political ritual of the Inauguration was a symbolic watershed in the change of the guard and the life of the national religion. To the extent that ritual symbolism can create substantial changes in national perspective, the Clinton Inauguration of 1993 will be remembered as a spectacular departure from the dominant Anglo culture so often represented in Inauguration ceremonies and will be remembered as one of the most profound ritual events in the life of the national civil religion.

CONCLUSION

The ritual aspects of the Presidential initiation cycle constitute an important focus for the identity of the the American people. As C. Kluckhohn noted in his general theory of ritual: "myths and rituals are adaptive from the point of view of the society in that they promote social solidarity, enhance the integration of society by providing a formalized statement of its ultimate value attitudes . . . thus protecting cultural continuity and stabilizing society" (Kluckhohn 1968:155). Members of American political culture calculate cultural time and national identity through these ritual events. The selection and Inauguration of the President indicates that the members of the culture are transformed. They are undergoing a change of status; clearly a publicly held ritual event which involves the majority of adult members of a society is an important aspect of social solidarity for any culture. The political rituals which endorse the legitimacy of members of the political elite have repercussions for all members of the culture, voters or not.

People of the United States are transformed by each Presidential election as the realities of power in the wider society change with the installation of a new President. A change of Presidents can signal a change of national mood or in cultural values that were previously held. Essentially after the candidates are selected, and before the election is held, the entire culture is in a liminal state. Then, before the President-elect is confirmed in January, the tension of the ritual fades while the country waits for installation. In this sense, it is clear that the Presidential election and installation cycle constitutes a rite of passage for the nation as a whole.

The relationship between symbols and field of action is clearly demonstrated here. The levers of Presidential power, such as Commander in Chief of the Armed Forces, Director of the Federal Budget, and a host of other executive functions do not accrue to the President-elect simply through the election itself. In order for the candidate to control the levers of power rather than simply gain access to office, the ritual of installation must first take place.

For a significant proportion of the people of the United States, the President's Inauguration serves as a public demonstration of the legitimacy of the entire process of political campaigning and electioneering. As the Inaugural Book of George Bush's accession to power explains:

> The Inauguration of an American president is at once symbol and political reality. It is the fusion, in splendid ceremony, of these two qualities that create the significance of each Inauguration.
>
> Conducted in the very seat of national power, the Inauguration celebrates a government established and empowered by the 'consent of the governed.' Attended by hundreds of thousands of private citizens and by all members of Congress, it suggests a nation united in a peaceful co-existence of political opponents.
>
> Since the first Inauguration, the ceremony has represented the orderly transfer of power and the institutional stability of the oldest democratic state. Each Inauguration thereby imparts a sense of renewal and hope to the people of the United States and to foreign observers who view the American presidency as an example of a leadership assumed in peace and unscarred by violent dissension (American Bicentennial Presidential Inauguration Committee 1989: 3).

A pointed question to ask about the Presidential Inauguration ritual is whether or not these ceremonies are monocultural or multicultural in scope and focus. To the extent that the United States is seen as a melting pot under the auspices of the Constitution, the President's Inauguration can be seen as a monocultural event. All of the various races, languages, ethnic groups, and religious are subsumed under a single political mantle. Thus, the Presidential Inauguration acts to re-enforce the integrity of the oneness of the American culture as a whole. In recent times, however, the Presidential Inauguration has become more multicultural in its focus and scope. For example, Miss Indian America was featured in the 1969 Inaugural and increasingly by particular ethnic and social groups have been identified within the context of the Inauguration. The references to the Constitution within the context of the Inauguration ritual itself are such attempts to achieve the goals stated in the national motto "E Pluribus Unum"; that is, out of many, one. There have been tacit recognitions on the part of the Presidential inaugurees through rhetoric that the United States is now an extremely multicultural society. But it is also clear that framework of difference is subordinate to similarity in the dominant cultural matrix.

While still strong in terms of values, the dominant culture must contend with a host of subcultures each claiming its own validity within the complex political whole. If the *raison d'etre* of the Presidential ritual cycle is the reintegration of the culture after significant political conflict, then the Inauguration ceremonies must reflect the multicultural nature of the new American society. Rituals of the installation of kings among the Zulu and Swazi show us that the Presidential Inauguration ritual itself is not a ritual of rebellion. That function is fulfilled by the Presidential campaigning and election process. Rather, the Inauguration functions as an attempt at inclusion and incorporation. Subgroups within the society are not allowed, nor are they expected to perform in such a way as to demonstrate symbolically the hostility which they most certainly feel toward the dominant political culture.

As Novak has observed: "If a nation is a religion, then all citizens need to be nourished by that religion. All need to see reflected in its liturgies and symbols a confirmation of the meaning and worth of their own lives. The most visible civil religion of the United States is remarkably snobbish and limited in the range of its official symbols" (Novak 1974:308). As the United States becomes a truly multicultural society, the rituals which underpin and legitimize power must become correspondingly multicultural in scope and premise. While there is no need to abandon the traditional rituals associated with the historic patterns of Inaugurations, the solidarity of the culture requires that the patterns of difference be recognized and validated through the national ritual cycle. Tokenism cannot accomplish this, nor can the realities of the emerging multicultural America be kept underground for long. The Presidency, the Constitution, and the Inauguration process have survived for over 200 years because they are changing and dynamic institutions. Symbols become substance because they are truly the representations which we make of ourselves, and they need to reflect the *zeitgeist* of contemporary America in a significant way.

The dominant Anglo culture has been able to mask the realities of a multi-cultural America through election and installation rituals up to this point. If the cycle of American Presidential ritual is truly to become an accurate representation of the cultures of America, integration of non-Anglos into the ritual process must continue to be a priority. Ritual process has the power to effect cultural change. Perhaps the symbolic unity of the Presidential cycle can be come a reality.

NOTES

First, I would like to thank Pam Frese for her editorial judgment and encouragement in the work. Her timely comments were excellent and her editorial efforts superb. Second, Dr. Abe Goh for his efforts in reviewing the section on Japan. Finally, I wish to thank the staff of Ohio State University (Mansfield campus) for their work on typing and research support. Thanks to you all.

1. Rituals of installation and selection have been the object of study since Gluckman's classical analysis of the Swazi *incwala* ritual (1963). The restudy of that same ritual by B. Lincoln (1989) and the analysis of rituals in the Israeli Labor Party as analyzed by M. Aronoff (1980) are two of the more important studies derived from that work. These political rituals constitute an important focus for the analysis of integration and consolidation of political power over time and act as a template upon which the right to rule or political legitimacy (Kertzer 1987; Weber 1968) is predicated. Traditional political rituals have been studied by A. Southall (1965), M. Fortes and E.E. Evans-Pitchard (1970), D. Hughes (1982), H. Kuper (1947), J. Middleton (1966) and a host of others. The study of modern political rituals as rituals of authorization can be traced directly to M. Abélès analysis (1988) of the pilgrimage and Inauguration of François Mitterand of France. In that article Abélès noted that political rituals in complex societies are critical aspects of political culture and important phenomena for study by political anthropologists. Other important contributions in this field include M. Abélès (1992), A. Bocock (1974), R.A. Kideckel (1983), J. Kubik (1989), and J. McLeod (1991a).

The relationships between political ritual, political rhetoric, and political symbolism have been identified and analyzed by D. Kertzer (1987). Civil religion has been examined by R. Bellah (1980), W.L. Bennett (1979, 1980), and D. Adams (1987). The relationships between symbol, ritual, and political culture have been explored by many analysts including F.G. Bailey (1981), A. Cohen (1975, 1979), J. Ellul (1967), R. Paine (1981), J. Scott (1990), and M. Swartz, V. Turner, and A. Tuden (1966). Perhaps the most familiar analysis of political symbolism and political ritual in the installation of the American presidency is M. Novak's (1974) *Choosing Our King*, in which he argues that the American President is an elected monarch.

2. The Fujiwaras were Regents to the Imperial throne, but the term "Shogun" did not become popular until the Edo period (1600-1868). However, it is the bifurcation of political/military and symbolic power which is my major point here. I am indebted to Abe Goh of Hiroshima University for pointing this out to me in a personal communication.

BIBLIOGRAPHY

Abélès, M.
   1988 "Modern Political Ritual: Ethnography of an Inauguration and a
   Pilgrimage by President Mitterand." *Current Anthropology* 29(3):391-404.

   1992 "Anthropology Politique de la Modernite!" *L'Homme* 121, 32(1):15-30
   (January-March).

Adams, D.
   1987 "Ronald Reagan's 'Revival': Voluntarism as a Theme in Reagan's Civil
   Religion." *Sociological Analysis* 40(1):17-29.

Almond, G., and G.B. Powell
   1966b *Comparative Politics*. Boston: Little Brown.

American Bicentennial Presidential Inauguration Committee
   1989 *200 Hundred Years of the American Presidency: The 1989 Inauguration
   Story*. Norfolk: Donning.

Aronoff, M.
   1980 "Ideology and Interest: The Dialectics of Politics." In *Political
   Anthropology Yearbook*. Vol. 1. M. Aranoff (ed.) New York: Crowell. Pp. 1-
   29.

Bailey, F.G.
   1969 *Strategems and Spoils*. New York: Schocken Books.

   1981 "Dimensions of Rhetoric in Conditions of Uncertainty. " In *Politically
   Speaking*. R. Paine (ed.) Philadelphia: Institute for the Study of Human Issues.

Barthes, R.
   1972 *Mythologies*. London: Jonathan Cape.

Beattie, J.
   1964 *Other Cultures*. New York: Free Press.

Bellah, R.
   1980 "Civil Religion in America." In *Beyond Belief: Essays on Religion in a
   Post Traditional World*. R. Bella (ed.) New York: Harper and Row. Pp. 168-192.

Bennett, W. L.
   1979 "Imitation, Ambiguity, and Drama in Political Life: Civil Religion and
   the Dilemmas of Public Morality." *Journal of Politics* 41:106-133.

   1980 "The Pardox of Public Discourse: A Framework for the Analysis of
   Political Accounts." *Journal of Politics* 42:792-817.

Birnbaum, N.
   1955 "Monarchs and Sociologists: A Reply to Professor Shils and Mr. Young."
   Sociological Review (NS) 3: 5-23.

Bloch, M.
   1977 "The Past and the Present in the Present." *Man* 12(3 & 4):278-292.

Boas, F.
   1986 [1978] *Anthropology and Modern Life*. New York: Dover Publications.

Bocock, R.
1974 *Ritual in Industrial Society*. London: Allen and Unwin.

Cohen, A.
1975 *Focaltown: The Management of Myths*. Manchester: Manchester University Press.

1979 "Political Symbolism." *Annual Reviews of Anthropology* 8:87-113.

Duncan, H.
1968 *Symbols in Society*. London: Oxford University Press.

Durbin, L.
1977 *Inaugural Cavalcade*. New York: Dodd, Mead.

Ellul, J.
1967 *The Political Illusion*. New York: Vintage.

Fairbank, J., E. Reischauer, and A. Craig
1978 *East Asia: Tradition and Transformation*. Boston: Houghton, Mifflin.

Firth R.
1973 *Symbols: Public and Private*. Ithaca: Cornell University Press.

Fortes, M., and E.E. Evans-Pritchard
1970 "Introduction." In *African Political Systems*. M. Fortes and E.E. Evans-Pritchard (eds.) London: Oxford University Press.

Fried, M.
1967 *The Evolution of Political Society*. New York: Random House.

Gibbon, E.
1952 *The Decline and Fall of the Roman Empire*. New York: Viking Press.

"George Washington: Journey to the Presidency."
1989 Washington, DC: Commission on the Bicentennial of the U.S. Constitution.

Gluckman, M.
1963 *Order and Rebellion in Tribal Africa*. London: Cohen and West.

1965 *Politics, Law, and Ritual in Primitive Society*. Manchester: Manchester University Press.

1970 "The Kingdom of the Zulu of South Africa." In *African Political Systems*. M. Fortes and E.E. Evans-Pritchard (eds.) London: Oxford University Press. Pp. 25-56.

Graves, R.
1970 *I, Claudius*. London: Book Club Books.

Herzog, H.
1987 "The Election Campaign as a Liminal Stage: Negotiation Over Meanings." *Sociological Review* 35:559-574.

Hughes, D.
1969 "Reciprocal Influence of Traditional and Democratic Leadership Roles on Ponape." *Ethnology* 8(3):278-291.

1982 "Continuity of Indigenous Ponapean Social Structure and Stratification."
Oceania 53(1):5-18.

Inaugural Committee (U.S.)
1977 *"A New Spirit, a New Commitment, a New America": The Inauguration of
President Jimmy Carter and Vice President Walter F. Mondale: The Official 1977
Inaugural Book.* New York: Bantam Books.

The Inaugural Story: 1789-1969
1969 Editors of American Heritage Magazine and the 1969 Inaugural Book
Committee. Norfolk: American Heritage Publishing.

Jennings, I.
1972 *The Queen's Government.* London: Pelican

Kertzer, D.
1987 *Ritual, Politics, and Power.* New Haven: Yale University Press.

Kideckel, R.A.
1983 "Secular Ritual and Social Change: A Romanian Case." *Anthropological
Quarterly* 56:69-75.

Kluckhohn, C.
1968 "Myth and Ritual: A General Theory." In *Studies on Mythology.* Robert
Georges (ed.) Homewood, IL: Dorsey Press. Pp. 142-167.

Kubik, J.
1989 "John Paul II's First Visit to Poland and the Collapse of the Official
Marxist-Leninist Discourse." Working Paper Series. Center for Research on
Politics and Social Organization. Cambridge: Harvard University.

Kuper, H.
1947 *An African Aristocracy: Rank Among the Swazi of Bechuanaland.*
London: Oxford University Press.

La Fontaine, J.
1985 *Initiation.* London: Pelican.

Lincoln, B.
1989 *Discourse and the Construction of Society.* London: Oxford University
Press.

Mair, L.
1970 *Primitive Government.* London: Pelican Books.

Marx, K.
1964 *Karl Marx: Selected Writings in Sociology and Social History.*
M. Bottomore and M. Rubel (eds.) New York: McGraw Hill.

McLeod, J.
1990a "Deconstructing Bush: Political Rhetoric and the Bush Campaign."
International Journal of Moral and Social Studies 5(1):1-22.

1990b "Ritual in Corporate Culture Studies." *The Journal of Ritual Studies*
4(1):85-97.

1991a "Ritual and Rhetoric in Presidential Politics." *Central Issues in Anthropology* 9 (Spring).

1991b "The Cult of the Divine America: Ritual, Symbol, and Mystification in American Political Culture." *International Journal of Moral and Social Studies* 6(2):1-24.

1993 "Rhetoric and Ritual in the Age of Teledemocracy: The American Presidential Campaign of 1992." *The Canadian Journal of Rhetorical Studies*, 3:1-31. (Carleton University for Rhetorical Studies)

McLeod, J., and Abe Goh
1991 "Worldviews, Ritual, and Rhetoric in Presidential Politics." *Speech Communication Education* 4:43-60. (Tokyo University)

Middleton, J.
1966 *The Lugbara of Uganda*. New York: Holt, Rinehart, and Winston.

Moore, S.F. and B. Myerhoff
1977 *Secular Ritual*. Amsterdam: Van Gorcum.

Novak, M.
1974 *Choosing Our King: Powerful Symbols in Presidential Politics*. New York: Macmillan.

Oberg, A.
1970 "The Kingdom of the Ankole in Uganda." In *African Political Systems*. M. Fortes and E.E. Evans-Pritchard (eds.) London: Oxford University Press. Pp. 121-164.

Ohnuki-Tierney, E.
1991 "The Emperor of Japan as Deity (Kami)." *Ethnology* 30(18):199-215.

Ortner, S.
1973 "On Key Symbols." *American Anthropologist* 75(5):1338-1346.

Paine, R.
1981 *Politically Speaking*. Philadelphia: Institute for Human Issues.

Richards, A.
1982 *Chisungu*. London: Tavistock.

Scott, J.
1990 *Domination and the Arts of Resistance: Hidden Transcripts*. New Haven: Yale University Press.

Shils, E., and M. Young
1953 "The Meaning of the Coronation." *Sociological Review* (NS) 1:63-81.

Southall, A.
1965 "A Critique of the Typology of African States and Political Systems." In *Political Systems and the Distribution of Power*. M. Banton (ed.) London: ASA Monographs Series. Pp. 119-130.

Southwold, M.
    1968 "The History of a History: Royal Succession in Buganda." In *History and Social Anthropology*. I.M. Lewis (ed.) A.S.A. Monograph No. 7. London: Tavistock.   Pp. 128-149.

Swartz, M., V. Turner, and A. Tuden
    1966 *Political Anthropology*. Chicago: Aldine.

Turner, V.
    1967 *The Forest of Symbols*. Ithaca: Cornell University Press.

    1974 *Dramas, Fields & Metaphors*. Ithaca: Cornell University Press.

Warner, W.L.
    1959 *The Living and the Dead*. New Haven: Yale University Press.

Weber, M.
    1968 *Max Weber on Charisma and Institution Building*. Chicago: University of Chicago Press.

Wenke, R.
    1990 *Patterns in Prehistory*. London: Oxford University Press.

Yamaguchi, M.
    1972 "Kingship as a System of Myth: An Essay in Synthesis." *Diogenes* 78(3): 43-70.

Index

Alcoholism, and ritual drinking, 166, 171-74

American culture: elite as ethnographic subject in, 178-79; gender metaphors in, 95-97; language and identity in, 123-24; as melting pot, 44-45; multiculturalism of, 44-45, 151-54, 213. *See also* Anglo-American culture

American Eskimos. *See* Inupiat Eskimos

American Indians. *See* Native Americans; Waccamaw Sioux

Angelou, Maya, 214

Anglo-American culture, 110 n.1, 192 n.1; gendered domains in, 94-98, 105-10; nature and culture in, 94-98, 110

Asian immigrants, 149-50, 159, 160. *See also* Punjabi-Mexican community

Azusa Street revival, Los Angeles, 65

Barr, Roseanne, 208

Biethnic community. *See* Punjabi-Mexican community

Black churches. *See* Testimony service

Borderlands, Mexican, 121-22, 136 n.7

Borderlands, U.S., 135 n.5; deportation and immigration practices in, 122-23; economy of, 121-24. *See also* Mexican-Hispanic community

Bush, George, 208

Calendric cycles, 126-33

Carrington, John, 180

Carter, Jimmy, 208

Catholic church, 38, 120, 131, 147

Celebratory ritual: communal drinking as, 161-63; and historical change, 145; versus play, 152. *See also specific ethnic community*

Cemeteries, 100-101, 110 n.3

Ceremony, versus ritual, 197-98

Ceremony of homecoming, 54-55

Cherokees, 76, 79

Chief Freeman, 79, 81

City of God, 55-56, 57

Civic ritual, 55

Civil religion, and political ritual, 214, 217 n.1

Civil Rights Act of 1964, 78, 81

Civitas, 55-56

Simpson-Rodino Immigration
Reform and Control Act
(IRCA), 123
Singing. *See* Ritual songs
Sisala of Ghana, 10
Social class rituals. *See* Coronation
in San Antonio
Social drama, phases of, 76-77
Social order: as model for reality,
190; in ritualized social events,
177; and socially-approved
proper relations, 121. *See also*
Class; Gender
Songs, sacred. *See* Ritual songs
Southern Presbyterianism: City of
God in, 55, 56-57; communal
obligations in, 51; Covenant
people doctrine in, 50, 52-54,
56-57; family of faith idea in,
53, 56; family-ancestor tradition
in, 52-54; homecoming
ceremony in, 54; individual
vocation in, 51; kindred tradition
in, 51-55; Pilgrimage complex
in, 50, 53; symbolism in, 50-51
Spanish-Pakistanis, 149
Spassfest festival, 38
Spectacle, ritualized. *See*
Coronation in San Antonio
Spirit possession, 10
St. George's Greek Orthodox
church, 40
Stereotypes, and ethnic identity, 44
Stories-telling, 62
Structuralist theory, and Inupiat
culture, 26-33 Superabundance,
cultural role of, 30
Swazi Incwala ritual, 203-4, 217
n.1
Symbolism: and economic factors,
200-201; as ethnic markers, 42;

and false consciousness, 199-
200; and group identity, 36-38,
39; and monarchy, 199; in
political ritual, 197-202, 204,
208-9

Testimony service: cadential rite in,
66-68; coherence factor in, 66;
communitas in, 64, 69; I-Thou
relation in, 64, 68; singing in,
62-64, 65-68; singing-testifying
isochronism in, 65-70; story-
telling in, 62
Theocracy, 55-56
Town, as religious entity, 55-56,
57
Trobriand mortuary ritual, 93

Waccamaw Siouan Development
Association (WSDA), 79, 81
Waccamaw Sioux: racial harmony
of, 86; and school desegration,
78-80. *See also* Powwow
Whaling festival, 15, 20-25;
structural analysis of, 26-33;
whale as spirit in, 17-18; and
whaling hunt, 15-19; woman as
shaman in, 17, 22, 24. *See also*
Inupiat Eskimos
Women: as creators of cultural
identity, 133-34; and family
identity, 94; in funeral ritual,
98; as inhabitant of borderlands,
153-54; mediating role of, 153-
54; spiritual role of, 17, 22, 24;
as wage earners, 120-21, 134
n.3. *See also* Gender

Zulu kingship, 210

About the Contributors

John M. Coggeshall received a Ph.D. in Anthropology from Southern Illinois University (Carbondale) and currently serves as an Associate Professor of Anthropology at Clemson University. Coggeshall's publications include *Vernacular Architecture in Southern Illinois* (with Jo Anne Nast), *Transcending Boundaries: Multidisciplinary Approaches to the Study of Gender* (coedited with Pamela R. Frese), and articles on American folklore and prisoner culture appearing in the *Journal of American Folklore, Anthropology Today*, and *Southern Folklore Quarterly*.

Madeline Duntley teaches Ritual Studies and Religion in America at The College of Wooster, Wooster, Ohio. Duntley is a founding and contributing editor of the *Journal of Ritual Studies* and she has a special interest in ritual theory and historical method. Duntley wrote an article on ritual in the United States for the *Anthropology of Religion: A Handbook of Method and Theory* (Stephen Glazier, ed.) and did fieldwork among Seattle's Asian-American urban Christians for *The Gods of the City: Religion and the Contemporary Urban Landscape* (Robert A. Orsi, ed.). Currently, Dr. Duntley is writing *Ritual, Nonconformity, and Religious Liberty*, a book addressing the role of ritual and marginality in religious liberty debates.

Pamela R. Frese received her Ph.D. from the University of Virginia and is an Associate Professor in the sociology and anthropology department at the College of Wooster, Wooster, Ohio. In addition to *Transcending Boundaries* (coedited with John M. Coggeshall), Frese has conducted research and published on Anglo-American lifecycle rituals and ritual symbolism, marriage rituals in world cultures, American food beliefs and practices, and the gendered symbolism in American yard decorations. Her work appears in *The Encyclopedia of Religion* (Mircea Eliade, ed.), *Food and Foodways,* and *Visual Anthropology*. She is completing a manuscript on the historic and contemporary symbolism in the Anglo-American wedding ritual.

Michaele Thurgood Haynes is a doctoral student in anthropology at the University of Texas at Austin. Her dissertation topic is the San Antonio Coronation, the subject of her essay. She is interested in material culture, specifically personal appearance, as a reflection of relationships on both macro and micro levels and as means of enacting relations. She has presented papers on changes in political organization as seen in the clothing of Delaware Indians, on clothing choices made by frontier women, and on clothing made of natural products such as citrus peel as part of a community-based agricultural fair. "Delaware Clothing as Indicator of Personal Identity" was published in *New Jersey Folklife*, vol. xiv, 1988.

Karen Leonard is a Professor of anthropology at the University of California, Irvine. Her Ph.D. was in history, and she publishes on the social history and anthropology of India and on Asian-Americans in California. Dr. Leonard's work is primarily on caste, ethnicity, and family and life history. Related publications include: *Making Ethnic Choices: California's Punjabi-Mexican-Americans*; "Immigrant Punjabis in Early Twentieth-Century California" in *Social and Gender Boundaries in the United States* (Sucheng Chan, ed.); "Pioneer Voices from California: Reflections on Race, Religion, and Ethnicity" in *The Sikh Diaspora: Migration and the Experience beyond Punjab* (N. Gerald Barrier and Verne A. Dusenbery, eds.); "Ethnic Identity and Gender: South Asians in the United States" in *Ethnicity, Identity, and Migration* (Milton Israel and N.K. Wagle, eds.); "Finding One's Own Place: the Imposition of Asian Landscapes on Rural California" in *Culture, Power, Place: Explorations in Critical Anthropology* (James Ferguson, Akhil Gupta, and Roger Rouse, eds.).

Patricia B. Lerch earned her doctoral degree from Ohio State University and is an Associate Professor of anthropology at University of North Carolina, Wilmington. Her research and publications cover spiritism in Brazil, tourism in Barbados, and the Waccamaw Indians of North Carolina. Her most recent publications include: "State Recognized Indians of North Carolina, Including a History of the Waccamaw Sioux" in *Indians of the Southeastern U.S. in the Late 20th Century* (J. Anthony Paredes ed.); "Tourism as a Factor in Development: Implications for Gender and Work in Barbados" (with D. Levy) in *Gender and Society* 5 (March 1991, No. 1:6567-85); "Predicting Success in Barbardos' Tourist Industry" (with D. Levy) in *Human Organization* 49 (Winter 1990, No. 4:355-363); and "An Explanation for the Predominance of Women in the Umbanda Cults of Porto Alegre, Brazile" in *Urban Anthropology* (1982, 11:237-261).

Rachel Mason received her Ph.D. in anthropology at the University of Virginia. Her contribution in this volume is adapted from her dissertation, also entitled "Fishing and Drinking in Kodiak, Alaska." Research interests include secular ritual, occupational subcultures, and social interpretations of disaster. In addition to dissertation fieldwork in Kodiak, which focused on alcohol consumption and fishermen's identity, she has, since 1989, contributed to several applied studies of the social impacts of the Exxon Valdez oil spill in rural Alaska. She currently teaches anthropology and sociology at Kodiak College and also works for the Subsistence Division of the Alaska Department of Fish & Game.

J. R. McLeod is Associate Professor of Anthropology at Ohio State University, Mansfield. His research interests include the anthropology of power, complex institutional systems, and the study of political symbolism, ritual, and rhetoric. He is the author of numerous articles on political culture and power, including "Deconstructing Bush: Political Rhetoric and the Bush Campaign" (*International Journal of Moral and Social Studies,* 5:1, Spring 1990) and "The Labour Party and Administration in East London, England" (*Journal of Anthropology*, 4(2), Winter 1985).

Gwen Kennedy Neville is Elizabeth Root Paden Professor of Sociology at Southwestern University in Georgetown, Texas. She holds the B.A. degree in English from Mary Baldwin College and the M.A. and Ph.D. degrees from the University of Florida in Anthropology. She has conducted fieldwork in the Borders region of Scotland and among Scottish descendants in North Carolina in studies of the Southern Presbyterians. Her long-term research on family and religious gatherings in the American South has been published in a number of articles in professional and scholarly journals and in a recent book *Kinship and Pilgrimage: Rituals of Reunion in American Protestant Culture.* Forthcoming is a book on civic ritual in Scotland entitled *The Mother Town: Symbol, Ritual and Experience in the Scottish Borders.* Other projects include research under the auspices of the Lilly Endowment on Mainline Protestantism in American Life; consultantship with the World Council of Churches Division of Education; and ethnographic studies of Catholic parishes in Central Texas sponsored by the Council of Catholic Bishops. Gwen Neville is also co-author of two books on religious socialization in America: *Generation to Generation* and *Learning Through Liturgy*.

Emiko Ohnuki-Tierney, a native of Japan, is Vilas Research Professor at the University of Wisconsin, Madison. She began her work with the Sakhalin Ainu which resulted in *Illness and Healing Among the Sakhalin Ainu, The Ainu of the Northwest Coast of Southern Sakhalin*, and *Sakhalin Ainu Folklore*. She has since then turned her attention to Japanese culture and first focused on cultural underpinnings of contemporary Japanese health care and illness perception in her *Illness and Culture in Contemporary Japan*. Beginning with *The Monkey as Mirror: Symbolic Transformations in Japanese History and Ritual*, whose central focus is on the Japanese conception of self and other and its historical transformations, her research has focused on long-term historical changes and stabilities in Japanese culture. Her most recent book is *Rice as Self: Japanese Identities Through Time.*

Jon Michael Spencer is Director of African and Afro-American Studies at the University of North Carolina at Chapel Hill. His training is in music (M.A., Ph.D.), and he holds a theological degree from Duke University. He is the author of five books, the most recent being *Black Hymnody: A Hymnological History of the African American Church.* He is the founding editor of the academic journal *Black Sacred Music: A Journal of Theomusicology,* published semi-annually by Duke University Press.

Edith Turner teaches anthropology at the University of Virginia. Her special field is symbolism, ritual, and healing. She has done fieldwork among the Ndembu of Zambia and the Inupiat Eskimos of Northern Alaska. Turner is the author of *Image and Pilgrimage, The Spirit and the Drum, Experiencing Ritual,* and a number of articles on performance, ritual, and healing. She is now working on a book on Inupiat "spirituality"—their own term.

Carlos G. Vélez-Ibáñez received the Ph.D. in Anthropology from the University of California, San Diego. He specializes in urban and political anthropology with areas of interest in Latin America, India, and the U.S. Southwest. He has numerous publications including *Bonds of Mutual Trust: The Cultural Systems of Rotating Credit Associations Among Urban Mexicans and Chicanos; Rituals of Marginality: Politics, Process, and Cultural Change in Central Urban Mexico; La Política de Lucha y Resistencia: Procesos y Cambios Culturales en el Centro Urbano de México, 1969-1974;* and *Lazos de Confianza: Los Sistemas Culturales de Asociaciones Rotativas de Credito Entre Mexicanos y Chicanos Urbanos* (*Economica,* forthcoming). He is currently finishing several monographs on the U.S. Mexican Borderlands, one of them titled "Plural Strategies of Survival and Cultural Formation in U.S. Mexican Households in a Region of Dynamic Transformation: The U.S.-Mexico Borderlands," in *Diagnosing America: Anthropology and Public Engagement.*